The Legal Image of China in Chinese Legal Tradition

Xiaobo Dong · Yiran Luo

The Legal Image of China in Chinese Legal Tradition

Springer

Xiaobo Dong
Nanjing Normal University
Nanjing, Jiangsu, China

Yiran Luo
Nanjing Normal University
Nanjing, Jiangsu, China

ISBN 978-981-96-5796-4 ISBN 978-981-96-5797-1 (eBook)
https://doi.org/10.1007/978-981-96-5797-1

This Springer imprint is published by the registered company Springer Nature Singapore Pte Ltd.
The registered company address is: 152 Beach Road, #21-01/04 Gateway East, Singapore 189721, Singapore

Preface

The Chinese legal tradition, steeped in millennia of history, encompasses a wealth of legal thoughts and profound political wisdom that have profoundly influenced and shaped contemporary Chinese legal culture. This rich heritage, encapsulated in ancient Chinese classics, offers a unique lens through which to examine the evolution of China's legal image.

The study of China's legal image within this tradition necessitates a comprehensive and interdisciplinary approach. By examining the spread of ancient Chinese classics beyond their native borders, this book seeks to unveil the complex factors shaping China's legal reputation in the Western world over the past few centuries. This exploration delves into the historical, cultural, and political contexts surrounding the Spreading of Chinese legal texts and their reception by Western audiences. It aims to uncover the underlying causes and consequences of the twists and turns in China's legal image, offering insights into the construction of legal narratives and the interplay between different legal systems and cultures.

By exploring the Spreading of Chinese classics, the book also sheds light on the formation of China's extraterritorial legal images and the cultural origins of contemporary Chinese rule of law thought. It highlights the dynamic interplay between traditional legal concepts and modern legal reforms, providing a nuanced understanding of China's evolving legal landscape. This book serves as a valuable resource for general readers, students of relevant majors and professions, and anyone seeking a deeper understanding of Chinese legal culture and legal philosophy. It offers a feasible path for exploring China's rule of law concepts and culture in the New Era, fostering a greater appreciation for the complexities and richness of China's legal heritage.

In the process of crafting this book, we were fortunate to benefit from the selfless aid and robust backing of our dedicated research team. Their diligent efforts in gathering and organizing a wealth of valuable research data have significantly contributed to the sturdy groundwork of this publication. We extend our heartfelt appreciation to Fan Jiahui, Shao Chen, Sun Nuoxi, Zhang Yinjia, and Zhou Juanjuan for their generous commitment and seamless collaboration.

Nanjing, China

Xiaobo Dong
Yiran Luo

Competing Interests The authors have no competing interests to declare that are relevant to the content of this manuscript.

Contents

About the Authors

Xiaobo Dong is Distinguished Professor of Jilin International Studies University and Professor at School of Foreign Languages and Cultures of Nanjing Normal University, Deputy Director of the Belt and Road Rule of Law Research Center at Academy of China's Modernization of Rule of Law and Researcher at Jiangsu Academy of Talent Development Strategy. He is also Director and Chief Expert of Jiangsu International Rule of Law Research Center, as well as Chief Expert on major programs of the National Social Science Fund of China. His research interests include history of Sino-west civilization exchanges, legal linguistics, legal translation, language policy and planning, cross-cultural communication, as well as area studies. In recent years, he has published over 350 interdisciplinary academic papers and articles in prominent journals and more than 70 books, including academic monographs, edited volumes, and translations.

Yiran Luo is Ph.D. Candidate at School of Foreign Languages and Cultures of Nanjing Normal University and Lecturer of School of Foreign Language of Jinling Institute of Technology. Her research interests include Sino-west civilization exchanges, legal linguistics, as well as translation of Chinese legal classics.

Chapter 1
Chinese Legal Tradition

Abstract Since ancient times, China has developed a distinctive Chinese legal system within the global legal framework, nurturing rich and profound legal culture. The ancient legal classics, as the carrier of Chinese legal wisdom, provide a significant avenue for exploring Chinese legal culture. Western awareness of Chinese legal culture dates back to the late sixteenth century. The translation of traditional Chinese legal classics began in 1810 with the English translation of *Ta Tsing Leu Lee* by Sir George Thomas Staunton. Up to now, the foreign translation of legal classics has gone through a history of more than 200 years. To actively carry out the translation and research of legal classics is helpful to grasp the initiative of the translation of legal classics, reduce cultural misunderstandings and misinterpretations of foreign translators in the translation process, and faithfully preserve the genuine essence of Chinese legal classics.

1.1 The Origin, Lineage, and Influence of Chinese Legal System

The Chinese legal system is a general term of the laws in the feudal period of China and the legal systems of East Asian countries that were developed under the specific social and historical conditions in ancient China, with the combination of rites and laws as the fundamental feature, the written criminal code as the core content, and the *T'ang Code* as the typical representative. The Chinese legal system has its roots in the cultural heritage of the Chinese nation, embodying the fusion of ancient wisdom and the crystallization of their governance experiences. Throughout its extensive historical development, the Chinese legal system has played a significant role in maintaining national stability and unity, fostering national cohesion, and promoting Chinese civilization.

The term "legal system" refers to "the combination of the inherent laws of a certain country with laws adopted from foreign countries, or with laws developed over an extended period of domestic history to form a unique system (Chen, 1980)". In 1884, Hozumi Nobushige, a pioneering figure in Japanese jurisprudence, published a paper

X. Dong and Y. Luo, *The Legal Image of China in Chinese Legal Tradition*,
https://doi.org/10.1007/978-981-96-5797-1_1

titled "On the Five Legal Family" in the *Journal of the Jurisprudence Association*, dividing the world legal system into "Indian Legal Family", "Chinese Legal Family", "Islamic Legal Family", "English Family", and "Roman Legal Family", setting a precedent for the study of the world legal system. As the only legal system in the world that did not break down due to the change of dynasties and was not involved in other legal systems, the Chinese legal system developed for over 2000 years, starting with the *Book of Law* compiled by Li Kui in the Warring States Period (481BC-221BC), it reached a perfect stage in the Sui and Tang Dynasties through the evolution and development of the Qin, Han, Wei, Jin, Southern, and Northern Dynasties, and then it was carried on by the Song, Yuan, Ming, and Qing Dynasties. At the end of the Qing Dynasty, when a prominent Chinese politician and jurist Shen Jiaben and others amended the law, it was dissolved.

In ancient history, the Chinese legal system played a crucial role as the precursor of legislative frameworks in East Asian nations. In a long period of time, the principles of the Chinese legal system have evolved into a common legal ideology among East Asian nations, with its influence once extending to Southeast Asia and beyond. Liang Qichao, a Chinese politician, social and political activist, journalist, and intellectual, highlighted in his article "On China's Enactment of Gains and Losses of History" that the states of Goryeo, Japan, and Annam countries were all influenced by our country's legal system in that era (Zhang, 2016). Legal historian Yang Honglie (2015) emphasized that "when comparing the histories of various legal systems, the Chinese legal system has endured for over a thousand years, outlasting the most ancient legal systems in Egypt and Mesopotamia, and its influence spread to the East Asian countries such as Korea, Japan, Ryukyu, Annam, and the Western Regions, while the influence of the Egyptian and Mesopotamia legal systems was limited to a small area. Therefore, it is appropriate to assert that the Chinese legal system ranks among the world's largest legal systems".

Viewed through ancient history, there are profound historical factors that contributed to the formation of the Chinese legal system.

First and foremost, the similarity in national realities paves the way for the development of the Chinese legal system. There are significant similarities between ancient East Asian countries and China: they both existed self-sufficient feudal, small-peasant economies; their political systems were predominantly centralized feudal monarchies; in ideology, the Confucian rule were respected. The alignment of national realities has facilitated smoother exchanges and mutual understanding among countries effectively, eliminated the incompatibility of East Asian countries in transplanting Chinese laws, and enabled the assimilation and internalization of Chinese legal culture. This process has not only enriched the connotation of the Chinese legal system but also contributed to the development of a diverse and integrated East Asian legal culture that is harmonious yet distinct. At the same time, it also paves the way for the formation of the East Asian legal culture community.

Furthermore, political vassalage played a crucial role in establishing the foundation of the Chinese legal system. Throughout history, there were such connections between the member states of the Chinese legal system and the home country. During certain historical eras, these East Asian states were vassals of China and received titles from the Central Dynasty. For example, in the Han Dynasty, Japan dispatched diplomatic envoys to present tributes and show their respect. In the second year of Emperor Guangwu's reign (57 A.D.), according to the *Book of the Later Han*, which is one of the Twenty-Four Histories covering the history of the Han Dynasty from 6 to 189 CE (known as the Later or Eastern Han period), Japan dispatched envoys to the Han court. Emperor Guangwu, the founder of the Han Dynasty, honored these envoys by granting them a golden seal and giving Japan the name "Wa (倭)", the oldest name for Japan often used by ancient Chinese and Korean scholars, as a symbol of his appreciation. Historically, the vassal relationships between the countries of the Chinese legal system has greatly reduced the resistance to the spread of Chinese legal culture from top to bottom and laid a solid foundation for the formation of the East Asian legal culture community.

Thirdly, government-sponsored official exchanges and educational activities have considerably accelerated the development of the Chinese legal system. Ancient China's institutions and culture, as the cradle of the Chinese legal system, were notably advanced and superior to that of other contemporary East Asian countries. This led neighboring nations to take a keen interest in China's legal system, prompting them to send envoys and students to learn Chinese legal system and culture. Japanese Oriental historian Kuwabara Jitsuzo, in his article titled "The Laws and Decrees of the Chrysanthemum Dynasty and the Tang Dynasty", highlighted the substantial influence of Tang Dynasty culture on East Asian nations. During this era, students from Japan, Silla, Gaochang, Tubo, and other countries actively participated in the exchange of cultural knowledge. Government-led official exchanges and educational programs far exceeded private exchanges in both scale and standard, accelerating the spread and adoption of Chinese legal culture in East Asia and ensuring a stable, rapid, and high-quality development of the East Asian legal culture community.

The guiding ideology of the Chinese legal system is deeply rooted in Chinese Confucianism, which originated in pre-Qin Dynasty. It encompasses several key principles:

To begin with, the philosophy of the "unity of heaven and man" *(Tian Ren He Yi)*. In this worldview, the Chinese legal system emphasizes the harmony and alignment between celestial principles and human actions, stressing the compatibility of human conduct with virtuous ideals. As a result, this framework naturally gives rise to fundamental legal principles, including "the interaction between heaven and mankind *(Tian Ren Gan Ying)*", "virtue matching heaven *(Yi De Pei Tian)*", "morality given priority over penalty" *(De Zhu Xing Fu)* and "wise virtue and careful punishment" *(Ming De Shen Fa)*.

Secondly, humanistic ethics. Confucian "benevolence" *(Ren Ai)* places significant emphasis on the benevolence of heaven and earth, which profoundly influences the ideology and legislative and judicial practices of the Chinese legal system. It can be manifested in the harmonious integration of etiquette and laws, the prioritization of education and human studies, a focus on this life, the leniency of punishments, the value of people's lives, the light corvee and low tax, the simplicity of government, and the transparency of prison administration. In terms of the judiciary, the fundamental idea of judicious penalties and careful use of the death penalty plays a vital role in China's traditional legal culture. As noted by American scholars D. Bodde and C. Morris in their *Law in Imperial China*, the ancient Chinese law were, in some aspects, considered to be more rational and humane compared to those of Western countries.

Thirdly, the quest for a harmonious concept of "non-litigation *(Wu Song)*". The thought of "harmony" in Chinese traditional culture origins primarily from the philosophies of Taoist, Laozi, and Zhuangzi. Ideas of "the unity of heaven and man", "Taoism and nature", and "All things are one with me" embody the harmonious view of heaven and man. In ancient legal culture, there is a traditional thought of weariness of litigation. Confucius once said, "I am in the same boat as anyone else when it comes to litigated cases. The critical point is that litigation should be entirely avoided!" *Zhu Zi Jia Xun* also pointed out that "Family members should never spark lawsuits through quarrels, as this harms the family". Wang Shijin in Ming Dynasty shared the belief that "It is paradise when people live peacefully, pay their taxes and services, and there are no disputes or lawsuits". Since ancient times, Chinese people has the long-standing aspiration for a serene and conflict-free society.

Fourthly, in legislation, a blend of statutory law and case law prevails. Historically, legal codes like the *T'ang Code*, *Sung Criminal Code*, *Criminal Law of the Ming Dynasty*, and *Ta Tsing Leu Lee* form a continuous lineage, symbolizing the advanced legal culture of the Eastern world. Their profound influence extends to Japan, Korea, and Vietnam. Since the Western Han Dynasty, a large number of case laws have been applied. For instance, *the Spring and Autumn Annals* became the legal basis for hearing litigation and sentencing in the Western Han Dynasty; the Jin Dynasty employed "the system of deliberation and discussion"; the Tang Dynasty established code with many records of court cases; and the Ming Dynasty instituted its distinct law known as *Da Gao*.

Fifthly, concerning legal oversight, most ancient Chinese Dynasties prioritized supervision and established a top-down judicial supervision system to varying extents. During the Qin Dynasty, officials were appointed to inspect from the central government to local administrations. In the Sui, Tang, and Five Dynasties periods, the censorate acted as a central administrative supervisory body and a key judicial organ, responsible for rectifying, impeaching officials, and maintaining discipline. As for the Ming Dynasty, the censorate was further developed and tasked with supervisory duties, impeachments, and providing recommendations.

The rich heritage of traditional Chinese culture forms the spiritual core of the Chinese nation. China's legal system is deeply rooted in ancient legal traditions and cultural heritage, ensuring continuity throughout history. Historically, legal culture represents the accumulated values and practices of a nation, including the preservation of its traditions. Traditional legal culture is the source of water in the history of China's rule of law. Modern construction of the rule of law is intricately tied to the social and cultural context, inevitably guided by the principles and concepts of traditional legal culture.

1.2 The Spread of Chinese Legal Tradition in the West

As the Chinese legal system emerged and progressed, our ancestors gathered vast governance experience spanning thousands of years. They encapsulated profound insights within legal classics. The internal structure of legal culture embodies duality: one is the legal culture of institutional form, such as legal norms and legal system, while the other is the ideological legal culture, such as legal doctrine, psychology, customary practices, and so on. Legal classics, serving as the carrier of legal culture, naturally consist of two parts: substantive systems and codes, alongside conceptual legal thoughts and doctrines.

Legal classics encompass a vast spectrum beyond criminal laws, extending into ideologies, culture, and societal spheres. They should comprise written materials derived from legislative, judicial, law popularization, interpretation, and academic activities, including political legal codes, administrative and judicial documents, trial archives, legal literature, practical references, village rules and folk conventions, and guides for the convenience of the people, etc. They should also cover the material and content of law in history, philosophy, literature, art, and other cultural classics. According to *Chinese Ancient Books*, the total number of ancient Chinese books is 200,000, of which there are nearly 800 kinds of "criminal law". The *Bibliography of Chinese Legal History* edited by Zhang Weiren cataloged 2352 books based on norm, systems, theories, and practices, establishing it as the most extensive and detailed catalogue of legal documents so far. The cultural classics involving the content of jurisprudence are even more numerous and difficult to count.

In a narrow sense, "legal classics" refer to ancient codes and laws formulated and acknowledged by the state and enforced by the state including formal codes and various supplementary forms. According to the incomplete statistics of the literature records, there are 160 types of legal codes, ranging from the *Nine Chapter Law* to the *Ta Tsing Leu Lee*. While "律 *(Lü)*" was the primary form of ancient law and usually acted as the relatively stable national law, it was supplemented and restricted by other legal formats like "令 *(Ling)*", "科 *(Ke)*", and "比 *(Bi)*" during the Han Dynasty, and later by "格 *(Ge)*" and "式 *(Shi)*" during the Sui and Tang Dynasties. Additionally, the Five Dynasties and the Song Dynasty had "敕 *(Chi)*", and the Ming and Qing Dynasties introduced "例*(Li)*" as an supplementary form. These additional legal framework, more adaptable than traditional laws, addressed contemporary circumstances and global contexts. Over millennium, China's legal system has evolved, leaving behind an extensive collection of legal classics that shed light on the nation's legal history, encapsulate the essence of Chinese legal principles, and significantly influence legal culture of China and even the entire East Asia region.

Throughout the course of human cultural exchanges, translation has consistently acted as a crucial link facilitating communication across different languages. Before the sixteenth and seventeenth centuries, Europeans began to understand China's legal culture gradually through the introduction of missionaries and Jesuits, as well as the travel notes of Marco Polo, Matteo Ricci, and Zeng Dezhao, etc. However, these early descriptions and travelogues lacked direct references to original Chinese legal classics, casting doubt on the accuracy of their content as seen from today's perspective. From the sixteenth and seventeenth centuries onward to the present era, cultural exchanges between China and other countries have gradually evolved despite encountering various obstacles. A pivotal moment occurred in 1779 when the French translated an abridged version of the Chinese forensic work *Collected Cases of Injustice Rectified*, publishing it in the *Journal of Chinese History, Art and Science* in Paris. This marked the beginning of its journey to Europe, subsequently translated into Dutch, English, German, and other languages; in 1810, the United Kingdom witnessed the first publication of the English translation of the *Ta Tsing Leu Lee*, which sparked a century-long period of European and American scholarly exploration into Chinese law. Notably, in 1997, American scholar Wallace Johnson completed the inaugural comprehensive translation of the *T'ang Code* (Volume II) into Western languages. Furthermore, in 2005, Professor Jiang Yonglin from Boston University in the United States led the publication of the official English translation of the *Criminal Law of the Ming Dynasty*. Summarizing the trajectory of legal classics disseminating beyond their origins to the present era, it can be broadly delineated in three key phases.

1.2.1 The Phase of Understanding for Missionary and Profit-Making Purposes

Initially, missionaries, trader, and Jesuits ventured into China with dual aims: engaging in trade and spreading their religious beliefs. They devoted themselves to learning the Chinese language, understanding the intricacies of Chinese culture, and exploring classical works to comprehend the essence of Chinese culture and the preferences of its people. Their primary objectives were to effectively communicate their beliefs and seek financial gains. Living in China for extended periods, these foreigners had clear goals and gained profound insights into the language and customs of the Chinese people. Consequently, they shared their experiences orally with their fellow countrymen or chronicled their impressions of life in China through travelogues. Through these efforts, the mysterious facade veiling China, the "ancient enigmatic oriental country", began to dissipate, fostering a deeper understanding of China in the Western world. Marco Polo, the Italian traveler who spent 17 years in China, praised the country's prosperity and progress in his travelogue. He vividly described well-organized marketplaces and the efficient functioning of judicial systems. Subsequently, Spaniard Mendoza authored *Historia del Gran Reino de la China*, drawing from the travelogue of multiple Europeans to outline ancient Chinese legal culture. This Spreading of China's political system and laws to Europe ignited a fascination with China among Europeans at that time. In the latter half of the sixteenth century, Jesuit Matteo Ricci provided positive accounts of various facets of ancient Chinese political and legal culture. By the nineteenth century, clashed between foreign sailors, merchants in China's coastal areas, and local inhabitants led to sporadic criminal cases involving foreigners. This prompted Europeans and Americans to study *Ta Tsing Leu Lee* concerning such incidents. Following the Opium War, the Western presence in China expanded with the establishment of factories and churches, resulting in civil disputes. The sections in the *Ta Tsing Leu Lee* dealing with the resolution of civil disputes intrigued Westerners. However, Western perceptions of the *Ta Tsing Leu Le* remained critical during this period, largely due to the underlying colonial motives behind its translation by Westerners.

1.2.2 The Phase of Incomplete Translations by Sinologists

Historically, sinologists disseminate Chinese legal classics overseas primarily through compiled, selected, or abridged translations, aligning with their intent to translate these classics. Sinologists are foreign scholars engaged in the study of humanities and social sciences in ancient, modern, or contemporary China, such as Matteo Ricci, also belong to the ranks. Some early sinologists condense parts of the Chinese legal system, acquainting the Western world with China's societal norms through publications like the *Chinese Repository*. The prevalence of early Chinese legal classics abroad was mainly in the form of compiled, selected, or abridged translations. Here are several reasons. Firstly, sinologists aim to "assimilate" Chinese culture, guided by a strong sense of Western cultural centrism. Consequently, they selectively translate parts that intrigued them. Notably, the editorial enthusiasm for such reports reveals disdain for numerous death penalty cases, frequent executions, and the brutality of public executions in ancient China, as seen in accompanying commentaries on a few reports. Secondly, most Chinese legal classics are written in ancient languages, featuring lengthy, intricate, and expansive content. Translation demands significant time and effort, resulting in increased complexity. As a result, complete translations of legal classics are scarce. Sir George Thomas Staunton, in the preface of his translation of *Ta Tsing Leu Lee*, candidly expressed the challenges, "the language of the text of obscure, and the structure is complex". These key factors impede overseas readers from gaining a comprehensive understanding of Chinese legal classics due to their incomplete presentation abroad.

1.2.3 The Phase of Spreading of Full Translations and Research Dissertations

Full translations of Chinese legal classics and research papers written by scholars from China and sinologists have had limited exposure outside their native regions. While full translations of Chinese legal classics in foreign languages are scarce, scholarly research findings on these classics are primarily presented in dissertations. For instance, Wallace Johnson, known for translating the complete English version of the *T'ang Code*, took the translation and introduction of its initial three chapters as his doctoral dissertation. Another instance is the book *Recent American Academic Writings on Traditional Chinese Law*, compiling 12 papers authored by American scholars on the history of Chinese law, published in English journal. Notably, the "Library of Chinese Classics" project, launched in 1995, stands as China's significant national initiative to systematically introduce foreign language versions of representative cultural classics worldwide. The project aims to select 100 notable classic works from China's pre-Qin Dynasty to modern times across diverse fields like culture, history, philosophy, economy, military affairs, science, and technology. However, the absence of legal classics among the chosen works highlighting the pressing need for more robust translation efforts in legal classics. Due to the limited knowledge of Chinese legal classics and traditional legal wisdom among international audiences, scholars advocate for broader translation efforts. They propose expanding translation histories to include not only the Four Books and The Five Classics but also incorporating Chinese law, medicine, history, ethnic classics, scientific and technological works, along with other renowned literary pieces in overseas countries within the framework of the Translation History of Chinese Cultural Classics.

Among Chinese legal classics, four important representative works of the Chinese legal system have been published in full translation overseas, namely *Ta Tsing Leu Lee*, *Collected Cases of Injustice Rectified*, The *T'ang Code*, and *Criminal Law of the Ming Dynasty*, which plays an important role in promoting legal classics and is conductive to overseas reader, scholars, and sinologists, providing a comprehensive view of the Chinese legal system. They also provides first-hand materials for more researchers who are interested in the traditional Chinese legal system. However, both domestically and globally, research on translating legal classics has not received sufficient attention. So far, there are still many problems to be solved.

Firstly, the current translations are insufficient to meet the research demands, resulting in a focus on only a few major codes in present-stage translation studies. Despite the wealth of legal codes in China, there is a scarcity of available translation research materials. This scarcity is particularly evident in primary legal codes, and numerous legal thoughts and cultural writings remain untranslated. This highlights the pressing need for additional translations in these crucial areas.

Furthermore, there's a notable absence of systematic and thorough research into translating legal classics. Upon consulting papers addressing the translation of legal classics in China, many primarily delve into examining translated words, sentences, and chapters. These discussions largely revolve around textual-level conversion issues. However, these papers tend to overlook broader aspects such as the impact of Spreading, cultural influence, and historical significance of the translated texts. As a result, the exploration often stays limited within the textual context, lacking a comprehensive investigation into the crucial task of translating legal classics. This gap hampers efforts in fostering mutual appreciation between civilizations and promoting the exchange and communication of legal culture.

Thirdly, there is a significant shortage of professional legal translation talents. The translation of ancient legal classics involves both intralingual and interlingual translation, and the translator not only needs to have rich professional knowledge of law and foreign languages, but also needs to have high attainments of ancient Chinese. Therefore, the translation of legal classics has a high requirement for the accuracy of translation. The translation of legal classic is difficult, time-consuming, and difficult to produce results, which makes many translators and scholars discouraged.

1.3 The Modern Significance of Re-Exploring the Legal Tradition

Legal classics serve as a reflection of traditional Chinese law. Historically, upon initial contact between Westerners and the Chinese legal system, biases are prevalent against its traditional form. At times, these legal classics are purposely manipulated to diminish the image of ancient China. Presently, significant prejudices persist in the Western perspective toward the traditional Chinese legal system, often holding a critical view. Hence, the translation of Chinese legal classics has become increasingly urgent. It's crucial for Chinese traditional legal culture to gain recognition and for a comprehensive portrayal of China's concept of rule of law while reshaping its legal system. This emphasizes the necessity of translating these foreign texts in contemporary times. The translation of *Criminal Law of the Ming Dynasty* serves as an example. Its status in Western academic circles was once contentious, often viewed by most Western scholars as tools of the Ming empire's power, considered high oppressive and authoritative. Such perceptions ingrained serious biases against the traditional Chinese legal system among some Western scholars. Jiang Yonglin, aiming to counter these Western prejudices, translated the *Criminal Law of the Ming Dynasty*, reshaping them into classics within Western academia and jurisprudence. In this new era, proactive efforts to provide an objective research corpus for overseas scholars are crucial. Such initiatives help in dismantling global prejudices against the traditional Chinese legal system.

1.3.1 To Build a New Cultural Space for the Rule of Law

As humanity transitioned from barbarism to civilization, our world underwent significant qualitative shifts. The natural and material realm remains our primary domain, and the cultural sphere represents an inseparable secondary space intertwined with our material world. In the 1970s and 1980s, Juri Lotman, the founder of Soviet cultural semiotics, introduced the theory of cultural space. His goal is to comprehend cultural phenomena through signs, explore the essence of culture, and establish a multi-tiered, three-dimensional cultural sign system.

According to Lotman's theory, symbols give rise to text, text molds culture, and culture generates what he termed the semiosphere, which refers to "the consequence of human symbolic thought and behaviors reshaping the natural world, creating an organized, multi-level space established throughout human history (Kang, 2006)". Among these components, text stands out as "the carrier of complete meaning and function", being pivotal in constructing cultural space. The Chinese legal system stretches for thousands of years, leaving countless legal classics, which are foundational texts in shaping Chinese legal culture. Amid the global expansion of the rule of law, the translation of these legal classics holds immense practical significance and contemporary value to the construction of a new cultural space of rule of law.

1.3.2 To Strengthen a Greater Say on the Rule of Law

According to records, the ancient Miao people document the early use of the "*Wu Xing*" (five forms of punishment), indicating that there were laws. Over thousands of years, an East Asian legal culture circle has been formed with ancient Chinese law as its core. The Chinese legal culture space, which embodies the spirit, civilization, and practice of the rule of law in China and the whole East Asia, is flourishing. However, as the Qing Dynasty declined, the influence of Chinese legal culture gradually diminished. During a period of national reform and transformation, traditional Chinese legal customs succumbed to the pervasive impact of modern Western legal norms. This trend was further propelled by the spread of Western education and knowledge in the East. The dominance of Western legal concepts over traditional Eastern ones became an inevitable part of modernizing our nation's legal framework. Since the founding of New China, there has been an exploration of a path toward a legal system that upholds distinctively Chinese characteristics. General Secretary Xi Jinping stressed the inseparable link between the Chinese rule of law and the nation's 5000 years of civilization. The vitality of China's cultural space of rule of law depends on its historical foundations, often found within the forgotten and neglected legal classics. Hence, the urgent task of rejuvenating and redefining the traditional cultural space of the rule law necessitates a renewed translation effort for these legal classics.

Since modern times, Western sinologists and scholars have been at the forefront of translating and interpreting ancient Chinese legal classics and have understood and recognized Chinese legal culture from the angle of "others". The relevant translations and research results are guided by the theory and practical experience of the construction of cultural space of Western perspectives. The image of Chinese legal culture presented to the international community is often a "westernized" image with several misunderstandings, misinterpretations, and even prejudices. Cultural exchanges and mutual understanding thrive on the basis of equal discourse rights between the two sides. We should attach importance to the retranslation and research of legal classics, break away from the interpretation and evaluation system dominated by Western legal culture, interpret the original Chinese traditional rule of law from a local and modern perspective, and take its essence and discard its dregs. Only by firmly grasping the initiative to interpret our own culture can we truly enhance China's right to speak on rule of law. Therefore, the translation and research of legal classics shoulder the historical responsibility of unearthing new values in traditional legal culture, clarifying fresh interpretations of ancient legal philosophies, reviving ancient practices in the rule of law, and shaping a renewed image of Chinese legal culture.

1.3.3 *To Enhance the Cultural Identity of the Rule of Law*

"Cultures evolve and grow, with the past laying the foundation for the new. Understanding our history thoroughly ensures a more reliable translation to new ideas, emphasizing respect for the unresponsive past (Lotman, 1990)". As historical texts, on the one hand, legal classics act as repositories of historical facts, preserving and reconstructing past legal practices, objectively documenting both successes and failures. On the other hand, they can convey information, project the views, ideas and assumptions hidden behind objective events into the context of the new era, and generate new meanings through interactions with fresh ideas. Confidence in one's culture stems from a steadfast cultural identity, which requires a comprehensive understanding of our cultural heritage. Retranslating classics emerges as a critical tool for comprehending history and nurturing cultural identity.

To translate and study of traditional legal classics, it's crucial to approach the matter from both historical and contemporary angles. Initially, decoding the intricate text requires a deep dive into its ideological, political, social, religious, and philosophical dimensions, using the language and logic of the original text. This process aims to authentically restore the genuine essence of the legal text. Furthermore, when examining these classics from a contemporary standpoint, it's important to set aside any preconceived notions and thoroughly scrutinize the inherited legal principles. By employing modern research methodologies, we deconstruct these valuable assets of legal wisdom passed down by our ancestors. This endeavor seeks to bridge the past and present, distilling the core of legal culture that resonates with current societal needs, contributes to national rejuvenation, and explores innovative pathways to construct a space for Chinese legal culture. These profound traditional notions and concepts within legal culture form the bedrock for establishing a new legal cultural space. The consensus derived from extracting and understanding these concepts represents the genuine identity of legal culture with Chinese characteristics.

1.3.4 *To Shape the Common Legal Cultural Memory*

Lotman (2000) suggested that the development of cultural symbols proceeds precisely according to the laws of memory, and the past does not perish, does not become extinct. The past, selected and intricately encoded, is preserved and will reveal itself again under certain conditions, establishing a cultural realm for the rule of law requires a comprehensive exploration of the temporal dimension. Simply examining legal culture without acknowledging time or comparing different periods cannot adequately shape this new sphere. Legal classics are texts with high cultural memory capacity, and the information contained in the past context will be activated in the modern context, thus producing new meanings and influences. For instance, concepts like "law-based governance", "putting people first", and "administering by law and virtue" in traditional legal culture significantly contribute not only to China's modernization of legal principles but also to shaping our comprehension of "law". These concepts profoundly impact our collective memory of Chinese legal culture.

As Lotman (1990) argued that, the content of memory is in the past, but it is the tool of thinking in the present. Without these memories, contemplating the "now" or the events "at this time" becomes an impossible task. History isn't simply a trace of the past, but also a positive mechanism of the present. In this new historical context, retranslating legal classics not only allows us to trace the historical path of our predecessors in shaping the rule of law but also provides an opportunity to glean insights from the past. These retranslations offer valuable reference points for addressing contemporary challenges in China's modernization of the rule of law, drawing from historical experiences and lessons. Through the dialogue between the "past" and the "present", we vividly witness the emergence, evolution, prosperity, and decline of the Chinese rule of law cultural space. Our collective historical memory urges reflection on the core of "community" identity and motivates us to solve inherent contemporary issues. Furthermore, by continuously exploring and shaping a new shared memory within the realm of the rule of law culture, we aim to unite the great spirit of the Chinese nation, fostering enduring vitality.

To build a socialist legal system with Chinese characteristics is to vigorously promote the modernization of the rule of law in China, which is rooted in the rich soil of Chinese legal culture. In the era of globalization, pivotal aspects such as interpreting legal culture through retranslating legal classics, shaping China's legal discourse, strengthening the cultural identity of the legal system, and forming a shared legal cultural heritage stand as crucial endeavors to bolster China's legal development and amplify its global influence. Drawing insights from traditional legal culture, blending ancient wisdom with modern perspectives, narrating distinctive "Chinese stories" in a manner that resonates with Chinese values, all contribute to crafting a fresh cultural realm for the rule of law.

1.4 Summary

The rejuvenation of Chinese legal system in the contemporary era is deeply linked with the infusion and nurturing of traditional legal culture. The translation of legal classics serves a crucial role in shaping, disseminating, and classicizing the memory of traditional legal culture. Internally, this translation enriches research materials for domestic scholars, fostering multifaceted academic innovation. It also contributes to popularizing traditional legal culture, deepening understanding among the Chinese populace, and boosting their cultural confidence in modernizing China's legal system.

Externally, legal classics, serving as primary sources for understanding Chines legal culture beyond borders and shaping the image of China's legal principle, embody distinctive legal wisdom. In the translation and Spreading of ancient Chinese cultural classics, Western professional sinologists have been dominant, while Chinese scholars entered this arena much later.

Hence, actively engaging in translating and researching legal classics will help secure control over the translation of these texts. It will address cultural misunderstandings and misinterpretations by foreign translators and strive to accurately portray Chinese legal classics. This, in turn, fosters acceptance and recognition of Chinese legal culture globally, creating a conductive environment and establishing a solid ideological foundation for the revival of the Chinese legal system. Simultaneously, this effort will reverse one-sided and stereotypical impressions of the Chinese legal system held by the international community, dispel long-accumulated prejudices, actively disseminate the core values of Chinese legal culture, promote equal exchanges between the Chinese legal system and others, gradually realize the transmission of Chinese law to the West in the mutual learning among civilizations, bolster China's influence in global rule-of-law constructions, and ultimately contribute China's wisdom the global community of rule of law with a shared future.

References

Chen, C. (1980). A preliminary exploration of the characteristics of the Chinese genealogy of law. *Chinese Journal of Law, 01*, 6.

Kang, C. (2006). *Culture and its space for survival and development: A study on Lotman's cultural semiotics, 35*. HoHai University Press.

Lotman, Y. M. (1990). *Universe of the mind: A semiotic theory of culture*. I.B. Tauris & Co., Ltd.

Yang, H. (2015). *The influence of Chinese Law in East Asian countries*. The Commercial Press.

Zhang, J. (2016). *Chinese legal history*. China University of Political Science And Law Press.

Chapter 2
Chinese Legal Classics and National Image

Abstract Law serves as a rich vessel of cultural significance. Chinese legal civilization, steeped in a profound heritage and unique allure, has produced numerous legal classics attributed to sages. These classics are wellsprings of legal ingenuity, guiding the Chinese nation toward building a harmonious, prosperous, and influential society. The study of the spread and influence of Chinese legal classics outside the region can make us go out of the dual thinking of "East and West" and "modern and traditional", examine the value of Chinese culture within the scope of world culture, re-examine the influence and modern value of ancient Chinese culture from a global perspective, and reveal the universal significance of Chinese culture (Zhang, Introduction to study on the twentieth century's extraterritorial spread and influence of ancient Chinese cultural classics (volume 1), 1, Elephant Press, 2018). Throughout the history of legal exchanges between China and the West, Western sinologists are key in translating Chinese law. While they significantly promote Chinese legal culture globally, their translations often contained "misinterpretations" that, to some extent, catered to the cultural needs of the West and maintained cultural dominance. Therefore, for an authentic portrayal of Chinese legal systems and civilization and to globally project Chinese legal culture in the modern era while correcting stereotypical impressions shaped by Western sinologists, thorough research and retranslation of the Chinese legal classics are essential. Emphasis should be placed on the selection of translation texts, translators, and translation strategies.

2.1 The Global Significance of Chinese Legal Culture

In the context of Sino-Western legal and civilizational exchanges, "legal orientalism" refers to the shaping of a country's legal image using law as a global discourse, essentially portraying self-construction and world-building through legal perspectives. Before the nineteenth century, Western Sinological studies' focus was primarily on Chinese history, philosophy, and customs. It wasn't until the late Qing Dynasty, amid significant global shifts like the Industrial Revolution, Europe's technological advancement, the rise of capitalism, and colonial expansions, that the study of

X. Dong and Y. Luo, *The Legal Image of China in Chinese Legal Tradition*,
https://doi.org/10.1007/978-981-96-5797-1_2

Chinese law became imperative. This was due to the clash between the distinct legal systems and concepts of the East and West, especially when interest diverged (Karen Turner et al. 2004). French translation theorist Antoine Berman (1992), in *Experience of the Foreign: Culture and Translation in Romantic Germany*, suggests that translation serves as a form of communication. Translation's primary role involves fostering dialogue between different nations and people, aiming not just to convey the original text but also to illustrate the disparities between the original text and the target language. This process enriches both the language and culture of the target country.

Whether viewed critically or favorably, Chinese legal culture, often perceived as the "other" in contrast to Western culture, has been variously portrayed or misinterpreted in Western eyes. However, these interpretations do not alter its inherent value in world cultural history. In a way, this highlights the significance of translating Chinese legal classics, as it represents Chinese legal culture's substantial influence on shaping Western culture, thereby signifying its global importance.

General Secretary Xi Jinping (2021) emphasized China's rich legal heritage, noting its unique legal system within the global legal framework. Evolving from the Qin Dynasty and flourishing during the Sui and Tang Dynasties, exemplified by the *Tang's Code*, the influence of the Chinese legal system waned after the Qing Dynasty. Unlike other systems like civil law, common law, or Islamic law, China's legal system reflects the nation's distinct historical conditions, showcasing remarkable creativity a deep-rooted legal civilization. It encapsulates the essence and wisdom of the Chinese people, embodying invaluable concepts worth preserving. The revitalization of China in the new era draws strength from traditional legal culture. The translation of legal classics is pivotal in preserving, disseminating, and venerating this cultural legacy (Hu & Dong, 2020a, 2020b). Serving as primary resources for foreigners to comprehend Chinese legal culture and envision China's legal framework, these classics carry distinct national legal wisdom. In the translation and Spreading of ancient Chinese cultural classics, Western sinologists have historically dominated the field, while Chinese scholars have joined the discourse relatively later (Dong & Zhang, 2021). Actively undertaking the translation and research of legal classics can empower us to lead in introducing these works globally. This initiative aims to rectify cultural misinterpretations during translation, restore the authentic essence of Chinese legal classics, foster international acceptance and appreciation of Chinese legal culture, facilitate equitable exchanges between Chinese and other legal systems, and gradually enable the transmission of the Chinese law to the West through mutual understanding and cultural exchanges. Such efforts significantly contribute to enhancing China's global influence in the realm of legal constructions, enriching the collective global legal community with the wisdom derived from China (Dong, 2021).

2.2 China's Legal Image: The "Other" Behind Western Discourse

The perception of Chinese law in the Western world through translation discourse has a significant global context, evolving from initially positive to alternating positive and negative images, and eventually to a predominantly negative one. Said's concept of "Orientalism" represents a historical narrative constructed by Westerners, shaped by colonial expansion. The creation of a global "civilizational hierarchy" distinguishes superiority and inferiority among cultures (Barr, 2014). Non-Western nations or regions have come to align themselves within this East–West dichotomy and Western-centric world order, adhering to a dichotomous value system based on notions of progress/stagnation, freedom/authoritarianism, civilization/barbarism. This structure reinforces the perception of the West's superiority in terms of modern progress, freedom, and civilization, while positioning other cultures as inferior under the hegemony of Western norms (Jiang, 2010).

2.2.1 From "Utopia" to "Backwardness, Barbarism and Cruelty"

The construction of China's legal image has no subjective in history. The formation of "legal orientalism" and self-orientalization is closely linked to the translation and legal practices surrounding Chinese legal classics by the Western world for over 400 years. Historical accounts detailing legal interactions between China and foreign nations reveal an extensive history of translating ancient Chinese legal culture and its legal systems. China's ancient legal culture and legal system have attracted great attention from Western travelers, diplomatic envoys, scholars, merchants, missionaries, and politicians since the sixteenth and seventeenth centuries.

In 1585, Spanish missionary Mendoza (1945–1618) penned *History of the Great and Mighty Kingdom of China*, expressing profound admiration for China's scientific advancements, political system, social order, judicial structure, and social welfare institutions. He emphasized China's strong legal system, acknowledging the strict justice and maintenance of social order through methods like torture, though less humane. China's administrative system functioned in a manner akin to a parliamentary structure, where seasoned and esteemed parliamentarians deliberated collectively on governmental affairs. China is regarded as an immensely powerful kingdom and is considered one of the best-governed nations known worldwide (Zhou, 2006). Voltaire also lauded the Chinese emperor, laws, and Confucianism in dedicate chapters of his *Dictionnaire Philosophique* and *An Essay on Universal History, the Manners*. Meanwhile, Jesuits, led by Matteo Ricci, entered China in the late sixteenth century, initiating the introduction of Chinese culture to Europe. Ricci spoke favorably of ancient China's political and legal culture, highlighting the historical Chinese preference for monarchical government, the Ministry of Justice's role in handling criminal cases, and regional judicial departments. He emphasized punishments for officials violating the law and the restriction on judges presiding over cases in their home provinces. Ricci admired Chinese customs and laws, aligning with the ethical principles of Confucianism. He believed that the Chinese etiquette and law infused with the Confucianism made China more civilized than Europe. Ricci also studied China's imperial examination system, even recommending a similar model to Europe's ruling class. In summary, historical sources of that era depicted China as a nation with an advanced legal system and a flourishing culture.

However, this positive image has gradually changed with the passage of time, and the Western understanding and perception of Chinese law have also changed. In the late period of the Enlightenment, the concept of "Oriental Despotism" began assimilating China's image. Thinkers like Montesquieu, Nicolas Boulanger, and Hegel, prominent in their academic writings, labeled China as an autocracy, and the image of the barbaric Chinese empire was formed in the late eighteenth and early nineteenth centuries. In the nineteenth century, Western portrayals of barbaric China were laden with ambiguity, arbitrariness, generalities, and a fusion of ideologies, thoughts, and even fantasy and imagination. At that time, Westerners opened a lot of newspapers and periodicals in China. Notably, Chinese Repository, the first mature periodical, was published from May 1832 to December 1851, with a total of 20 volumes. It had a relatively large influence and, significantly contributed to altering Western perspectives on Chinese law. Most discussions about Chinese law in this journal had a negative undertone. Legal historian Li Xiuqing (2015a; b) roughly summed up the basic characteristics of Chinese criminal law written by foreigners, that is, "conviction and sentencing are uncertain; violent crimes, especially homicide, is very common; there are cruel punishments like beheading, lynching, abusing torture, etc.". In 1871, Holcmbe, Chester, the first counselor of the United States in China, wrote in The Real China-man that "the practical workings of Chinese courts of law show that bribery, extortion, and cruel injustice are not merely possible, but easy and common under the most elaborate system that can be devised (Tian & Li, 2007)". Similar descriptions were found in various works of that era. Westerners viewed Chinese laws as cruel and unreasonable, lacking fairness and integrity in enforcement (Willoughby 1957). Post the Opium War, more Westerners perceived a deteriorating society in China, marked by a corrupt, incompetent government, a dark judiciary, and moral decay. Their depiction of Chinese law was selective and one-sided. At that time, many Westerners residing in Guangzhou, China, had first-hand experience of the Chinese prison system because of the alienation of Chinese law, they tended to describe the prison life as dark and dreadful. These prisons were perceived as the epitome of cruelty and darkness in China's feudal society (Tian & Li, 2007).

Western perceptions of Chinese law have oscillated from one extreme to another. This shift in understanding is not without basis. The concept of legal Orientalism promotes the notion that the Western world represents the pinnacle of global civilized order. With the West symbolizing "progress" and "civilization", while the "East" embodies "backwardness" and "barbarism". After Macartney mission's visit to China, disparaging comments about China's image became widespread in Britain, leading to a prevalent discourse denouncing China's laws as barbaric and regressive.[1]

2.2.2 The Masked Ideologies

The translations and assessments of Chinese legal classics by Westerners hold a significant role in shaping the Western perception of China. Foreign images are never free and objective products, but the imaginary production of the self on the other, the creative fabrication of the other according to the needs of the self, as well as the projection of the image-maker's own desires (Jiang, 2014). This is true for how Westerners have viewed Chinese law and culture. The idealization of Chinese law in the West can be attributed to two key reasons. Firstly, the Chinese legal system historically held a position of significance globally. Its civilization, particularly during the Tang Dynasty, was influential, extending its legal principles to Southeast Asian nations. The self-contained nature of ancient China's economic growth further contributed to the uniqueness of its legal culture, unaffected by external legal traditions. Fueled by Confucian culture, the Chinese legal system developed independently, boasting a comprehensive legal structure on par with contemporary systems. Secondly, the allure of China's legal image aligns with the "utopian" yearning at the heart of European thought. Plato's "Republic" embodies the cherished desires of Westerners and often manifests in distant lands. There are striking similarities between accounts of China in Renaissance travel writings and the ideals of Utopia. From Marco Polo's narratives to Mendoza's historical works, the depiction of China gradually approached the Western ideal of a utopia—a place where justice and happiness for humanity were thought to be realized or approached.

The Marxist thinker Plekhanov (1962) observed that the prevailing system of thought in a specific era is a reflection of the social psyche of that time. It's shaped partly by the prevailing economic conditions and, significantly, by the overall societal framework founded upon that economic structure. In the mid-eighteenth century, the onset of the capitalist Industrial Revolution initiated a new phase in Western expansion, shifting from cooperative trade to imperialist colonialism, while China's authoritarianism extended its influence on all aspects of political rule, ideology, and culture. This regime of authority isolated China's legal culture from the world's legal culture, making it distinctly unique. However, this isolation also led to conservatism

[1] In the 1760s, the Industrial Revolution took place in Britain, and capitalism was on the rise. With the development of commodity economy, Britain urgently needed to open up new markets and vast raw material sources. Britain initiated Macartney's mission to China in 1793, with the purpose of opening Chinese markets and expanding foreign trade, which was not achieved due to the discomfort between China and Britain over etiquette, but Macartney gained insights into the Qing government's military capabilities during his travels in mainland China. Twenty years later, Britain dispatched another mission led by Amherst, yet it encountered similar disputes over etiquette and failed to achieve its objectives. It wasn't until 1860 that Britain commenced the Opium War, and opened the door to China with cannons, ultimately achieving its original goal.

and limited cultural exchanges, hampering China's social and cultural evolution. Different from China's culture of harmony, when the West achieved rapid economic development, it had to carry out its external expansion. Therefore, in order to find the right reasons for its own purposes, China became the "other" denied and excluded by Western ideology, a representation of backwardness in contrast to the West's perceived superiority. This portray positioned Europe at the center of the world. In his book Legal Orientalism, Teemu Ruskola demonstrated how over the course of the nineteenth century a diffuse set of European prejudices about Chinese law developed into an American ideology and practice of empire, entailing the extraterritorial application of American law in a very different, lawless Orient (Ruskola, 2016).

In general, a translator's motivations and goals are shaped by personal intentions, yet they are strongly influenced by the prevailing zeitgeist. As a result, their translation objectives are inevitably colored by the period's distinct characteristics (Zhu & Yuan, 2021). During Macartney's visit to China, financial support was provided by the British East India Company. Similarly, when Sir George Thomas Staunton translated *Ta Tsing Leu Lee*, he was employed by the same company, serving as a Guangzhou clerk. His translations mirrored the company's agenda in pursuing economic interests in China. At the linguistic level, Staunton opted for "metaphorical equivalence" rather than seeking alignment between seemingly disparate linguistic or cultural systems. This choice aimed to enable the British to swiftly understand and navigate Chinese laws, enhancing their capacity to wield this "discourse power". In doing so, he partially sacrificed the authenticity and precision of the translated text. Staunton reconstructed the original text by employing established Western legal concepts, styles, and terminology rather than a literal translation, intending to render it more compatible with the logical frameworks and perceptual sensibilities of Westerner. Consequently, this adaptation made it more accessible for the British to comprehend, paving the way for their advantage in subsequent legal conflicts between English and Chinese perspectives.[2]

In the eighteenth and nineteenth centuries, there was a prevailing concept of "oriental despotism" dominating European thought. Several prominent European thinkers, ranging from Montesquieu to Hegel, began to describe China as a civilization vastly different from, and far behind, Western European countries. Their perspectives were based on their own legal history, interpreting Chinese law through the lens of Western law. China was depicted as a negative example, embodying everything they sought to avoid or did not acknowledge in Western civilization. At that time, Western society, eager to define itself, sought identification through the contrast with an "other".

In the history of Western modernization and the thinking structure of modernity, a set of Western "civilization" has been used to assess the international behavior and legal rights of countries worldwide. "Civilization" is perceived as a stage of social

[2] Stanton's translation of *Ta Tsing Leu Lee* served not only to explore Chinese legal culture but also to safeguard the interests of merchants in China. This translation not only unveiled crucial insights about the functioning of Chinese societal laws to the Western world but also provided a significant pretext for the West to establish extraterritorial rights in China.

advancement contrasting with "barbarism", and a set of "civilization" discourse system was constructed by connecting it with racial distinctions, foreign policy, international law, and global order. Under this framework, the portrayal of Chinese law becomes the mirror image of the "other" in Western modern culture. It represents a complete body of knowledge on the "other" within Western modernity, a discourse that wields influence. When Western perception labels Chinese law as "barbaric" or "backward", this discourse permeates globally, transforming these perceptions into an epistemology that aligns with Western legal rationality rather than factual reality. Consequently, this discourse justifies China's exclusion from the rights and interests of international law.

2.3 Image Reconstruction Through Texts, Translators, and Strategic Selection

Since the late twentieth century, the rise of China is undoubtedly the most important event of this century. Not only has China emerged as a significant political and economic power, but also aims to showcase its cultural richness and diversity worldwide. One crucial task in the endeavor involves retranslating ancient Chinese legal classics, which carries the essence of Chinese civilization. This effort is aimed at offering the world a more comprehensive and accurate understanding of the traditions and cultural heritage of the Chinese people.

2.3.1 Text Selection

"Classics refer to significant books and documents written throughout history that have been passed down through generations (Zhao, 2014)". The selection of the original text to be translated is the primary problem that all translators have to face, and the translation of classics is no exception. In China's vast history, ancient legal classics are abundant and divers. Legal culture operates on two levels: one is institutional, including legal norms and systems, and the other involves conceptual aspects like legal doctrines, psychology, and customs (Liang, 1992). Similarly, legal classics also have two levels of content composition, one is of legal system and code, and the other is of legal thought and doctrine. Records show around 160 types of codes, ranging from the *Nine Chapter Law* to *Ta Tsing Leu Lee* (Hou et al., 1997). Different dynasties witnessed various supplementary legal forms. For example, during different periods like pre-Qin to Ming, Qing, different legal forms emerged such as Qin for the Lv (law), different forms of orders and decrees named Ming, Zhi and Zhao, Shi (provisions and procedures concerning trial principles and investigation, inquest, trial and sealing of cases), legal questions and answers, and Ting Xing Shi (the court action that refers to the established rule or old rule), and other supplementary forms to law and orders named Cheng and Ke (课); Han for the Lv, Ling, and supplementary forms of Ke (科), Pin, Bi; Jin for the Lv, Ling, Gu Shi (a form of invoking former practices); Sui and Tang for the Lv, Ling, Ge, Shi; Song in addition emphasized Bian Chi (editing rescripts), Duan Li (precedent case), and Zhi Hui (commands). The Yuan Dynasty stressed Tiao (rules) and Duan Li; Ming and Qing Dynasties highlighted the compilation of cases, Yu Zhi (decrees), Gao, proclamations, local regulations, village rules and covenants (Yang, 2002). However, many historical forms of law haven't been fully preserved or transmitted due to various historical reasons. Additionally, the feudal dynasties in China were unified multi-ethnic states with the Huaxia people as the main body. Although the Han people played a major role in the creation of the Chinese legal system, many ethnic minorities also made their own contributions, and brilliant achievements were made in ethnic legislation. Notable achievements in national legislation, especially during the Qing Dynasty, such as the *Mongolia Law*, *Tibet Law*, *Uygur Region Administration Policy*, represent invaluable additions to the rich wisdom of the Chinese legal system.

In essence, the realm of Chinese legal classics is expansive, encompassing numerous books. While translating all of them into foreign languages for global Spreading is an admirable aspiration, it's an extensive undertaking that cannot be swiftly accomplished. Therefore, it's vital to prioritize the selection of classics that best encapsulate Chinese legal culture and project an accurate image of China for translation. In the early stages of translating Chinese legal classics, as most translators were foreigners, they held the authority to choose texts for translation. Despite four significant works being fully translated abroad, namely the *Ta Tsing Leu Lee*, *Collected Cases of Injustice Rectified*, *T'ang Code*, and *Criminal Law of the Ming Dynasty*, which greatly aided in popularizing legal classics and offering foreign readers, scholars, and sinologists valuable insights into the comprehensive Chinese legal system, the selection process was sometimes swayed by translators' ideologies, translation motives, personal preference, and occasionally colonial intentions. Consequently, certain texts chosen may not authentically represent the profound wisdom of Chinese law or accurately mirror China's genuine image.

2.3.2 Translator Selection

French postmodern scholar Foucault once stated, "Discourse is power", signifying that those who possess power and knowledge shape history. The construction of the legal image is fundamentally a system of discourse composed of knowledge, ideas, concepts, and values. Over time, the portrayal of China's legal image has been largely influenced by the West, where developed countries serve as both primary creators of global legal discourse and controllers of channels through which legal concepts are disseminated. The hegemony formed by manipulating content and Spreading methods has effectively established the dominance of Western legal discourse (Hu & Dong, 2020a, 2020b). The way and path of Chinese legal image communication in the nineteenth century has given us a full Enlightenment: correcting historical misinterpretations in the "othering" of China's legal image is a comprehensive endeavor. Translation and Spreading hold significant historical missions and contemporary value. However, translating ancient Chinese law encounters numerous challenges due to cultural disparities between Chinese and Western languages. Sir George Thomas Staunton (2015) despite his efforts, acknowledged the complexities in translating the text due to its obscure language and intricate structure. Publications from that era, including newspapers and magazines, often contained biases and misconceptions in their portrayal of Chinese law. For instance, in *Chinese Repository*, the term "Yi Mu (夷目)", used to refer to a foreign leader in an official order, was inaccurately translated as "the barbarian eye", for the single character "夷" means "foreigner" and "目" means "eye" in English. Moreover, in reviewing the Records of the Three Kingdoms, there were instances where the author confused it with *The Romance of the Three Kingdoms* (Li, 2015a, 2015b). Such issues stemmed from inherent limitations in the knowledge, perspectives, language, cultural disparities, and ideologies of editors and authors. The translation and Spreading of "Chinese knowledge" by Westerners, particularly the cultural terminology with Chinese characteristics, tend to be misinterpreted. These limitations significantly impact the representation of China's legal image, highlighting the drawbacks in shaping the "other" in the portrayal of Chinese law.

To promote the "going out" of Chinese legal discourse in the new era, it is necessary to emancipate the mind and establish the concept of international legal translation talent (Dong 2018). The translation of legal classics should adhere to the concept of self-orientation, bring together and rely on foreign sinologists, jurists, and translators engaged in Chinese-foreign translation work. Such collaboration aims to delve into the essence of traditional Chinese legal culture, spotlighting its unique value and concepts within the international community. Concurrently, it is necessary to reinforce partnerships with leading international translation institutions and professional legal translation organizations, establish specialized institutes for high-end legal translation that embody distinctive Chinese traits, and focus on training and continuous education for high-level legal translators, including overseas sinologists, jurists, and translators, so as to improve their understanding of China's socio-cultural landscape, legal framework, and proficiency in both Chinese and foreign language, address challenges encountered in cross-cultural exchanges and bilingual translations, and thus create a collaborative platform where Chinese and foreign legal translation experts complement each other's strengths, share resources, and work closely together. This expanded collaboration fosters a comprehensive and robust network of high-level "Chinese-foreign" legal translation professionals, laying a solid foundation for advancing China's legal translation and enhancing its global legal image.

2.3.3 Translation Strategy Selection

Given the distinctions between Chinese and Western languages, especially in their legal cultural contexts, merely choosing legal classics and translators isn't enough to ensure the successful transmission of Chinese legal culture through translations. The pivotal aspect lies in the strategic decisions made during the translation process, aiming to construct an impartial and genuine representation of Chinese law.

The German theologian and philosopher Friedrich Schleiermacher, in his 1813 treatise "On the Different Methods of Translating", outlined two methods of translation: Either the translator leaves the writer alone as much as possible and allows the reader to approach the writer, or he leaves the reader alone as much as possible and let the author get closer to the reader, which are commonly known as "author-centered" and "reader-centered". Later, Lawrence Venuti, a translator, proposed "domestication translation" and "foreignization translation" on this basis. In the history of translating legal classics, foreign translators often lean toward "domestication" strategy. For instance, while translating the *Ta Tsing Leu Lee*, Sir George Thomas Staunton completely interprets and replaces certain Chinese legal names and terms with Western legal terms (Hu & Dong, 2021). Foreign translators tend to interpret Chinese classics based on their familiar cultural and worldview contexts. Their translations conform to Western language norms, making them more easily comprehensible to Western reader, essentially presenting "transparent" translations. The primary goals behind such translations include introducing Chinese culture to the West, satiating Western reader's curiosity, and serving the colonial agendas seeking to understand China while constructing hegemony over discourse. These "domestication" translations effectively fulfill these objectives.

In fact, translation is seen as a means of cultural Spreading rather than cultural transplanting. When translating legal classics, the role of the translator extends beyond conveying the literal content of the original work; they become agents of civilization diffusion. The objective of translation lies in fostering people's comprehension and absorption of diverse civilizations, rather than domesticating foreign cultures. General Secretary Xi Jinping (2018) stressed that we should adhere to extensive consultation, joint contribution and shared benefits in global governance, steadily reform and improve the global governance system, and push all countries to jointly build a community with a shared future for humanity. In a sense, the translation executed using the domestication strategy remains part of the Western cultural system. As a result, interpretations of Chinese culture and its image within such translations often fail to transcend Western cultural boundaries and independently convey the essence of Chinese legal civilization.

The "foreignization" approach not only upholds the uniqueness of Chinese legal civilization but also facilitates Western readers in comprehending the intricacies of Chinese legal culture, promoting mutual appreciation and understanding between the two cultures. As translators convey information, their primary focus should be on preserving the authenticity of the content. They must stay true to the humanistic essence and subtle nuances of the original language. This involves responsibly presenting various aspects of Chinese legal culture accurately to Western audiences. Additionally, it's their duty to faithfully introduce and impart the cultural richness of the Chinese language to Western readers, considering the unfamiliar traits and distinct national sentiments embedded in the Chinese language. Sun Zhili (2002), a translation theorist, highlighted in an article that "foreignization" serves as an effective method to ensure accuracy in translation. He stressed that while language can be adapted, cultural aspects should remain unchanged. He suggested avoiding domestication unless absolutely necessary, emphasizing that cultural facsimile stands as the core principle of translation.

In summary, adopting the "foreignization" strategy in translating legal classics not only involves objectively and accurately representing the essence of Chinese law but also aims to convey the depth and richness of Chinese legal civilization to Western readers. Its significance goes beyond portraying the image of Chinese law; it involves transplanting the profound legal and cultural aspects of the Chinese language into another language. This approach facilitates the transmission of Chinese legal concepts to the West, promotes mutual appreciation between civilizations, widens the inclusivity of Western culture, and contributes to its enrichment. As society progresses in various aspects such as economics, culture, science, and technology, global cultures are diversifying. Different cultures are showing mutual respect, tolerance, and a willingness to absorb from one another. "Foreignization" translation, as an effective method for advancing cultural exchanges between nations, seems an inevitable trend that will continue to gain momentum.

2.4 Summary

In the history of legal exchanges between China and the West, Western sinologists have primarily led the translation of traditional Chinese law. Despite the profound heritage and unique charm of Chinese legal civilization, the Western translation discourse has shaped the image of Chinese law. Initially portrayed as a "utopia" and a "republic", it shifted over time to notions of "backwardness", "barbarism", and "cruelty" in modern times, filled with Western imaginations and prejudices. These descriptions were constructed to align with the needs of the Western cultural system itself. While significantly promoting Chinese legal culture globally, it's commonplace for translations to involve "misinterpretation", often serving Western cultural hegemony in a certain sense. The vastness and complexity of Chinese legal classics pose a challenge. In the contemporary era, it's crucial to reevaluate Chinese culture in the broader global context, reassess the influence and contemporary significance of ancient Chinese culture, and study the extraterritorial Spreading and impact of Chinese legal classics. Priority should be given to selecting classics that best represent Chinese legal culture and embody China's image. International cooperation is key. Collaboration among sinologists, jurists, and translators involved in Chinese and foreign translation work should be strengthened. Employing the foreignization translation strategy in translating legal classics can break free from the dual thinking of "East and West" and "modern and traditional" and help to construct an objective, authentic, and positive image of Chinese law while unveiling the global significance of Chinese legal culture.

References

Antoine, B. (1992). *Experience of the foreign: Culture and translation in romantic Germany*. State University of New York Press.

Barr, A. H. (2014). Cultural differences and translation strategies. *Literature and Art Newspaper*, August 20.

Dong, X., & Zhang, Y. (2021). Emphasizing the translation of legal classics and contributing to the revival of the Chinese legal system. *Chinese Social Sciences Today*, February 2.

Dong, X. (2021). The translation and introduction of ancient Chinese Legal Classics. *Guangming Daily*, May 22.

Dong, X. Legal translation contributes Chinese wisdom to global governance. *Chinese Social Sciences Today*, June 26.

Hou, W., Zhang, L., & Jia, G. (1997). *Journal of Northeast Normal University (Philosophy and Social Sciences), 03*, 57–61.

Hu, B., & Dong, X. (2020). From "being told by others": On the overseas publicity of China's legal image in the 19th century from the perspective of orientalism. *Law and Modernization* 06.

Hu, B., & Dong, X. (2020). Translation of legal classics helps construct cultural memory. *Chinese Social Sciences Today*, March 27.

Hu, B., & Dong, X. (2021). Is it cultural communication or cultural hegemony: An analysis of the cultural misleading in the first English Translation of *Ta Tsing Leu Lee*. *Chinese Culture Research, 02*, 163.

Jiang, Z. (2010). *Scratches on our minds American images of China*. People's Publishing House.

Jiang, Z. (2014). *The western mirror, the Eastern Image*, 6. Central Compilation & Translation Press.

Karen, T. (2004). *Recent American academic writings on traditional Chinese law*, 657. Gao, H., & He, W., Trans. Tsinghua University Press.

Li, X. (2015a). *Perception and reception: Western understanding of the 19th century Chinese legal system based on the Chinese repository, 58*. SDX Joint Publishing Company.

Li, X. (2015b). *Perception and reception: Western understanding of the 19th century Chinese legal system based on the Chinese repository, 56*. SDX Joint Publishing Company.

Liang, L. (1992). *Traditional Chinese legal culture and modernization of the legal system, 3*. China University of Political Science and Law Press.

Plekhanov. (1962). Selected Philosophical Works of Plekhanov (Volume III) (p. 195). Sanlian Bookstore.

Rainer, S., & John, B. (1992). *Theories of translation: An anthology of essays from Dryden to Derrida*. The University of Chicago.

Ruskola. (2016). *Legal orientalism*, 9. Wei, L., Trans. China University of Political Science and Law Press.

Sir, G., & Thomas, S. (2015). *Memoirs of the chief incidents of the public life of Sir George Thomas Staunton, Bart*, 219. Qu, W., Trans. Shanghai People's Press.

Sun, Z. (2002). China's literary translation: From domestication to foreignization. *Chinese Translators Journal*, 01.

Tian, T., & Li, Z. (2007). *Contact and confrontation: Chinese legal system in the eyes of westerners since 16th century, 102*. Peking University Press.

Willoughby. (1957). Privileges and Interests of Outsiders in China (p. 368). Translated by Wang Shaofang. Sanlian Bookstore.

Xi, J. (2018). *H.E. Xi Jinping, President of the People's Republic of China, at the 18th meeting of the council of heads of member states of the Shanghai Cooperation Organization.*

Xin, J. (2021). Resolute adherence to the path of socialist rule of law with Chinese characteristics and providing a strong guarantee of the rule of law for the comprehensive construction of a modernized socialist country. Qstheory. Retrieved August 13, 2021, from http://www.qstheory.cn/dukan/qs/2021-02/28/c_1127146541.htm

Yang, Y. (2002). An important area of misunderstanding in the study of the genealogy of Chinese law—doubts about "all laws were incorporated into one and there was no difference between civil and criminal laws." *Social Sciences in China, 06*, 78–94.

Zhao, C. (2014). *A study of English translation of Chinese cultural classics in the 19th century.* Nankai University.

Zhou, N. (2006). *The distant celestial empire: Western images of China (Volume 1), 54.* Peking University Press.

Zhu, Z., & Yuan, J. (2021). How the cultural values guiding sinologists' English translation of Chinese classics affect China's image in the Western countries. *Chinese Translators Journal* 02.

Chapter 3
Visual Analysis of the Domestic Studies of Chinese Legal Classics Spreading

Abstract Scholarly attention toward Chinese legal classics and their translations has notably increased due to initiatives like "introduce the Chinese culture abroad" and "tell China's stories well". The knowledge base of a research field is closely linked to the body of literature within that domain. Despite this interest, few articles have employed visual measurement tools to analyze research literature on translating legal classics comprehensively. To bridge this gap, this chapter uses Cite Space version 5.6 R5 as a research tool and extracts data from the China National Knowledge Infrastructure (CNKI), encompassing journals, doctoral and master's theses, conferences, and newspapers. The analysis aims to delve into several facets, including yearly publication volumes, primary authors, issuing institutions, highly cited literature, keyword co-occurrences, keyword time zones, keyword time zones, keyword clusters, and burst terms. By providing a comprehensive and objective overview, this study endeavors to accurately portray the fundamental characteristics, research trends, frontiers, and key themes in legal classics research in China from 1983 to 2021. The objective is to offer valuable insights and references to support future research endeavors centered on translating Chinese legal classics.

3.1 Data Sources and Research Methodology

The Contemporary Chinese Dictionary (2016) defines "classics" as "important documents that record ancient decrees and systems, generally referring to ancient books". In a narrow sense, legal classics encompass ancient codes and laws formulated or recognized by the state and enforced through state coercion, including formal codes and their various supplementary forms (Dong, 2021). Based on this definition, this study utilizes CNKI as the data source and employs the advanced search function. Initially, set the search conditions as the Term = "法律典籍(legal classics) /古代法律(ancient law) /中华法系(Chinese legal system)" containing "英译(English translation) /翻译(translation) /外译(C-E translation)". Then, focusing on specific titles of legal classics like "*Ta Tsing Leu Lee*", "*Collected Cases of Injustice Rectified*", "*The T'ang Code*", "*Criminal Law of the Ming Dynasty*", "*Xing-an-hui-lan (Conspectus*

X. Dong and Y. Luo, *The Legal Image of China in Chinese Legal Tradition*,
https://doi.org/10.1007/978-981-96-5797-1_3

of Penal Cases)", etc., coupled with "英译(English translation) /翻译(translation) / 外译(C-E translation)", for a comprehensive exploration of the field of legal classics translation research. After the search, 186 valid samples were obtained by excluding duplicates, non-English foreign language literature, translation manuscripts, literary works, and news reports. After converting the data in Cite Space, the Time Span was selected from 1983 to 2021, and the Time Slice was selected as 1 year, that is, the data of every 1 year was analyzed.

3.2 Basic Characteristics of the Study

In the upcoming section, we'll examine Chinese legal classic translation research based on four aspects: annual publication volume analysis, prolific authors analysis, publication institutions examination, and highly cited literature statistics.

3.2.1 Analysis of Annual Publication Volume

Figure 3.1 illustrates the trends in literature output related to the study of legal classic translation, divided into three distinct phases. The initial period (1983–2001) saw only 12 articles, mostly discussing historical events such as late Qing Dynasty law revisions and translation, British Ambassador Macartney's visit to China and other historical events. The establishment of the Institute for Chinese Ancient Legal Documents at China University of Political Science and Law in 1984 laid foundation for collecting and studying Chinese legal classics. During this phase, fewer documents focused specifically on the "translation of legal classics" theme, instead exploring broader literary, historical, and philosophical topics, including Confucianism, Buddhism, and Taoism classics.

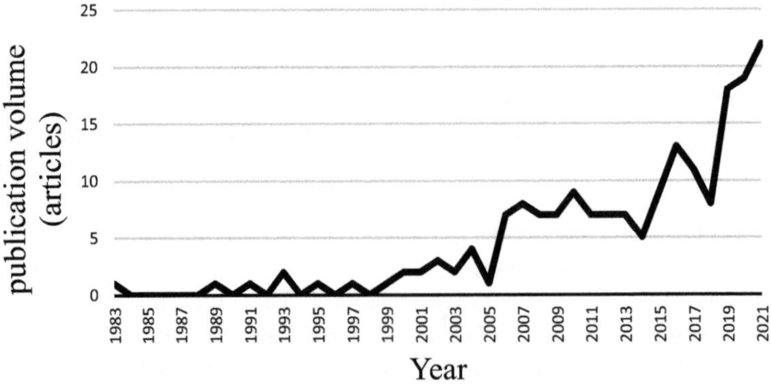

Fig. 3.1 Line graph of annual publications on the study of translation of legal classics (1983–2021)

The second phase (2022–2013) experienced a notable surge with 69 published articles. Researchers began highlighting representative works of the Chinese legal system such as *Ta Tsing Leu Lee*, *Collected Cases of Injustice Rectified*, *The T'ang Code*, and *Criminal Law of the Ming Dynasty*, gaining increased attention. Wang Jian's (2002) summary of Sir George Thomas Staunton's translation of the *Ta Tsing Leu Lee* marked the initiation of legal classics translation research. Another significant development was Liu Yingchun's (2008) focus on the *The T'ang Code* as a research corpus, beginning systematic studies in this area. This surge in publications was influenced by national policies, academic interest, and institutional support, aligning with China's "go global" strategy outlined in the 16th National Congress report (Jiang, 2002). The proposal of "Culture going global" as an important component of the "go global" strategy was put forward. In 2004, the Central Committee of the Communist Party of China (2004) issued a document supporting research projects that play a significant role in promoting the national spirit and preserving the national culture. In 2007, report to the Seventeenth National Congress of the Communist Party of China emphasized the need to have a comprehensive understanding of traditional Chinese culture and to strengthen international cultural exchanges (Hu, 2007). Many scholars have recognized that literary classics represent just a portion of the expansive Chinese cultural heritage, not its entirety. In 2005, Southwest University of Political Science and Law established the Legal Language, Culture, and Translation Research Center. Subsequently, in 2013, a project entitled "Comparative Research on the English Translation of *Ta Tsing Leu Lee*", led by Professor Xiong Demi, a member of the center, was approved as a National Social Science Foundation of China (NSSFC) Annual Program.

The third phase (2014–2021) demonstrated consistent growth, peaking in 2021. This increase was driven by government policies, widespread media coverage, and academic conference. The 19th National Congress emphasized the need to "tell China's stories well, present a true, multi-dimensional, and panoramic view of China (Xi, 2017)". In 2021, the Publicity Department of the Central Committee of the Communist Party of China and the Ministry of Justice of the People's Republic of China issued a document pointing that we should "focus on telling the story of China's rule of law well" and highlight "China's excellent traditional legal culture". Media outlets, including *People's Daily* and *Guangming Daily*, contributed by emphasizing the unique features, cultural heritage, and importance of the Chinese legal system, advocating for its global Spreading. The Specialized Committee on English Translation of Classics of Association for Comparative Studies of English and Chinese organized national seminars, engaging scholars in legal classics translation research and aligning their academic pursuits with national development objectives, thereby broadening horizons in this field.

3.2.2 Analysis of Prolific Authors

As depicted in Fig. 3.2, at present, the authors who have published more papers in the field of translation of legal classics in China include Dong Xiaobo, Xiong Demi, Qu Wensheng, He Qinhua, Hu Bo, and Zhang Yafang.

Translation studies of legal classics have formed two main research growth rings. The first is the research ring composed by Dong Xiaobo, Hu Bo, and Zhang Yafang. Their research not only analyzes the words, sentences, paragraphs, and chapters of the translated text, but also discusses the historical value, cultural exchange, and mutual learning of civilizations. The second is the research ring formed by Xiong Demi, whose research mainly scrutinizes English versions of Chinese legal classics from the perspective of translation comparison and translation criticism, and points out the pathway and practical implications for this field of study.

Qu Wensheng and He Qinhua merge linguistic forms with socio-historical contexts within translations and extend their research vision from the translation of legal classics to the historical field of Sino-foreign relations and exchanges. This specialized research necessitates interdisciplinary skills encompassing proficiency in ancient Chinese, foreign languages, translation studies, and legal expertise. As a result, prolific authors often possess interdisciplinary backgrounds, typically rooted in law and translation studies or affiliated with political and legal universities. While

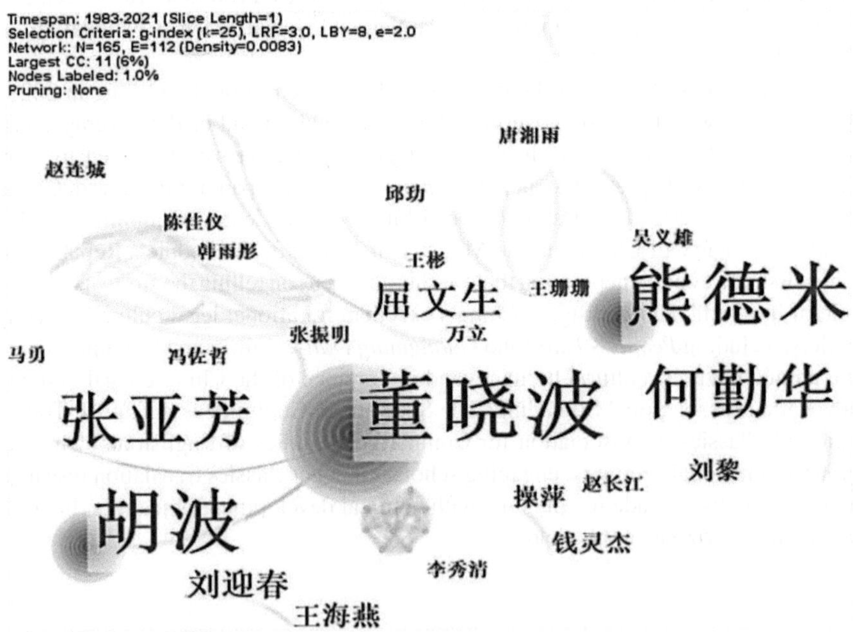

Fig. 3.2 the Co-occurrence map of authors in the translation studies of legal classics

individual publications predominate, collaborate efforts among researchers are also evident in this domain.

3.2.3 *Analysis of Publishing Institutions*

In Fig. 3.3, the main research institutions focused on translating legal classics are predominantly situated within the foreign language departments of normal universities and colleges specialized in political science and law. Notable establishments include Nanjing Normal University, Southwest University of Political Science and Law, Peking University, Hangzhou Normal University, Zhejiang Gongshang University, East China University of Political Science and Law. Among these, Nanjing Normal University and Southwest University of Political Science and Law formed two research rings. Furthermore, the History Research in China Academy of Social Sciences has made significant contributions to the exploration of translating legal classics.

This concentration of research institutions has evolved for two main reasons. Firstly, the translation of legal classics is intricately linked with linguistics and translation studies, thus assigning a central role to the School of Foreign Languages. Secondly, the study of translating legal classics intersects with disciplines such as jurisprudence and legal history, prompting research initiatives within historical research institutes and universities. These academic faculties and institutions boast a robust research foundation and serve as primary hubs for investigating the translation of lcgal classics.

Fig. 3.3 the Co-occurrence map of research institutions for translation of legal classics translation

3.2.4 *Analysis of Highly Cited Literature*

According to Table 3.1, Qu Wensheng, Hou Yi, Wang Bin, Liu Yingchun, Wang Haiyan, Qiu Le, and Zhao Changjiang are the main cited authors. Their early publications garnered higher citations, which laid a strong foundation for later research. Qu Wensheng (2010) analyzes Morrison's *Wuche yunfu* (a bilingual dictionary of Chinese and English) from the aspects of criminal, civil and commercial matters, litigation system, basic legal words, etc., and summarizes Morrison's translation strategy as prioritizing maintenance while supplementing with replacements. Hou Yi (2009) introduces the origin and purpose of Sir George Thomas Staunton's translation of the *Ta Tsing Leu Lee* and points out that his English version announces the end of an era and the beginning of a new one, signifying the spread of Western learning and legal principles toward the East.

A thorough review of these scholar's articles reveals that they either made a groundbreaking, macroscopic, and overview introduction to legal classics translation, or made a case analysis and objective evaluation of a translation, or analyzed the translation background, purpose, strategy, communication, and influence from the perspectives of historical contexts, translation style, and social value.

3.3 Panoramic Display of Research Hotspots

Examining keyword co-occurrence, keyword clustering, and emerging words offers a comprehensive insight in to the focus of legal translation research.

3.3.1 *Analysis of Keyword Co-Occurrence*

As illustrated in Fig. 3.4, the graph generates 339 nodes interconnected by 671 edges, with a density of 0.0117. The keywords that appear more frequently are: Sir George Thomas Staunton (斯当东/小斯当东), the English Translation of *Ta Tsing Leu Lee* (《大清律例》/大清律例/《大清律例》英译本), translation, Macartney (马戛尔尼), Thomas (托马斯), Emperor Qianlong (乾隆皇帝/乾隆帝), translation strategy (翻译策略), *Collected Cases of Injustice Rectified* (《洗冤集录》), and Sino-British relations (中英关系).

To present the primary areas of focus in legal classics translation research more distinctly, the top 10 keywords with both high frequency and centrality were extracted using Cite Space's Export function (see Table 3.2).

In Table 3.2, the top 4 keywords—"*Ta Tsing Leu Lee*", "translation", "Sir George Thomas Staunton", and "Macartney"—consistently hold high ranks in both centrality and word frequency. The English translation of *Ta Tsing Leu Lee* signifies the initial

Table 3.1 Statistics of highly cited literature in the translation studies of Chinese legal classics

Number	Citation counts	Author	Article title	Journal title (year/ issue)
1	28	Qu Wensheng (屈文生)	Early English Translations of Chinese Legal Term: A Study Based on Robert Morrison's Wuche yunfu	Historical Research (2010/05)
2	27	Hou Yi (侯毅)	The First European Attempt at Translating a Complete Chinese Legal Classic: Stanton and the Translation of the *Ta Tsing Leu Lee*	Historical Archives (2009/04)
3	16	Wang Bin (王彬)	Thick·Dealienation·Omission: Filtering Traditional Chinese Medicine Culture in the Translation of *Collected Cases of Injustice Rectified*	Chinese Translators Journal (2017/05)
3	16	Liu Yingchun, Wang Haiyan (刘迎春，王海燕)	Applying the Principle of Consistency to the English Translation of Ancient Chinese Legal Text – A Critique of Johnson's Translation of the *Tang Code*	Foreign Languages and Their Teaching (2018/12)
4	13	Liu Yingchun, Wang Haiyan (刘迎春，王海燕)	Compensation in the English Translation of Ancient Chinese Legal Texts	Foreign Languages in China (2009/06)
5	11	Qiu Le (邱玏)	A Brief Review of the First English Translation of *The His Yüan Lu, or Instructions to Coroners*	Chinese Journal of Integrated Traditional and Western Medicine(2011/04)
5	11	Liu Yingchun (刘迎春)	An Intertextual Approach to Translating Ancient Chinese Legal Texts into English – A Case Study of *The Tang Code*	PhD thesis, Soochow University, (2008/03)
6	10	Qu Wensheng, Wan Li (屈文生，万立)	What Has Motivated English Translation of the Codes of Pre-modern Chinese Dynasties	Chinese Translators Journal (2019/01)
7	9	Zhao Changjiang (赵长江)	The First Direct Dialogue in the History of Chinese and British Cultural Communication – Studies on the English Version of *Ta Tsing Leu Lee*	Journal of Xi'an International Studies University (2012/03)

(continued)

Table 3.1 (continued)

Number	Citation counts	Author	Article title	Journal title (year/issue)
8	7	Zhao Changjiang (赵长江)	The Duality of Legal Text Translation: Cultural Exchange and Information Leakage – A Case Study of the 1810 English Translation of *Ta Tsing Leu Lee*	Minority Translators Journal (2012/03)
9	6	Liu Yingchun, Wang Haiyan (刘迎春，王海燕)	Translation: The Path of Ancient Chinese Legal Culture towards the World	Foreign Language Education (2013/06)

Fig. 3.4 The co-occurrence map of keywords in the study of legal classics translation

introduction of the Chinese legal code to the Western world, offering a comprehensive grasp of the traditional Chinese legal system (Wang 2001). As a result, considerable attention is directed toward both the translated work and its translator, Sir George Thomas Staunton. The term "Macartney" refers to a British mission to the Qing Dynasty in 1791, where both Stanton's father and son were involved—the elder Stanton served as Macartney's aide-de-camp, while the younger Stanton trained in Chinese translation. These prominent keywords indicate that earlier comprehensive translations significantly influence translation research. Additionally, the background, experiences, and actions of the translator attract substantial attention in the study of translating legal classics. Beyond the top four keywords, discrepancies exist between the centrality and frequency of terms like "Thomas", "Emperor Qianlong",

Table 3.2 Centrality and frequency of keywords in the study of legal classics translation

Number	Citation counts	Author	Article title	Journal title (year/issue)
1	28	Qu Wensheng (屈文生)	Early English Translations of Chinese Legal Term: A Study Based on Robert Morrison's Wuche yunfu	Historical Research (2010/05)
2	27	Hou Yi (侯毅)	The First European Attempt at Translating a Complete Chinese Legal Classic: Stanton and the Translation of the *Ta Tsing Leu Lee*	Historical Archives (2009/04)
3	16	Wang Bin (王彬)	Thick·Dealienation·Omission: Filtering Traditional Chinese Medicine Culture in the Translation of *Collected Cases of Injustice Rectified*	Chinese Translators Journal (2017/05)
3	16	Liu Yingchun, Wang Haiyan (刘迎春，王海燕)	Applying the Principle of Consistency to the English Translation of Ancient Chinese Legal Text – A Critique of Johnson's Translation of the *Tang Code*	Foreign Languages and Their Teaching (2018/12)
4	13	Liu Yingchun, Wang Haiyan (刘迎春,, 王海燕)	Compensation in the English Translation of Ancient Chinese Legal Texts	Foreign Languages in China (2009/06)
5	11	Qiu Le (邱玏)	A Brief Review of the First English Translation of *The His Yüan Lu, or Instructions to Coroners*	Chinese Journal of Integrated Traditional and Western Medicine (2011/04)
5	11	Liu Yingchun (刘迎春)	An Intertextual Approach to Translating Ancient Chinese Legal Texts into English – A Case Study of *The Tang Code*	PhD thesis, Soochow University, (2008/03)
6	10	Qu Wensheng, Wan Li (屈文生，万立)	What Has Motivated English Translation of the Codes of Pre-modern Chinese Dynasties	Chinese Translators Journal (2019/01)
7	9	Zhao Changjiang (赵长江)	The First Direct Dialogue in the History of Chinese and British Cultural Communication – Studies on the English Version of *Ta Tsing Leu Lee*	Journal of Xi'an International Studies University (2012/03)

(continued)

Table 3.2 (continued)

Number	Citation counts	Author	Article title	Journal title (year/issue)
8	7	Zhao Changjiang (赵长江)	The Duality of Legal Text Translation: Cultural Exchange and Information Leakage – A Case Study of the 1810 English Translation of *Ta Tsing Leu Lee*	Minority Translators Journal (2012/03)
9	6	Liu Yingchun, Wang Haiyan (刘迎春，王海燕)	Translation: The Path of Ancient Chinese Legal Culture towards the World	Foreign Language Education (2013/06)

"Sino-British relations", and "Amherst". Although these words appear frequently, their centrality is less pronounced. Conversely, terms such as "translation of classics" and "ancient law" exhibit strong centrality despite their lower frequency. Overall, the research predominantly revolves around three key aspects of "Ta Tsing Leu Lee", "Sir George Thomas Staunton", and "translation".

3.3.2 Analysis of Keyword Cluster

As illustrated in Fig. 3.5, the top 8 clusters identified are: translation, legal translation, Macartney, Sir Thomas Francis Wade, Ta Tsing Leu Lee, Chinese legal image, and expression.

According to the clustering results, combined with the above analysis of high centrality and high-frequency keywords, the research on translation of legal classics mainly focuses on the following topics.

Research on Translators

The act of translation by translators relies on their comprehension, forming a continuous merging of the translator's perspective with that of the original text. Throughout this process, elements such as the translator's background, identity, and experiences significantly shape the chosen translation strategies. Some scholars concentrate their focus on translators, particularly emphasizing Sir George Thomas Staunton, an important figure in modern Sino-British relations. Cao Ping and Qian Lingjie (2020) provide an impartial assessment of Sir George Thomas Staunton, viewing his work through the lens of the translator's habitus theory. They suggest that within the academic habitus, Staunton prioritizes practicality but overlooks the readability and accuracy of the translated text due to political habitus. Zhao Changjiang (2012) suggests that Stanton's translation of *Ta Tsing Leu Lee* results from a blend of accidental and inevitable, subjective, and objective factors. Qu Wensheng and Wan Li (2019) examine four translators—Sir George Thomas Staunton, William C. Jones, Zhuang Weisi, and Jiang Yonglin, and point out their varying motives in translating

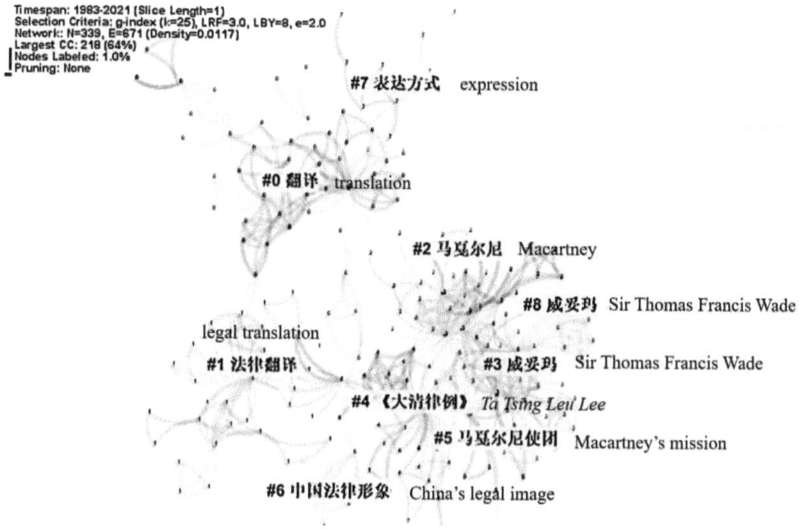

Fig. 3.5 Clustering map of keywords in the study of legal classics translation

the three codes: Stanton's aim was to gain an advantage in Anglo-Chinese trade; William C. Jones sought to correct and showcase the original code; Zhuang Weisi's translation of *The T'ang Code* was for the study of Chinese law; Jiang Yonglin translated *Criminal Law of the Ming Dynasty* to fill gaps in English translations of China's feudal codes. These descriptive translation studies, which focus on the behavior of translators, reveal patterns in their conduct: Stanton, juggling multiple identities such as tea merchant, emissary, China expert, diplomat, and member of parliament, was influenced by the "invisible hand" of social ideology; William C. Jones, a researcher of Chinese law, complements the study of Chinese and comparative jurisprudence through his translation of *Ta Tsing Leu Lee;* Zhuang Weisi, an American sinologist, balances in-depth legal study with accessible translation, intriguing readers in Chinese culture and philosophy; Jiang Yonglin, building upon the groundwork laid by previous translators and drawing from Chinese scholar's deep understanding of Chinese culture, advances the essence of legal translations into the era of academic intercultural exchange.

Research on Translation Strategies and Techniques

The focus of research on translation strategies and techniques revolves around the translation strategies of legal terms and culture-loaded words in legal classics. Kan Jian (2016) provides an overview of Stanton's English translation strategies, which include foreignization, domestication, footnotes, and transliteration. Li Yiyun and Wu Yulian (2021) argue that translation by Herbert Allen Giles and Brian E. McKnight of the *Collected Cases of Injustice Rectified* involve strategies like combining domestication and foreignization, deepening and superficialization. Li Hongkun (2013), using culturally loaded words from *The T'ang Code*, proposes specific translation strategies like amplification, annotation, transliteration, transliteration with annotation, literal translation with annotation, and explanation translation. These refined strategies enrich the "toolkit" for translating legal classics. Besides examining a translator's in translation behavior, researchers have also explored their extratranslational behavior, that is, the sociolinguistic behavior of altering the original text's meaning with strategies such as deviation, variation, and transliteration (Zhou, 2014). According to Hu Bo and Dong Xiaobo (2021), Stanton employed omission translation to avoid or filter certain legal terms carrying traditional Chinese cultural information. Stanton replaced Chinese legal terms with concepts from the common law system using the matching meanings method and adjusts the structure of *Ta Tsing Leu Lee* using flexible translation methods. This kind of analysis, characterized by logic, thinking and analysis, highlights the problem consciousness and promotes the standardization process of ancient legal translation.

Research on Translation and Spreading of Legal Classics

It primarily focuses on how translated texts are interpreted, received, and disseminated in various cultural contexts. Wang Hao (2018) thoroughly examines the trajectory of translating and exporting legal classics, highlighting the significance of works like *Collected Cases of Injustice Rectified* and *Ta Tsing Leu Lee*, highly valued in Western circle. Wang advocates for a consistent and structured export of legal classics to bolster the global influence of Chinese legal culture. Dong Xiaobo and Zhang Yafang (2021) highlight that translations of legal classics by Western scholars often present a biased and stereotypical portrayal of traditional Chinese legal culture abroad. They stress the necessity of proactive measures to restore an authentic representation of these legal codes. Hu Bo and Dong Xiaobo (2021) argue that intentional alterations in Stanton's translations represent a form of cultural dominance and power manipulation. Beneath this discourse lies an underlying intention to influence Chinese legal life through the Spreading of translated texts. It can be seen that the complex power structure and cultural mechanisms shaped in the multi-dimensional interaction of "translator translating, translation Spreading, reader acceptance" has urged researchers to explore these dynamics further through sociology, history, and culturology research paths.

Research on Translation Comparison and Translation Criticism

Translation comparison mainly describes and analyzes the similarities and differences between two or more translation, while translation criticism assesses translated texts based on the original content (Yang, 2009). Because there are relatively few legal classics with multiple translations, the main focus of translation comparison and criticism lies on the English translation of *Ta Tsing Leu Lee*. Xiong Demi (2018) analyzed the close relationship between law and culture, the shared traits and unique aspects of Eastern and Western legal cultures, as well as the commonness and individuality of English and Chinese legal languages, and call on experts and scholars to scrutinize and oversee the quality of existing translations, so as to improve the effect of disseminating legal classics abroad. Zhang Li (2018), through a comparison of Stanton's and William's translations, categorizes Stanton's translation as instrumental and William's as documentary. By analyzing linguistic aspects within both translations of *Ta Tsing Leu Lee*, Zhang identifies and evaluates mistakes, deviations, and other shortcomings in the translation process. This analysis aims to rectify and outline general principles, ultimately aiming to improve translation quality and standardize translation practices in the field of legal classics.

3.3.3 Analysis of Burst Terms

The analysis of burst terms can present the research frontiers of this field in different time periods. Illustrated in Fig. 3.6, burst terms can be divided into three categories.

The fist category is mainly characters, such as "Stanton (斯当东)", "Morrison (马礼逊)", and "Protestant missionary (新教传教士)". Stanton was the initial translator of *Ta Tsing Leu Lee*, and the Strength of this term is 0.9006. Although Morrison didn't directly translate Chinese legal classics, his work in *A Dictionary of the Chinese Language* contained numerous legal terms, offering valuable historical insights into the Chinese legal system. The term "Protestant missionary" signified a group arrived in China for missionary work, cultural immersion, and scholarly study, with a higher Strength rating of 1.274. The second category includes terms like "*Ta Tsing Leu Lee* (大清律例)" and "Sino-British relation (中英关系)", which means scholars are no

Top 10 Keywords with the Strongest Citation Bursts

Keywords		Year	Strength	Begin	End	1983—2021
Staunton	斯当东	1983	0.9006	1995	1996	
Morrison	马礼逊	1983	1.2702	2000	2001	
Protestant missionary	新教传教士	1983	1.274	2005	2006	
Ta Tsing Leu Lee	《大清律例》	1983	0.9308	2006	2007	
Sino-British relations	中英关系	1983	1.3721	2008	2010	
Amherst	阿美士德	1983	2.0741	2008	2010	
Macartney's mission	马戛尔尼使团	1983	1.646	2008	2010	
ancient laws	古代法律	1983	1.1066	2008	2009	
legal translation	法律翻译	1983	1.2144	2012	2013	
Tiansheng Statues	天圣令	1983	0.963	2013	2014	

Fig. 3.6 Map of burst terms in translation studies of legal classics (Note: "Keywords" refers to burst terms, "Year" indicates the time when the term first appeared, "Strength" refers to the intensity of burst terms, "Begin" and "End" respectively refer to the time when a term becomes burstness or not, and the thick line beneath the time period refers to the term's duration.)

longer limited to questions like "who translated" or "who disseminated", but begin to explore more specific issues of the quality of translations and their influence on Sino-British relations. Notably, "Amherst (阿美士德)" emerges with the highest Strength of 2.0741, followed by "Macartney's mission (马戛尔尼使团)" at 1.646. Macartney and Amherst served as key British ambassadors in China during that period. Stanton notably participated in both Macartney's and Amherst's missions, distinguishing him as the sole British representative. The third category encompasses terms like "ancient laws (古代法律)", "legal translations (法律翻译)", and "Tiansheng Statues (天圣令)". Scholars have redirected their focus toward the study of legal translations. The emergence of "Tiansheng Statues (天圣令)", which means scholars have redirected their focus toward the study of legal translations. The emergence of "Tiansheng Statues" as a burst term is primarily attributed to the initiation of a reading class by the History Research in China Academy of Social Sciences (CASS) on the Tiansheng Statues in 2009.

3.4 Conclusions and Research Outlook

The translation of legal classics represents a significant challenge due to the intricate historical and cultural nuances embedded within these texts. This section will explore the current state of research in this field, highlighting limitations and identifying areas for future exploration.

3.4.1 Research Conclusions

After reviewing 186-related literature pieces on legal classics translation within the CNKI, various issues have surfaced the realm of legal classics translation research.

First, the limited research outcomes primarily stem from the lack of available translated legal classics for study. Despite China's efforts through major projects like the "Library of Chinese Classics", the "China Book International", and the "Chinese Academic Translation" initiatives to globally introduce cultural classics, actual translations of legal classics are absent. Consequently, research efforts remain confined to analyzing existing translations, restricting their impact to a small audience, and limiting their influence. Furthermore, the majority of researchers come from political and law universities, with fewer participants from institutions focusing on foreign languages. The absence of a collaborative research team encompassing political and law universities, foreign language institutions, and normal universities results in fragmented and homogeneous research outcomes, making it difficult to form a sustained and stable research system.

Second, research endeavors need to deepen both in depth and breadth. In terms of depth, while the primary focus remains on the English translation of the *Ta Tsing Leu Lee*, abridged translations like the condensed translation by George Jamieson and

James William Jamieson published in *China Review*, and Félix's French translation based on the English version, have not garnered in adequate attention. Furthermore, despite being published later, Jiang Yonglin's translation of *Criminal Law of the Ming Dynasty* offers a scholarly and profound translation strategy, yet it remains an underexplored source of research material deserving further investigation due to its classical attributes. Concerning breadth, individual research on classics and their translations has persisted for years, yet efforts toward integration or a synthesized view are lacking (Wang, 2017). Additionally, certain disciplines such as sociology, communication, and overseas sinology, crucial for comprehensive research, have been somewhat absent, hindering a more holistic approach to this study.

Third, the lack of empirical research presents a significant challenge. When it comes to translation research, methods encompass both theoretical approaches like experience summarization and inductive thinking, as well as empirical methods such as corpora and experimental research techniques (Yang, 2009). Legal classics, mainly existing in printed collections, carry a profound historical and humanistic essence. However, several existing translations are published overseas and stored in international libraries, complicating research efforts. Consequently, ongoing research predominantly revolves around textual analysis and theoretical discussions. Yet, establishing a comprehensive research framework for translating legal classics requires empirical studies and a fusion of qualitative and quantitative methodologies. Urgently, there's a need to establish relevant corpora and the glossary. These resources will not only quantitatively portray translator styles and translation patterns but also visually demonstrate changes in the translations of ancient legal terms, providing guidance for translation practices.

3.4.2 Research Outlook

Based on the outcomes of the preceding research, future studies on legal classics translation should emphasize the following aspects:

Research on the Planning of Translation of Legal Classics

Dong Xiaobo and Hu Bo (2018) proposed a comprehensive framework for translation planning, spanning national, industry, academic, and media domains. Drawing on this framework, there's a necessity to establish a government-led translation planning structure specifically focused on translating legal classics. To initiate this, experts and scholars are called upon to form a translation and research team within specialized centers or institutes to create a roadmap for translating legal classics. On the one hand, it corrects and retranslates the intentional rewriting in Western translations, and on the other hand, it makes clear the selection criteria to select, compile, and fully translate more classics highlighting excellent traditional legal culture. This approach, anchored in a rich and diverse corpus, aims to enhance the capacity for translating legal classics and advance the outcomes of legal classics translation research.

Research on the Paratexts of Translation of Legal Classics
Paratext plays a crucial role in enhancing, explaining, refining, and validating the original text of the translation (Pellatt V 2013). In several published translations, translators have utilized forewords, acknowledgments, introductions, and other paratext to express the diverse perspective of Chinese law and history, providing both popular and scholarly commentary or reproducing the context of disseminating traditional Chinese legal culture abroad. Consequently, they supplement and broaden essential information for readers, catering to different levels of engagement with the translations. By employing methods such as close textual analysis and comparison, one can better interpret the profound meaning of paratext as an independent literary form. This approach aids in understanding the translation's intention behind the translation and discerning the distinct roles of paratext in shaping the relationship between the translator and the reader.

Research on the Standardization of English Translation of Ancient Legal Terms
Translating ancient legal terms into English presents significant challenges for translators. It requires a deep grasp of intricate legal vocabulary, comprehension of the underlying legal culture, and consideration of the target readers' understanding. Western translators are not only influenced by their own religious, ideological, cultural backgrounds, readers, and reception environment, but also by broader Sino-Western cultural contexts. Consequently, their English translation may sometimes contain subtle biases or obscured intentions. A more comprehensive validation of existing translations is crucial. This process should carefully address linguistic and cultural disparities between the source and target languages. It involves making necessary adjustments, adeptly converting internal discourse to external discourse (Zhao, 2021), ensuring faithful conceptual interpretation, and maintaining consistency in linguistic symbols. These refinements aim to establish a more rational and standardized set of "revamped" ancient legal terminologies. Additionally, delving into a unified and standardized system for legal terminology deserves further investigation.

Translation and Research on Traditional Legal Culture
The ancient legal classics contain profound insights from our Chinese forebears on society, law, culture, and philosophy, offering invaluable wisdom. Principles such as "prudent punishment", "respecting the old and caring for the young", "mitigated punishments for the disabled or invalid criminals", "making judgement based on law", and so on all reflect the wisdom ingrained in our traditional legal culture. To thoroughly explore these traditions, on the one hand, it's crucial to explore, inherit, and translate traditional legal culture under the new era and new historical context, such as the concept of "non-litigation (*Wu Song*)" from the *Sung Criminal Code* and "separate proceedings between the criminal and the people (*Xing Min Fen Su*)" in the Yuan Dynasty Constitution; on the other hand, attention should be directed to the "introduction" after "translation". This entails considering the cultural and social aspects of terms, evaluating their audience, channels, and impact stemming

from existing translation and introduction practices. By distilling valuable experiences and drawing inspiration, identifying instances where the essence of tradition legal culture aligns with global acceptance in the modern era becomes pivotal. Effectively introducing traditional legal culture into the international arena is crucial for enhancing its visibility and influence.

Research on the Translators of Legal Classics

Apart from Stanton, there are other translators worth exploring. For instance, Jiang Yonglin was recommended to Harvard Law School by Zhuang Weisi, the translator of *The T'ang Code*, and also supported William C. Jones in translating *Ta Tsing Leu Lee*. From the perspective of academic pedigree, he belongs to the numerous translators who have ventured beyond their homeland while preserving their roots. With a comprehensive grasp of the original text, Jiang Yonglin supplemented cultural nuances to the code to meet the readers' needs, thus facilitating cultural dialogue through translation. From the perspective of translation sociology, there is a need to further investigate the cultural identity of these translators and the translated texts. This can be done by employing translation theories such as multiculturalism and critical theories of translator behavior. Additionally, it can benefit from relevant theories in comparative literature, narrative, sociology, and reception aesthetics.

Interdisciplinary Research on Translation of Legal Classics

The research on translating legal classics greatly benefits from interdisciplinary approaches. To delve into the core ideas within legal classics, invigorate their relevance, and infuse them with contemporary significance, it's crucial to incorporate theories from various disciplines to enrich the research perspectives. For instance, adopting a historical perspective allows us to trace the evolution of ancient legal terms' translation. From a Spreading viewpoint, examining the journey of legal classics' translations helps objectively assess their impact and standing. Alternatively, through an image study lens, one can explore how translators constructed, disseminated, and altered China's legal image abroad. Similarly, viewing it through semiotics unveils the symbolic significance of ancient legal terms, enabling the establishment of a bridge between bilingual symbolic systems. These diverse approaches provide the study of legal classics with profound academic depth and substance.

Empirical Research on Translation of Legal Classics

The digitization of classics using modern technology aligns with the direction of the "Internet Plus" era. Establishing a legal classic corpus or an electronic platform, whether Internet-based or utilizing big data, will significantly facilitate research. Taking the translation of legal terms as an example, researchers can use a Chinese-English corpus to swiftly identify corresponding translations for terms and assess their variations. By analyzing the frequency of these translation, their literature sources, and example sentences, researchers can make informed decisions on the suitable translation. Furthermore, in terms of translation comparison, utilizing tools like the UCREL semantic analysis system (USAS) allows researchers to replicate power relations found in two English translation of *Ta Tsing Leu Lee*. This is accomplished by comparing them based on the total number of power relations and several subordinate semantic domains. Similarly, creating a multilingual parallel corpus of *Collected Cases of Injustice Rectified* aids in exploring a translator's style through quantitative comparisons at lexical, syntactic, and discourse levels.

Research on Translation of Legal Classics and Cultivation of Research Teams Although many universities in China offer master's and doctoral programs in translation, a notable trend exists where graduates from master's programs tend to move into business-related fields, while those from doctoral programs predominantly pursue research in literary translation. Unfortunately, this leads to a scarcity of individuals involved in translating and researching legal classics. To sustainably generate research outcomes, universities must proactively take up the responsibility of nurturing talents focused on translating and researching legal classic. This initiative calls for innovative changes in curricula, teaching methodologies, and assessment approaches. Consequently, researchers need to evaluate the current state of talent cultivation in translating and researching legal classics in Chinese universities and design a practical development program.

3.5 Summary

This chapter visually presents the trends and current status of research on translating legal classics. Translating legal classics holds the responsibility of preserving the essence of legal culture and showcasing confidence in legal culture. How to effectively promote the Spreading of these invaluable legal classics globally is a question of our times, a duty of the translators, and a responsibility of scholars. Analysis reveals that research in this field, after its initial stages, has seen an increase in outcomes, diverse perspectives, and deeper content. This not only highlights the ongoing mission of improving research but also calls for researchers to adopt a forward-thinking approach in the context of modern Chinese studies abroad. It demands enhanced foresight, depth, breadth, theoretical understanding, practical relevance, and continuity. Thus, striving to present a comprehensive and genuine portrayal of traditional Chinese law to the global audience in a more vivid and complete manner.

References

Cao, P., & Qian, L. (2020). On George Thomas Staunton's translation of *Ta TsingLeu Lee* from the perspective of translator's habitus. *Journal of Xi'an Aeronautical Institute* 06.

Dictionary Editing Office, Institute of Linguistics, Chinese Academy of Social Sciences. (2016). *Xiandai Hanyu Cidian (7th edition)*, 291. Commercial Press.

Dong, X., & Hu, B. (2018). Translation planning research based on "the belt and road initiative": Content and framework. *Foreign Language Research* 03.

Dong, X., & Zhang, Y. (2021). Translation and research of traditional Chinese legal classics. *China Legal Science* 03.

Dong, X. (2021). The translation and spreading of ancient Chinese legal classics. *Guangming Daily*, May 22.

Hou, Y. (2009). The first comprehensive translation attempt of Chinese legal classics by Europeans—Stanton and the translation of the *Ta Tsing Leu Lee.* Historical Archives 04.

Hu, B., & Dong, X (2021). Is it cultural communication or cultural hegemony: An analysis of the cultural misleading in the first English translation of *Ta Tsing Leu Lee. Chinese Culture Research* 02.

Hu, J. (2007). Hold high the great banner of socialism with Chinese characteristics and strive for new victories in building a moderately prosperous society in all respects—Report to the seventeenth national congress of the communist party of China. *People's Daily*, October 15.

Jiang, Z. (2002). Build a well-off society in an all-round way and create a new situation in building socialism with Chinese characteristics—Report at 16th party congress. *People's Daily*, November 08.

Kan, J. (2016). *The research on English translation of criminal legal terminology in the Sir George Thomas Staunton's English Version of "Ta Tsing Leu Lee."* East China University of Political Science and Law.

Li, H. (2013). *Culture-loaded words in traditional legal Chinese: Its interpretation and English translation—Take The T'ang Code as an example.* Southwest University Of Political Science And Law.

Li, Y., & Wu, Y. (2021). Translation strategies and translators' motivation of culture-loaded words in *The Washing away of Wrongs*: Forensic medicine in thirteenth-century China. *Foreign Language Education & Research, 9*, 2.

Liu, Y. (2008). *An intertextual approach to translating ancient Chinese legal texts into English—A case study of The Tang Code.* Soochow University.

Pellatt, V. (2013). *Text, extratext, metatext and paratext in translation.* Cambridge Scholar Publishing.

Qu, W., & Wan, L. (2019). What has motivated English translation of the codes of pre-modern Chinese dynasties. *Chinese Translators Journal* 01.

Qu, W. (2010). Early English translations of Chinese legal terms: A study based on Robert Morrison's *Wuche yunfu. Historical Research* 05.

The Central Committee of the Communist Party of China. (2004). Proposals for further enriching the development of philosophy and social sciences. *People's Daily*, March 21.

Wang, H. (2018). The output track of translating Chinese legal literature and its enlightenment. *Political Science and Law* 11.

Wang, H. (2017). From Han Canon, ethnic canons to texts of sinological interests: The shifting foci of the three stages in the translation of Chinese classics. *Chinese Translators Journal* 05.

Wang, J. (2001). Eastward expansion of western law: An examination of the early history of correspondences between Chinese and western legal concepts. *Tsinghua Forum of Rule of Law* 01.

Wang, J. *The legal significance of bridging two worlds: The introduction of western methods and exploration of legal neologisms in Late Qing Dynasty, 10.* China University of Political Science and Law Press.

Xi, J. (2017). Secure a decisive victory in building a moderately prosperous society in all respects and strive for the great success of socialism with Chinese characteristics for a new era—Delivered at the 19th national congress of the communist party of China. *People's Daily*, October 28.

Xiong, D. (2018). An interpretive approach to different English versions of Chinese classics of legal culture from Ancient China. *Journal of Southwest University of Political Science and Law* 05.

Yang, M. (2009). On research methods in translation studies. *Journal of Chongqing University (Social Science Edition)* 04.

Zhang, L. (2018). *Translation of legal terminology in Chinese legal classics: A comparative study of two English translations of Da Qing Lü Li*. Southwest University.

Zhao, C. (2012). The first direct dialogue in the history of Chinese and British cultural communication—Studies on the English version of *Ta Tsing Leu Lee*. *Journal of Xi'an International Studies University* 03.

Zhao, J. (2021). Title translation in the perspective of re-instantiation: With the examples in Xi Jinping: The governance of China. *Journal of University of Science and Technology Beijing (Social Sciences Edition)* 01.

Zhou, L. (2014). *A theoretical framework for translator behavior criticism, 19*. The Commercial Press.

Chapter 4
China's Legal Image in Western World

Abstract "Legal Orientalism" is the application of "Orientalism" in the legal domain, which directly refers to the legal image of a nation. As a discourse system of the national legal image, it has its history and roots during the course of forming. Before the nineteenth century, China's legal image, other-shaped by the Western world, presented a utopian perfect imagination. In the nineteenth century, its Spreading in the Western world was gradually labeled as a typical example of "barbarism" and "backwardness". From the perspective of "Orientalism", the essence behind the "other-shaping" of China's legal image in the nineteenth century is imperialist ideology, which seeks extraterritorial rights, measures Chinese law according to occidental standards of "civilization", and safeguards commercial interests and hegemonic status of Western enterprises in China. "Oriental Legalism", as a transcendence of "legal orientalism", in the final analysis refers to the question of how to build the discourse system of Chinese rule of law. The "self-shaping" of China's legal image in the new era needs grand narrative, thereby building the concept of great translation and broad Spreading underpinned by a large pattern and vision.

4.1 Introduction

Said's Orientalism is a way of thinking, a discourse or a discipline. It is a narrative framework created by Westerners in the course of history and a mechanism used to describe, control, rebuild, and dominate the East. It can be applied to the study of politics, military, literature, culture, sociology, ideology, and many other fields. As Said (1999) said, "My contention is that without examining Orientalism as a discourse one cannot possibly understand the enormously systematic discipline". "Legal Orientalism" is the extension and practice of "Orientalism" in the legal domain by the American scholar Ruskola (2016), aiming for "a global mapping of discourses of world-making and self-making through law", that is, the shaping of the national legal image. Over recent years, with the continuous translation and extensive discussion of Ruskola's "Legal Orientalism" in China, Chinese scholars in the legal field have begun to fully describe and interpret the map of Legal Orientalism[1].

X. Dong and Y. Luo, *The Legal Image of China in Chinese Legal Tradition*,
https://doi.org/10.1007/978-981-96-5797-1_4

In general, the construction of national image is supported by a set of discourse system, which has two different ways, namely other-shaping and self-shaping. However, there has long been no autonomy over the shaping and extraterritorial Spreading of China's legal image. Before the nineteenth century, the study of Sinology in the West focused on Chinese history, philosophy, and customs. In the late Qing Dynasty, the world pattern underwent major changes. The Industrial Revolution promoted the technological and economic progress of European and American countries, leading to the rapid development of capitalism and the colonial expansion movements. Western powers urgently needed to open more trade markets and came to China one after another for benefits. Then, Turner (2004) pointed out that intense clashes happened to the very different legal systems and concepts of China and Western countries, and the study of law has become an important part of Chinese studies. Yu (2015) believed that, by the nineteenth century, Western knowledge of Chinese law had surpassed Chinese knowledge of European law, and the Chinese at that time might still disdain to understand Western legal systems. This cognitive bias in time and space has led to the shaping and extraterritorial Spreading of China's legal image arbitrarily or deliberately "dressed" by Westerners to a fair extent. As Ruskola (2016) points out in his representative work *Legal Orientalism*, that there is no discourse of rule-of-law that is not at the same time a discourse of Legal Orientalism—a set of usually unarticulated cultural assumptions about that which is not law, and about those who do not have it. In the ideological discourse structure of "legal orientalism", there is no doubt that China's legal image is "lawful-less" and "authoritarian" from the perspective of "the other". To explore how this discourse structure was formed, we have to go back to the "diffuse set of European prejudices about Chinese law throughout the nineteenth century", for any image construction will have its form of Spreading. This chapter, from the perspective of in-depth analysis of legal orientalism discourse, explores how Westerners in the nineteenth century constructed discourse expressions to shape China's legal image, and then finds out the real intention and thought behind this system through the ways of discourse Spreading, thus providing some inspiration and reference for the construction and extraterritorial Spreading of the image of China's rule of law in the new era.

4.2 The Nineteenth Century: The Watershed of the Extraterritorial Spreading of China's Legal Image

In the Western vision of "the other", the Chinese legal image has been dynamic and changing, showing a process of "ideologization".

Zhou (2006) points out that, around the year 1250 marked the beginning of the establishment of the Western economic system and, the world knowledge system, which also set an explaining frame for the study of China's image in the Western world. In the thirteenth century, the Mongol Empire opened up the Eurasian continent and voyagers traveled around the world, leaving behind lots of travel stories and travel literature, where originated China's legal image. For example, *The Travels of Marco Polo* written in 1298 is a representative. This work is mainly about wealth and monarchy, in which China is the "Great China Empire" with abundant materials, wise emperors, clean officials, a long history, and advanced technologies. Marco Polo highly praised the fifth emperor of the Yuan Dynasty Kublai Khan, because "the monarch cherishes the great benefit of his poor, and in return people love him and worship him like God" (Gong, 2004). Among popular books in Europe, *The Travels of Marco Polo* made the first explicit reference to the Chinese legal articles, "A man who steals a small thing which doesn't commit a capital offense, shall be hit seven times with a stick; two pieces for 17 times then; three pieces or less for 27 times; at most 107 times depending on the circumstances till death" (Ma, 2011). This can generally represent the legislation characteristics in the Yuan Dynasty. In 1585, *Annals of the Great Chinese Empire*, written by the Spaniard Mendoza based on his travels, was published in Rome and presented an empire with perfect systems (especially its political system) to the world. He pointed out the importance of the law in China, "With a strict administration of justice, the torture in China, though inhumane, ensures public order. China adopts parliamentary system in which experienced and respected interpreters work together to decide on government affairs. This mighty kingdom has the most perfect governance the world has ever seen" (Zhou, 2006). In the late sixteenth century, Jesuits represented by Mathew Ricci began to enter China and introduce Chinese culture to Europe. His writing narrates various forms of the political and legal culture of ancient China with approbation. He holds that the monarchy has been the only form of government that the Chinese people have appreciated since ancient times. Under this government, the Head of the Ministry of Justice is responsible for the investigation and punishment of criminal cases, and there are corresponding departments which carry out jurisdiction in each local government; but a judge cannot preside over a court in the province where he was born, and officials who break the law shall be punished (Gong, 2004). Mathew Ricci had the greatest esteem for Chinese etiquette. He fully agreed with the feudal ethics of Chinese Confucianism and believed that the Chinese etiquette imbued with the spirit of Confucianism made China more civilized than Europe. He also made a detailed investigation of Chinese imperial examination system and even recommended this system to the ruling class of Europe (Ma, 2011). In short, China, in this historical period according to almost all records, is depicted as a country with advanced legal system and flourishing culture. Of course, this is not the history in its entirety, nor is it the end of its Spreading.

Discourse is a rhetorical strategy and mode of thinking, which is dominant and can constitute a space of the ideology of Western modernity. In this space, the West and the East have undoubtedly become binary opposition, with the West being the representative of "progress" and "civilization", while the "East" being the embodiment of "backwardness" and "barbarism". At the beginning of the formation of the discourse structure of legal orientalism, the barbarism and backwardness of Chinese law have been magnified to give a nice contrast to the superiority of Western civilization and law. Such discourse, through continuous presentation, superposition, and continuation, has formed a complete set of disciplinary knowledge and exerted the power of the discourse system in the course of history. Not only does it create a hostility between East and West, but it can also be applied specifically to institutional expressions, such as legal exclusion of Chinese immigrants, to justify itself. From the late eighteenth century, especially after the Macartney Mission's visit to China, derogatory remarks about China's image began to prevail in Britain, and it became popular to denounce Chinese laws as barbaric and backward. As Zhou (2006) pointed out that, around 1750, China's image in the West saw great changes. "Sinomania" has witnessed the peak of beautified China's image in the West over the past five centuries, and a trend of vilifying China also appeared. Behind the reversal of China's image is not only the appearance of the rise of Western economic power and the decline of the Qing Empire, but also the ideological effects of the development of Western modernity and civilization progress. The eastern despotism in the eyes of the West originated in ancient Greece and flourished during the Renaissance. In the late period of the Enlightenment, China's image has been incorporated into the discourse of eastern despotism. The Enlightenment thinkers represented by Montesquieu, Nicolas Boulanger, and Hegel all asserted in their academic monographs that China was an autocratic country, and the image of the barbaric Chinese empire was formed at the end of eighteenth century and the beginning of nineteenth century. The transformation of China's legal image from "advanced" and "flourishing" to "backward" and "barbaric" also occurred, and it was particularly obvious in the nineteenth century. Therefore, the nineteenth century can be called "the watershed of the extraterritorial Spreading of China's legal image".

Of course, as for individuals in the West, some of them maintain a comprehensive and objective cognition of the East. In the early nineteenth century, represented by Sir George Thomas Staunton, he was not short of praise in the translator's preface to the *Ta Tsing Leu Lee*. Staunton (2015) pointed out that the *Ta Tsing Leu Lee* is undoubtedly a first class one among all the existing Chinese classical and modern publications that have not yet been translated into European languages, because it was formulated with absolute authority for its significant subject. This work is combined with two strengths featuring a relatively simple style and a concise form. However, after the First Opium War (1840–1842), more Westerners saw in China a dilapidated society, a corrupt and incompetent government, a dismal judicial system, and the moral decay of the country. As a result, in their works, China's legal image was overwhelming labeled with these stereotypes. At that time, many Westerners living in Guangzhou, China have also been to jail. As they didn't understand Chinese law, they saw Chinese law mostly from the prison, thus their memories and records are full of darkness and sorrow in Chinese prisons. Tian and Li (2007) wrote that "Chinese prisons" was called "牢狱(*Lao Yu*)", "监牢(*Jian Lao*)", or "牢房(*Lao Fang*)" in history, showing the cruelest and darkest part of judicial activities in Chinese feudal society.

Barbarism is a concept of anthropology, under the shadow of which China's image was shrouded by darkness. In the nineteenth century, Western descriptions of barbaric China were full of vagueness, randomness, generalities, and a combination of ideology, thought, and even fantasy and imagination. At that time, Westerners founded a lot of newspapers and periodicals in China, among which *The Chinese Repository* was the first mature English periodical. From its inception in May 1832 to its termination in December 1851, it had a total of 20 volumes before and after and had a relatively large influence in disseminating information. This journal is an important reader for understanding the transformation of China's legal image in the West, for its almost entirely negative introduction of Chinese law. Li Xiuqing (2015) roughly summarized the basic characteristics of Chinese criminal law in the foreign articles that there is no clear standards for conviction and sentencing; violent perpetrators, especially homicide, will be imposed cruel penalties, as seen in "斩刑(*Zhan Xing*)(beheading)" most commonly, "凌迟(*Ling Chi*)(death by a thousand cuts)", "枭首(*Xiao Shou*)(beheading and hanging the head in public in downtown)", and the abuse of torture. Although only a few comments were given on the report of death penalty cases in China, from those we can more or less see why the editors are keen to cover such stories—what implied between the lines is the construction of a picture of China featuring abundant death penalty cases and frequent executions, is the aversion to the cruelty of Chinese people and public executions of criminals, is the criticism of the indifferent onlookers.

From some studies on Chinese law, we can see some authors' comments on Chinese law as "barbaric" and "backward". For example, in 1871, Holcmbe, Chester, the chief counselor of the United States in China, wrote in his book *The Real China-Man*, "Judging from the actual operation of the Chinese courts, it is not only inevitable but too common in terms of corruption and bribery, extortion, irregularities for favoritism, and the persecution of the faithful and honest" (Tian & Li, 2007). Similar descriptions can be read in many more works. The laws of Chinese Empire then were synonymous with backwardness and barbarism for the Westerners. As Willoughby (1957) pointed out that these laws are cruel and unreasonable in some important respects. They have no faith in the fairness and integrity of Chinese courts.

4.3 The Basic Ways of Extraterritorial Spreading of China's Legal Image in the Nineteenth Century

The media are indispensable for Spreading, and there are different media in different eras. Zhou (2006) wrote that, in the Age of Discovery, eastern information in Europe spread in three forms and ways: the reports of official envoys and colonial governments, the rumors of merchants and sailors, and the letters of missionaries. Of these three, only the missionary's letters boast the richest, the most comprehensive, and the most humanistic content. Despite of its typical characteristics of fragmentation, this kind of information has contributed to the formation of eastern knowledge and discourse in the Western world, which led to the strengthening of China's legal image in the West. With the advance of discovery and the development of navigation technology, more and more Westerners began to set foot on the land of China, which brought changes not only in the form of information transmission but also in the narrative mode of China's legal image. The Industrial Revolution in Europe in the 1760s brought production technological innovation. One of the important changes is the progress of printing technology that witnessed movable type printing replacing traditional manual printing, thus mechanized production promoted the booming of the publishing industry, leading to the spread of knowledge and information and the transoceanic communication and understanding between different civilizations and cultures.

As Hu and Li (2017) said that, both China's self-image and other-image are the result of the construction and claim of meaning of the symbol systems such as social activities and language. In the nineteenth century, China's legal image was mainly transmitted to the world through language symbols and different forms of text, but before the nineteenth century, it also spread based on full translation, painting, and academic research. Compared with the previous superficial understanding, Westerners' understanding of Chinese law shows certain comprehensive and profound characteristics in this diversified form.

4.3.1 Codex Translation

Hu and Li (2017) pointed out that translation can not only directly participate in the construction of national image but also promote its Spreading. As a kind of cross-cultural behavior and activity, translation itself has the nature of Spreading, so what we need to consider is the targets, purpose, ways, and channels of Spreading. Westerners had a quite late understanding of Chinese law, even the British knew little about the operation of the Chinese legal system until the end of the eighteenth century (Su, 2003). Before Jr. Staunton translated the *Ta Tsing Leu Lee*, some people in the West began to introduce Chinese legal culture. The German Alexis Leontiev introduced some details of Qing penalty to the West, and in 1781 published in Berlin a German text, *The Laws of China*, which selectively translated fragments of Qing law (Tian & Li, 2007).

However, Western scholars generally believe that Jr. Staunton's translation of the *Ta Tsing Leu Lee* is the earliest and most complete translation of Chinese written codes by Westerners. Jr. Staunton's father, George Thomas Staunton, was secretary and director of the Macartney Mission. As a page boy, Jr. Staunton learned Chinese on the ships he accompanied his father to China and developed a strong interest in Chinese culture. In 1789, he was appointed Guangzhou Clerk of the East India Company. In 1807, he was appointed translator of Guangzhou Mercantile Museum. From 1789 to 1816, when he lived in Guangzhou, there were frequent trade disputes and legal conflicts between China and the West. Since Westerners did not know much about Chinese law, they believed that Chinese officials were too arbitrary in handling cases, so he thought it was necessary to introduce the *Ta Tsing Leu Lee* to Westerners. It took him more than eight years to complete the translation, then he transferred the rights to the Cadell and Davis Press in England, and the book was officially published in London in 1810.

The value of the *Ta Tsing Leu Lee* is highly recognized by Jr. Staunton, as Staunton (2015) said that because no other Chinese work can be translated to explain so concisely the unique system of the Chinese government, the basic principles of its organizational structure and domestic policy, the relation of the habits and character of the people to them, and their influence on the general condition of the Chinese people. This was the first time that he introduced China's written code to the West in a relatively complete and systematic way, and he is also known as "the first European translator of Chinese legal classics". As soon as the English translation of the *Ta Tsing Leu Lee* was published, it received wide attention in the West, including the *Edinburgh Review* and other magazines published its book reviews. Moreover, both the French and Italian editions of the book were quickly translated from English two years later in 1812. In 1876, Firas retranslated it into French. According to Budi and Morris (1995), Firas, a captain in the French Navy, wrote a translation of more than 1,500 pages in less than four years, but less of it has survived. In the 1920s, Blythe translated it again into French.

4.3.2 *Newspaper Review*

The publishing of English translation of the *Ta Tsing Leu Lee* played a direct role in its Spreading in the West and soon attracted the attention of British review journals. In his memoirs, Jr. Staunton copied several major book reviews, including the *Edinburgh Review*, the *Eclectic Review*, the *Monthly Review*, the *Critical Review*, the *British Critic,* and the *Journal Asiatique.* The reviews in these journals are not short of glowing words, such as, "In the case before us, we have reason not only to believe that the translation is absolutely fair and accurate, and we can find that the translator himself has such characteristics as forthrightness, calm judgment and so on"; "Sir George Jr. Staunton showed us a general picture of the Chinese system with clear, humble and wise strokes"; "qualified people like the translator of this book are rarer than hen's teeth; there are also few people like him who, regardless of fame and wealth, spend a large amount of time doing such work"; "our debt to the translator of this Chinese code is not diminished by our views on Chinese writing"; "he translated a large number of precious materials"; "I was surprised by the accuracy of the translation; I have not forgotten to say how much the author deserves the honor of publishing this important work". The comments of these magazines and periodicals played the role of "mouthpiece" and "amplifier" and boosted a second round of Spreading of the *Ta Tsing Leu Lee* in Britain and even Europe.

In addition, Westerners who came to China in the nineteenth century also set up newspapers both inside and outside China to introduce the realities of China to Westerners. Outside China, in 1807, the first Western missionary to China, the British Robert Morrison (1782–1834), came to China, and then the Malacca missionary William Milne (1785–1822). In 1815, they jointly printed and published *Chinese Monthly Magazine*, which was not only the first Chinese monthly magazine founded by missionaries outside China, but also the first modern Chinese newspaper aimed at Chinese people in the world. It mainly published religious and moral articles and some astronomical knowledge as well. Later, in Malacca, they founded a quarterly English journal, *The Indo-Chinese Gleaner*, which focused on news from China and neighboring countries, including the history, philosophy, literature of China and India, and other Chinese and Malay news translated into English.

In China, foreign newspapers and periodicals with different orientations and in different languages began to spring up: *Abelha da China* (founded on September 12, 1822) was the first Chinese newspaper founded by foreigners and published in Portuguese and was mainly read by Portuguese people in Macao; *The Canton Register* (founded in 1827), a commercial newspaper, was the first English newspaper published in China, mainly publishing price quotation; *Canton Miscellany* (founded in 1831) is the earliest English periodical published in China, publishing various subjects, including history, geography, literature, current affairs, and poetry; The Chinese Courier and Canton Gazette (founded on July 28, 1831) was the first English newspaper founded by Americans in China, mainly reporting business information; *The Chinese Repository* (founded in May 1832) was the first mature English periodical founded by foreigners in China, covering a wide range of contents, including politics, history, geography, trade, economy, law, religion, natural science and language, and its founder, E.C. Bridgman (1801–1861), the first American missionary in China, aimed not only at evangelism but also to shoulder the responsibility of introducing the current conditions of Chinese society (Li, 2015: 46–49); *The China Review* (1872–1901) was an English journal founded by the British in Hong Kong in the late nineteenth century and published a wide range of articles (Li, 2017a).

No matter how influential and how widely spread they are, these newspapers, both inside and outside China, more or less published some introduction to Chinese law and serve as a window for foreigners to understand Chinese legal culture. For example, the articles related to Chinese law (especially criminal law) in *The Indo-Chinese Gleaner* are scattered in each volume, which criticized and denied the excessive death penalty, cruel execution methods, illegal torture, local officials' dereliction of duty, constant judicial corruption and rape and murder cases, and moral deterioration (Li, 2017b); *Chinese Repository* reported China's legal situation sporadically, with specific content involving China's legislation, law enforcement, criminal law, litigation, prison, land system, etc. Among them, reports related to litigation are the most complex, while those of civil law such as land system are the simplest (Ibid.). After the English translation of *Ta Tsing Leu Lee* was published, its evaluation by the *Chinese Repository* was reflected in the article "Commentary on the Ta Tsing Leu Lee Translated by Thomas Staunton" serialized in three issues and the article "Characteristics, Current Realities, Policy, and Criminal Code of China", which was part of a series of articles called "Introduction to Contemporary China" serialized in four issues, etc. (Ibid.) As the editors and authors of *Chinese Repository* had high reputation and extensive contacts in both the clerical and secular circles, the scope of Spreading in the Spanish-speaking world was relatively wide. And some important journals of influence in Europe and America, such as *North American Review*, *Edinburgh Quarterly*, *Westminster Review*, *Blackwood Magazine*, published articles on China, and most of them also referred to the content of *Chinese Repository* (Ibid.), which inevitably increased the Spreading and attention of the *Ta Tsing Leu Lee* in the Spanish-speaking world. The content published by *China Review* has drawn attention to the implementation of Chinese laws, the attribution of judicial power, the various stages of criminal proceedings and prison conditions (Ibid.). In addition, "The Control and Enforcement of Chinese Laws" published in *China Review* in 1874, and the "Bao Gu System in Chinese Laws"[2] published in 1882 in *China Review*, are further introductions to the *Ta Tsing Leu Lee* (Zhang, 2011).

4.3.3 Memories and Experiences

As Su (2003) pointed out that, the reason why the memories and experiences listed as one of the channels for Westerners to understand Chinese law in the nineteenth century is because Western missionaries, diplomats, and other long-term expatriates wrote books and articles on China that essentially recorded or recalled what the author saw, heard, and experienced. From the style of writing, they are somewhat similar to the *Zhang Gu* (anecdotes about historical figures, rules, and regulations) of the Ming and Qing Dynasties in China. But generally, there is no small difference from the modern Western system of systematic social science research. The Portuguese Galeote Pereira and Friar Gaspar da Cruz are first to describe Chinese prisons and judicial procedures in Europe: Galeote Pereira spent much of his stay on the southern coast of China from 1549 to 1552 in prison; most of Friar Gaspar da Cruz's descriptions of Chinese prisons and judicial procedures are based on Galeote's experiences, and he himself had a short personal experience in Guangdong in 1556. Budi and Morris (1995) believed that their descriptions are brief but relatively accurate. In the early nineteenth century, the British living in Guangzhou constantly reported back to their country what they had seen in China. The British painter Thomas Allom once made an intuitive description of the judicial situation in Guangzhou. Through his depiction of Chinese pictures and scenes, it can be inferred that he had lived in China in the nineteenth century. And his work "flogging sinners" revealed the cruelty of grief, reflecting the cruelty of Chinese justice. Kirk, a Briton, describes the darkness and misery of Chinese prisons, with descriptions such as "stinking, like cages for animals in zoos" that make people repulsive and unpleasant (Tian & Li, 2007).

After the Second Opium War (1856), this kind of memories saw more and more gradually. Harry S. Parks, a British diplomat, wrote about his experiences as a prisoner in Beijing. In addition to describing deplorable prison conditions, Parks also revealed that prisoners were forced to pay for their living expenses, which also exposed flaws in the Chinese system of government. In 1859, D.J. McGowan, an American missionary, published a paper entitled "On the Exile of Convicts in China". The materials used in the paper was mostly what the author had seen and heard during his decades of living in China. He mainly discussed a punishment of deporting a prisoner to a remote place for hard labor called *Liu Xing* and compared the common one and military, one believing that there was no substantial difference between the two. The British consul, T. T. Meadows, wrote both the records and descriptions in detail in his "Guangzhou

Execution Records" how he witnessed the execution of 34 prisoners in Guangzhou on 30 July 1851 (Budi & Morris, 1995). In addition, DJ McGowan and T.T. Meadows are the authors of *The Light and Dark of Chinese Life* and *The Chinese and Their Rebellions*. The former has been published in Chinese, and except for the final chapter, other chapters were published independently in the *North China Herald* in Shanghai. Later, the title was changed to *People and their Way of Life in Modern China*, which was republished in the UK (Macgowan, 1998). Among them, five chapters directly related to Chinese law, including "Land and Land Law", "Punishment", "Lynching", "Money and Money Lending", and "Family and Family Life". There's also John Henry Gray's *China: A History of the Laws, Manners and Customs of the People*, much of what is said about judicial procedures and punishments that come from the author's experience (Budi & Morris, 1995).

4.3.4 Copperplate Etchings

In the early nineteenth century, in addition to the literal-dominated form of Spreading, some authors used the form of painting to introduce Chinese legal culture to the West. The aforementioned Thomas Arryn was a painter who once studied under the famous Western painter George Chinnery, and his painting *Wearing a flail for public display* was a very famous copperplate etching at that time. As Tian and Li (2007) described that, a man is wearing the pillory, and the official beside him is carrying a whip in the one hand and shackles in the other hand, executing the punishment of the prisoner. *The Punishments of China*, also known as *Twenty-Two Copperplate Etchings of Chinese Justice*, was published in London in 1801 by William Miller. The book includes a total collection of interrogation, arrest of criminals, inquisition by torture, and other punishments such as "笞(*Chi*)(whip with bamboo planks or wattles)", "杖(*Zhang*)(beat the prisoner on the back, buttocks, or legs with a large wattle or bamboo board)", "徒(*Tu*)(deprive the offender of his liberty for a certain period and force him to perform hard labor)", "流(*Liu*)(banish sinners to distant places)", "死(*Si*)(capital punishment)", and even other more unique tortures such as "割脚筋(*Ge Jiao Jin*)(cut the prisoner's hamstrings)", "伽床(*Jia Chuang*)(place the prisoner in a bed, his head, neck, chest, hands, legs and feet bound in chains, his belly pressed with a wooden beam and covered with a three-inch nail board)", "站笼(*Zhan Long*)(the cage is made of wood, with a flail on the top of the cage and a round hole on it, which can be put on the neck of the prisoner to make the prisoner stand upright in the cage; those who are punished in this way often die within a few days)". There are 22 illustrations in the book, and the original was made by copperplate printing, hand-colored, which gave a quite comprehensive description of the judicial situation and penal scenes during Qianlong period of the Qing Dynasty (Tian & Li, 2007). Of course, the scenes and characters depicted in these illustrations may not be completely consistent with the real situation in China, and some of them are even the author's imagination of the images of Chinese people based on the characteristics of Westerners. From the perspective of figures and costumes, those figures are completely consistent with the characteristics of Westerners. However, we have to admit that these paintings played an important role in the early introduction and Spreading of Chinese law.

4.3.5 *Academic Research*

Westerners' understanding of Chinese law must go through a process from the superficial to the deep, from the surface to the inside. Even in the period from the thirteenth to the sixteenth centuries, Western knowledge of Chinese law was still constantly improving, and groups coming to China, like the initial envoys, merchants, travelers, missionaries, and the Jesuits of the sixteenth century, were having more complete knowledge structure. For example, the French missionaries to China were strictly selected, they were not only knowledgeable, but also had specialized scientific and technical knowledge. In 1687, Jean de Fontaney, one of the six missionaries, in his letter to the Royal Academy of Sciences, mentioned his research program in China, which included such five subjects as astronomy and geography, Chinese chronology, literature, natural sciences and medicine, and the political, economic, and social situation of China (Ma, 2011).

Although the academic research at that time could not be compared with the one discussed in modern social sciences, it opened the curtain of the study of Chinese law and culture after all. Among the many Western writings on China in the nineteenth century, Ernest Alabaster was the pioneer of Chinese law study. He compiled *Notes and Commentaries on Chinese Criminal Law and Cognate Topics* (1899), which was regarded as the most authoritative Western study of Chinese law of the century (Su, 2003). The book, starting from the concept of Anglo-American law system, includes Lü(laws), Li(cases), other cases and six rules of law, and compacts them into a form similar to the textbooks of Anglo-American law schools (Tian & Li, 2007). D. Budi and C. Morris (1995) commented that his works are easy to understand, but his research on the institutional aspects of the Qing legal system is extremely sketchy, as opposed to ideology, which weakens his academic value.

4.4 The Other-Shaping of China's Legal Image from the Perspective of Orientalism

In his book *Orientalism*, Said (1999) wrote that I have found it useful here to employ Michel Foucault's notion of a discourse. "The Orient" is not a natural concept, but also a human creation. Such idea has its own history and traditions of thought, imagery and vocabulary. When East and West increasingly become a symbol of binary opposition, China's legal image is nothing but the knowledge and power relations constructed by Westerners between the real and the imaginary, and the subtle, unique, and various traces hidden under the individual, "show the 'order of discourse' in an apolitical gesture or a startling political ignorance, but this order itself is the trace of politics" (Xu & Yuan, 2001). The order of legal orientalist discourse is embodied in the forms and ways of the above-mentioned shaping and Spreading of China's legal image, all of which imply the political nature of discourse, translation, and Spreading.

4.4.1 The Perfect Imagination of Westerners

Before the nineteenth century, China's legal image presented a perfect utopian image in the West, mainly for two reasons.

First of all, it is a fact that the civilization behind the Chinese legal system has shown certain superiority in the world. Fairbank (1989) called such development model an "introversion demolition" one which differs from the Western style of external expansion and development. And such model thus formed a unique mode of production, social life, national system, and cultural system (Gong, 2004). The core idea of Confucian culture is to value peace and the Doctrine of the Mean. When Confucius and other schools tried to advise the rulers, they already understood that social solidarity is an important method and principle for the rulers to maintain pacifism. As a result, there is no possibility for Western polyarchy to appear nor proper environment for it to grow in China. This "introversion demolition" method produced two important results different from that of Europe: the developed ancient Chinese bureaucracy and the early prosperity of ancient Chinese culture and civilized art. Therefore, China reached a position of cultural superiority over all parts of East Asia, and its influence can still be felt that the Chinese people have a hidden sense of cultural superiority (Fairbank, 1989). The self-sufficiency of economic development in ancient China also gave birth to the uniqueness and isolation of legal culture, which made the Chinese legal system not affected by any other legal culture in the world. Thanks to the nourishment of Confucian culture, the Chinese legal system achieved independent development and formed a relatively complete legal system and legal department, whose development level was not inferior to that of any other contemporary legal system. For example, the legal culture reflected in the bronze ware of the Western Zhou Dynasty is comparable to the *Code of Hammurabi*; the bamboo slips of the Qin Dynasty (around the third century-BC), discovered in Yunmeng, Hubei Province, presented detailed laws and regulations, the diverse legal forms, accurate legal interpretations, scientific judicial expertise, and strict interrogation procedures, all of which eloquently demonstrate that the development level of the legal culture in the Qin Dynasty was almost a thousand years ahead of that of the Frank-Germanic people in the early feudal system of the West (Zang, 2007).

Secondly, the reason why China's beautiful legal image has been maintained in the Western world for nearly five centuries is that China's legal image conforms to the "utopian" impulse in the heart of the European spirit. Zhou (2006) pointed out that the study of utopian Chinese images in modern Western culture belongs to the study of the history of ideas, which focuses on the formation and evolution of symbolic systems that embody specific ideological values at the level of social collective psychology, and reveals their internal cultural logic as discourse activities. In the fourth century BC, Plato's *The Republic* was born in the declining Greek city-states. Plato analyzed the interconnectivity between individual justice and city-state justice, systematically expounded the concept of justice, and designed a beautiful blueprint for the ideal country, proposing that only in the "Republic" can true justice be realized. Thomas More inherited this "legacy" and wrote *Utopia* in the sixteenth century, which was praised by later critics as a continuation of *The Republic.* In his book, he depicted the image of the good people in Utopia, in contrast to the evil of the whole society at that time. If the "Utopia" is the "underlying code" buried in the consciousness of Westerners, then utopia is the long-cherished wish of Westerners; whether it is the republic or utopia, they appear in distant countries geographically. The development of navigation technology brought the world closer together, and when the distance is no longer far away, the dream may be truly realized. The great geographical discovery has found confidence for more people and strengthened their faith. Those idealistic navigators and travelers pin their cherished hopes on the "new world" they have discovered and described, and those utopian writers are also willing to place the utopian imagination on the world map of the travelers. They believe that rather than fabricating and imagining such an ideal country, it is better to materialize it in the real time, space, and world. There are common narrative modes and characteristics between travel texts and utopian ones in the Renaissance. Whether it is geographical location or political and religious system, China's image is in line with the characteristics of the Republic or utopia. From the travel notes of Marco Polo to the history of Mendoza, China's image is gradually approaching the Westerners' expectation of utopia, and China has approached or realized the goal of human justice and happiness in *The Republic.*

4.4.2 The Veiled Ideology

The turning point of China's image in the West appeared around 1750. On the surface, it was a change of Westerners' attitude toward China; in essence, it was the change of Westerners' imagination of China from a perfect utopian to an ideological image. Zhou (2006) wrote that, the relationship between the motivation and intention in China's image in Europe, should be looked from the starting point of modern history and modern spirit of the West. China's image in the West is a kind of fantasy about the cultural other projected by Western culture, and a way of self-examination, self-reflection, self-imagination, and self-writing of Western culture, showing the subconscious desire and terror of Western culture, and pointing to the imagination and ideological space of the Western cultural "other". In the middle of the eighteenth century, the capitalist Industrial Revolution began, and the Western expansion also changed from the era of mercantilist free cooperative trade to the era of imperialist colonial plunder trade. At the same time, China's absolutism has penetrated into all aspects of political rule, ideology, and culture. Such absolutism made China's legal culture unique and isolated from the whole world's legal culture. And this isolation continued to grow into a conservative and closed nature, blocking the possibility of legal cultural exchanges between China and the world. As a result, China did not keep up with the development of world civilization in time, and this conservatism also became a shackle on the progress of Chinese society and culture. Different from China's culture of harmony between man and nature, when the Western economy has achieved rapid development, it intended to carry out external expansion. Therefore, in order to find suitable reasons for its own purpose and cover up its real intention, China has become the "other" denied and excluded by Western ideology and a backward representative in mirror contrast of the other of the "Europe-centric world".

4.4.2.1 Seeking Extraterritoriality to Safeguard Commercial Interests

Jin (2017) believes that the discourse has the power to shape reality; when it has shaped and continue to shape reality, it is more than words, but at the same time a kind of social experience and historical fact. Shaping China's legal image as barbaric and backward is only the appearance of Westerners because by this they can achieve some purpose, and the essence behind this discourse is to meddle and interfere in China's legal life. Through the book Legal Orientalism, Ruskola (2016) also aims to demonstrate how, "throughout the nineteenth century, a diffuse set of European prejudices against Chinese law developed into an American ideology and practice of empire, entailing the extraterritorial application of a floating body of U.S. law in an otherwise lawless Orient".

If we simply regard Jr. Staunton's translation of the Ta Tsing Leu Lee as a kind of East–West cultural exchange, it will certainly ignore the more complex "conspiracy" in the historical context. The Industrial Revolution emerged in the middle of the eighteenth century, enabled the rapid rise of British economy and technology while inevitably leading to the readjustment and division of the European sphere of influence in the East. The Macartney Mission visited China with the financial assistance of the East India Company at that time, and Jr. Staunton worked for the East India Company as the Guangzhou clerk when he translated the Ta Tsing Leu Lee, so his translation must inevitably reflect the purpose of serving the economic interests of the company in China. Roman Alvarez and M. Carman-Africa Vidal (1996) argue that translation is a political act, which is not merely the production of two equivalent texts but a complex process of rewriting, and not only an overview of language and the entire history of people in the "other" world, but also the influence and balance of power between two different cultures. Andre Lefevere (1992), in Translation, Rewriting, and the Manipulation of Literary Fame, proposes that under different historical conditions, rewriting is primarily limited and manipulated by patronage, ideology, and poetics.

As a businessman, translator, and parliamentary interpreter, Jr. Staunton's translation of the Ta Tsing Leu Lee was inevitably influenced by the East India Company and mainstream British ideology. At the level of language rewriting, in order to enable British people to understand and master Chinese law more quickly so as to better manipulate this "discourse power", he chose to achieve "figurative equivalence" rather than seeking "seemingly incommensurable equivalence of language or cultural system". That is, to "sacrifice" part of the authenticity and accuracy of the translation and use the existing concepts and formats of Western law, as well as reconstructing the original language instead of literal translation. Qu (2019) argues that this is undoubtedly a rewriting of Chinese law, aiming to make Chinese law seem more in line with the logic and visual senses of Westerners, so as to facilitate British people to read and understand, and to take the initiative in the later conflicts involving law between Britain and China, which can indeed be confirmed by the later actions of Jr. Staunton. Because of his translation of the Ta Tsing Leu Lee, he became a recognized "expert in Chinese spirit" among the British people, and even enjoyed a certain reputation and influence in the British Parliament. In an 1810 letter to Jr. Staunton, the congregating priest Richny wrote that you have rich experience and been through numerous struggles, so you must know the politics of the Chinese officials; you are a formidable opponent for them (Tian & Li, 2007). The words "struggles" and "opponent" featuring conflicts and war used in the priest's speech and discourse are enough to show that the elites of British society back then only positioned the relationship between China and the West at the level of contradiction and opposition, and their real purpose was probably to "conquer", "defeat", and "control" China.

Li (2017a, 2017b, 2017c) points out that, in the course of the practice of legal imperialism, the seizing of extraterritorial privileges is a key factor, because extraterritoriality itself is a paradigm of this practice; its exercise has succeeded in extending the protection of Western legal authority to foreigners and their commercial interests within the boundaries of non-Western countries, and has correspondingly limited the scope of application of non-Western legal authority in this field. And that's exactly what happened. Legal imperialism is the legal projection of imperialism, which requires the subjective promotion of the leading country. In the nineteenth century, the "Empire on Which the Sun Never Sets" was another name for the British Empire, reflecting Britain's global colonization and hegemony, and Britain was naturally the leading country in seeking extraterritoriality in China. In 1833, under the pretext of China's backwardness, the then Member of the British Parliament, Jr. Staunton, proposed to the Parliament to set up a court in China to hear the cases of British people in China, and it was approved. Accordingly, the British Parliament enacted an act unilaterally giving the British consul in China the right to hear cases concerning British subjects, which was the first known bill that the British government passed to establish consular jurisdiction in China (Hou, 2009). There is, of course, no reason for Jr. Staunton's proposal. On the one hand, the Qing court was generally able to handle foreign-related cases equally and even treated foreigners much more leniently than Chinese (Morse, 2006). On the other hand, consular jurisdiction has long been abandoned in Europe. Although it was widely existed in the Middle Ages of Europe, after the seventeenth century, European countries abolished this system because of its serious infringement of national sovereignty (Hou, 2009). Ironically, in his original translation of the *Ta Tsing Leu Lee*, although Jr. Staunton's praised Chinese law and corrected the wrong perception of Chinese law by the West, in the end he still could not hide his showing off of the progress of Western legal system. And his imposing of the legal system of medieval Europe on China, fully exposed his true purpose. Namely, Western colonialists just want to weave a legal umbrella in China so as to find a reasonable foundation for their illegal activities. Jr. Staunton's translation of the Ta Tsing Leu Lee was not only for the study of Chinese legal culture, but to better safeguard the interests of businessmen in China. The translation of the Ta Tsing Leu Lee not only revealed to Western countries important secrets about the operation of laws in Chinese society, but also became an important basis and excuse for Western countries to establish extraterritoriality in China. Chinese scholar Wang Jian (2002) commented that the English translation and westward transmission of the Ta Tsing Leu Lee represented a peak in the achievement of the Catholic missionaries in the Ming and Qing Dynasties in spreading Chinese culture to the West and also heralded the end of an era and the beginning of a new era. Since then, Western culture and laws have been gradually introduced to China.

4.4.2.2 Taking Western Law as a Measuring Standard of Chinese Law to Maintain Hegemony

The emergence of law is a symbol of modernity. The spirit of modern "rule of law" has become the consensus of all countries in the world, and the "rule of law" built in the discourse background of modern civilized countries is rooted in the traditional connotation of European law (Li Yang 2017). Whether it is the memories and experiences of missionaries in China, or the selective reports and comments of Chinese and Western elites in newspapers, Turner (2004) pointed out that they are more or less wearing a "zoetrope" to observe the Chinese legal tradition. The "zoetrope" represents the development of modernity brought by the Renaissance and Enlightenment in Europe, and it's actually a mirror used to peer and measure other countries and regions, through which the West glorifies itself as a symbol of "civilization" and "progress" by the self-confirmation and self-legitimization. Since the sixteenth century, Western civilization has been dominant, relegating non-Western civilizations and their legal traditions to the museum of anthropology, and behind this phenomenon, there is an indisputable fact of hegemony (Lu, 2017). By the eighteenth and nineteenth centuries, the political imagination of "eastern despotism" began to occupy the mainstream, and a series of important European thinkers, from Montesquieu to Hegel, began to describe China as a civilization system completely different from and far behind the countries of Western Europe (Zheng, 2018). Obviously, they are based on the development of their own national legal history, using the concept of Western law to understand Chinese law, so China became a negative example, representing all the objects they do not want to be, or do not admit to be. At this time, eager to try, the Western civilization is in need of an other to identify itself (Li, 2017a, 2017b, 2017c).

Legal orientalism is a discourse construction, which uses a set of Western "civilization" to measure the international behavior and legal rights of all countries in the world in the history of Western modernization and the thinking structure of modernity. Liu (2014) argues that European intellectuals, including international jurists, regard "civilization" as a state of social progress relative to "barbarism" and construct a set of "civilized" discourse system by connecting "civilization" with ethnic differences, foreign policy, international law, and international order. Under such a set of discourse system, the Western world naturally regards itself as "civilized", and regards the East as "barbaric", "backward", and "uncivilized", thus constructing a hierarchical and orderly civilized world map, and they are convinced that it is their "sacred mission" to make their places "civilized".

In fact, barbarism is the common feature of the initial formation of laws in various countries, and any law must undergo a process of development from barbarism to moderation. In the opening of the first part of torture in *Discipline and Punish*, Foucault (1999) introduced the scene in which Damian, a French prisoner in the eighteenth century, was sentenced to publicly accept "torture" in front of the church gate in Paris for conspiring to stab the king. Compared with Western law, the laws of the Chinese Empire was in some ways more humane and reasonable. For example, theft in Qing Dynasty was generally not punishable by death, unless the value of stolen goods exceeded 120 taels of silver, or if the value of stolen goods was above 50 taels of silver for repeated or third theft; in England before the Industrial Revolution, however, the law provided for the death penalty for the theft of shop goods worth more than five shillings, and the law was not repealed until 1818 after Congress rejected it four times (Budi & Morris, 1995). In the world constructed by Western legal discourse, the "barbarity" of the laws of European countries is subjectively ignored, while the "barbarism" of Chinese laws is repeatedly amplified, which is often seen in the selective and concentrated reports of *The Chinese Repository*. This deliberate choice and preference for the dark side is exactly in line with their intention of running a journal: to reveal the serious problems and illnesses in Chinese law including criminal law and the society in order to attract the attention and self-healing of Western society, which at that time was taking the lead in carrying out legal reforms with increasing success (Li, 2015). However, the discourse expression that is separated from the real understanding of the cultural background of Chinese law will only cause a clear gap between the "civilization" of Western law and the "barbarism" of Chinese law.

Different laws reflect different ways of human life. Law or legal order is the core embodiment and concentrated essence of the world view of the creators of different civilizations. Therefore, different civilizations have different understandings of "law" (Ma, 2017). Such differences are based on different geographical environments, cultural foundations, living customs, and economic development. Different perspectives and starting points lead to different understandings; different civilizations give birth to different legal beliefs, and there is no natural universality, which is ultimately a type of hegemony. Since the nineteenth century, with the globalization of colonialism, the large-scale trade imperialism of the industrialized West against the rest of the world has been based on the institutionalized discipline of the unequal order, especially the unequal stage of economic development, on a worldwide scale

(Yin, 2017). In the international law system constructed by the West in the nineteenth century, the opposition between "civilization" and "barbarism" provided the imaginary basis and proof for the self-identification of Western modernity. It is also an effective "thought tool" for Western colonial expansion. In the gradual accumulation, repetition, and rewriting of discourse, an important standard has been formed to distinguish the status of different countries in the international community. The label of "civilization" has been recognized internationally, while the label of "barbarism" and "obscurantism" has been rejected. This "exclusive" circle has formed an unequal international relations dominated by the Western "civilized countries" and has exposed imperialism in the field of international politics. The ideology of hegemonism is only constructed by the Western world in order to maintain the needs of colonial expansion and foreign aggression, and Liu (2014) wrote that it is the Western powers who need to provide legal basis for their division of the world and enjoy privileges in colonial or semi-colonial countries under the banner of "civilization" and "international law" when they transition from liberal capitalism to imperialism at the end of the century.

References

Alvarez, R., & Vidal, M.C.-A. (1996). *Translating: A political act, translation, power, subversion.* Multilingual Matters Ltd.

Budi, D., & Morris, C. (1995). *Law in imperial China.* Zhu, Y., Trans. Nanjing: Jiangsu People's Publishing House.

Fairbank, J. King. (1989). *The Great Chinese Revolution 1800–1985.* Liu, Z., Trans. Beijing: International Cultural Publishing Company.

Foucault, M. (1999). *Surveiller Et Punir.* Liu, B., Yang, Y., Trans. Beijing: SDX Joint Publishing Company.

Gong, P. (2004). Legal exchanges between China and foreign countries before the 19th century. *Jin Ling Law Review.*

Hou, Y. (2009). The first attempt by Europeans to translate a complete Chinese legal text: Staunton and the translation of *Ta Tsing Leu Lee. Historical Archives* 4.

Hu, K., & Li, X. (2017). Corpus-based translation and Chinese image studies: connotation and meaning. *Foreign Languages Research* 4.

Jin, Z. (2017). The discourse and reality of the encounter between East and West: Notes on the *legal orientalism: China, the United States and modern law. Renmin University Law Review* 1.

Lefevere, A. (1992). *Translation, rewriting and the manipulation of literary fame.* Routledge.

Li, X. (2015). *Perception and reception: Western understanding of the 19th century Chinese legal system based on the Chinese repository.* Shanghai Joint Publishing Company.

Li, X. (2017). Western understanding of the 19th century Chinese justice based on *The China Review. Peking University Law Journal* 1.

Li, X. (2017). Western understanding of the early 19th century Chinese legal system based on *the Indo-Chinese Gleaner. Chinese Journal of Law* 4.

Li, Y. (2017). Another narrative of legal imperialism: Comments on the *Legal orientalism: China, the United States and modern law.* Renmin University Law Review 1.

Liu, W. (2014). "Civilizational" standards in European International Law at the end of the 19th century. *World History Studies* 1.

Lu, N. (2017). Towards eastern legalism: Comments on Ruskola's *legal orientalism. SJTU Law Review* 3.

Ma, H. (2011). *The silk road and the spreading of traditional Chinese legal culture.* Shanghai People's Publishing House.

Ma, J. (2017). The theoretical expression of the "imaginary" other and the "fictional" self: On *legal orientalism* and its repercussions in China. *SJTU Law Review* 3.

Macgowan, J. (1998). *The light and dark of Chinese life.* Zhu, T., & Ni, J., Trans. Beijing: Current Affairs Press.

Morse, H. B. (2006). *The international relations of the Chinese Empire.* Zhang, H., Trans. Shanghai: Shanghai Bookstore Publishing House.

Qu, W. (2019). A study on the English translation of Chinese feudal codes and the motivation for English translation. *Chinese Translators Journal* 1.

Ruskola, T. (2016). *Legal orientalism.* Wei, L., Trans. Beijing: China University of Politic Science and Law Press.

Said, E. W. (1999). *Orientalism.* Wang, Y., Trans. Beijing: SDX Joint Publishing Company.

Staunton, G. T. (2015). *Memoirs of Sir George Thomas Staunton.* Qu, W., Trans. Shanghai: Shanghai People's Publishing House.

Su, Y. (2003). Another perspective: The study of legal tradition of China in Britain and the United States in modern times. *Global Law Review* 1.

Tian, T., & Li, Z. (2007). *Contact and confrontation: Chinese legal system in the eyes of westerners since the 16th century.* Peking University Press.

Turner, K. (2004). *Recent American academic writings on traditional Chinese law.* Gao, H., Trans. Beijing: Tsinghua University publishing house co., ltd.

Wang, J. (2002). *The introduction of western laws to China: Investigation on the early history of correspondence between Chinese and western legal concepts.* Tsinghua University Publishing House.

Willoughby, W. W. (1957). *Foreign rights and interests in China.* Wang, S., Trans. Beijing: SDX Joint Publishing Company.

Xu, B., & Yuan, W. (2001). *The politics of languages and translation.* Beijing: Central Compilation & Translation Press.

Yin, Z. (2017). The third world as a subject: Legislators in action and the creation of a modern international order—Comments on the *legal orientalism: China, the United States and modern law.* Renmin University Law Review 1.

Yu, F. (2015). Chinese Law in the Eyes of the West. Zhejiang People's Congress Magazine 4.

Zang, J. (2007). *Review and prospect of the Chinese legal system.* China University of Political Science & Law Press.

Zhang, Z. (2011). The study of "Laws of Great Qing" in Britain and America in Late Qing Dynasty. *Journal of Beijing Institute of Technology (Social Sciences Edition)* 3.

Zheng, G. (2018). From Chinese rule of law to rule of law with Chinese characteristics: Lessons from *legal orientalism. Journal of Shanghai Institute of Political Science and Law* 2.

Zhou, N. (2006). *The celestial empire is far away: A study of western images of China* (Vol. I). Peking University Press.

Chapter 5
Image Construction in the Ancient Chinese Code

Abstract In ancient China, the special geographical location and the development process of legal civilization determined that the ancient people created a unique set of complex and detailed legal system in the long history. Since Qin and Han Dynasties, China has formed a legal governance society. The systematic evolution of ancient Chinese legal classics has a strong continuity, starting from the *Canon of Laws* of the Warring States Period to the *Ta Tsing Leu Lee* of over two thousand years later, and its systematic legislation technology was constantly improved. The stable value concept and the continuous improvement of legislation technology have created the highly legal civilization of ancient legal classics, which has become the symbol of the Chinese legal system. Qing Dynasty is the last unified absolute monarchy in China, and its national code *The Great Qing Legal Code* (also known as another translated version *Ta Tsing Leu Lee*), carrying rich connotations, inherited the legal tradition of China for thousands of years. This code can be regarded as the crystallization of ancient judicial culture and cultural tradition. In 1810, George Thomas Staunton translated the *Ta Tsing Leu Lee* into English and published it in London, which was the first time for Westerners to see the complete ancient Chinese code, and thus they had a direct understanding of the specific legal provisions of ancient China. From then on, Westerners' understanding and study of Chinese law have entered a new stage, representing a peak of Chinese culture spreading to the West since Ming and Qing Dynasties. In this chapter, we mainly introduce the inheritance and innovation of the *Ta Tsing Leu Lee* to the traditional Chinese legal culture, including the purpose of the English translation of the *Ta Tsing Leu Lee* and the story behind it, as well as the value of its English translation and its impact on the exchange of Chinese and Western legal civilizations.

X. Dong and Y. Luo, *The Legal Image of China in Chinese Legal Tradition*,
https://doi.org/10.1007/978-981-96-5797-1_5

5.1 *Ta Tsing Leu Lee*: An Epitome of Traditional Chinese Laws

Laws in China began with the early laws and penalties in the Shang Dynasty, followed by written criminal books *Jiu Xing* (*Nine Punishments*) and *Lü Xing* in the Zhou Dynasty. *Canon of Laws* written by Li Kui in the Warring States Period is the first known legal code, based on which Shang Yang, a representative legalist of Qin, reformed the Qin's legal system, and subdivided the abstract laws into rules emphasizing practical behavior. This form of laws and rules were named 律(*Lü*) in Chinese.

After the First Emperor of Qin unified the six countries, the Qin law was adopted by the whole of China at that time, and the laws of the ancient Chinese Dynasties were all originated from the Qin Law. Later, the reform of the legal system in ancient China had far-reaching influence in the Han, Tang, Song, Ming, and Qing Dynasties. The *Ta Tsing Leu Lee*, are regarded by later scholars as the epitome of the traditional Chinese feudal code, and it is the last participle code in the feudal society of more than 2000 years in China, which is in the same line with the ancient traditional legal system. The basic spirit and main system of the feudal laws established since the Han and Tang Dynasties have been fully embodied in the *Ta Tsing Leu Lee*. The formulation of the *Ta Tsing Leu Lee* fully considered the political practice and political characteristics of the Qing Dynasty, and made additions and subtractions according to the specific domestic and foreign situations at that time, and developed and innovated the laws of the previous generation in some specific systems.

From the first year of Shunzhi, the Qing Dynasty began to formulate the code by interpreting and revising the laws of the Ming Dynasty in detail. Through the efforts of the three emperors Shunzhi, Kangxi, and Yongzheng, the code gradually matured. After Emperor Qianlong ascended the throne, he continued to order ministers to re-formulate the former court rules and regulations, which was completed in the fifth year of Qianlong (1740 AD), and named the *Qing Ding Da Qing Lü Li* (*The Great Qing Code*). With its promulgation, the most systematic and representative written code of the Qing Dynasty was completed. Until the legal system reform at the end of the Qing Dynasty, the legal texts of the Qing Dynasty statutes did not change, and the adjustment of the legal system was mainly carried out in the form of adding and modifying provisions.

The *Ta Tsing Leu Lee* consists of 39 volumes, divided into three parts:

The first part is a law chart composed of 8 charts, namely "六赃(*Liu Zang*)(six crimes of illegally obtaining public or private property as stipulated in the *Tang Code*)", "纳赎诸例(*Na Shu Zhu Li*)(provisions on the number of redeemed silver in the criminal law of Qing Dynasty)", "徒限内老疾收赎(*Tu Xian Nei Lao Ji Shou Shu*)(if a person is under the age of 70 or has no physical disability when he is sentenced to prison after the crime, but reaches the age of 70 or has a sudden physical disability during the execution of the prison sentence, he is allowed to be redeemed on the basis of old age illness)", "诬轻为重收赎(*Wu Qing Wei Zhong Shou Shu*)(in the Qing Dynasty, false accusation was always a crime that was severely punished, and false accusation against others would be reversed, but the undecided false crime could be redeemed)", "过失杀伤收赎(*Guo Shi Sha Shang Shou Shu*)(For non-subjective intentional manslaughter, it is an unintentional mistake, so the method of redemption is also specially prescribed for such offenders, but unlike the above-mentioned articles, the money and property collected by the manslaughter person in accordance with the law must be paid to the victim.)", "五刑(*Wu Xing*)(five forms of punishment)", "狱具(*Yu Ju*)(the crime has been convicted)" and "服制(*Fu Zhi*)(the ancient system of clothing according to the status level)". Each chart is accompanied by the corresponding judicial interpretation, which stipulates the specific sentencing scale.

The second part consists of all 436 legal terms composed of 7 articles, and each article has the title of the law. For example, the first article is "名例律(*Ming Li Lü*)(General Law)", with a total of 46 law articles, mainly involving important legal systems such as "*Wu Xing*", "十恶(*Shi E*)(ten major crimes in ancient China that are not forgiven by ordinary amnesty)" and "八议(*Ba Yi*)(China's feudal criminal law stipulates that crimes against eight types of people must be handed over to the emperor for adjudication or punishment commuted according to law.)", and specific charges stipulated for "perpetrators", as well as various legal provisions on the punishment and exemption of punishment for the seven basic crime types convicted and sentenced.

The third part is the arrangement of specific legal provisions. According to the title of the specific provisions, it is arranged and combined by the names of the six sections of the Fiscal Law*(Lì Lü)*、Civil Law*(Hu Lü)*、Ritual Law*(Lǐ Lü)*、Military Law*(Bing Lü)*、Criminal Law*(Xing Lü)*、Law relative to Public Work*(Gong Lü)*, including "职制(*Zhi Zhi*)(one of the 12 titles of *Tang Code*, which refers to provisions on punishment and punishment of officials for violating the law)", "公式(*Gong Shi*)", "户役(*Hu Yi*)(household officers)", "田宅(*Tian Zhai*)(fields and houses)", "婚姻(*Hun Yin*)(marriage)", "仓库(*Cang Ku*)(warehouse)", "课程(*Ke Cheng*)(course)", "钱债(*Qian Zhai*)(monetary debts)", "市场(*Shi Chang*)(market)", "祭祀(*Ji Si*)(sacrificc)", "仪制(*Yi Zhi*)(the etiquette system and its specific provisions)", "宫卫(*Gong Wei*)(guards of the imperial court)", "军政(*Jun Zheng*)(military and governance)", "关津(*Guan Jin*)(an important route for land and water transportation)", "厩牧(*Jiu Mu*)(feeding and grazing)", "邮驿(*You Yi*)(post)", "贼盗(*Zei Dao*)(thieves and robbers)", "人命(*Ren Ming*)(human life)", "斗殴(*Dou Ou*)(brawl)", "骂咒(*Ma Zhou*)(abuse and curse)", "诉讼(*Su Song*)(litigation)", "受赃(*Shou Zang*)(offense of accepting stolen goods)", "诈伪(*Zha Wei*)(falsification)", "犯奸(*Fan Jian*)(committing adultery)", "杂犯(*Za Fan*)(charges other than those of the specific categories)", "捕亡(*Bu Wang*)(rules governing the pursuit of criminals and fugitive soldiers)", "断狱(*Duan Yu*)(hearing and deciding a case)", "营造(*Ying Zao*)(building)", and "河防(*He Fang*)(embankments of rivers)". All these amount to a total of 436 legal provisions and more than 1,800 articles which have the same legal effect as law stationery in accordance with the circumstances.

As the last feudal code in ancient Chinese history, the *Ta Tsing Leu Lee* has the following main features: First of all, the *Ta Tsing Leu Lee* includes both the laws*(Lü)* and the cases*(Li)* within a precise and thorough system. The integration of laws and cases is not the original creation of the Qing Dynasty lawmakers. Once the law is enacted, it is not easily changed, and the cases and examples can be used as the standard for determining the severity of punishment according to the specific circumstances. This is also the major characteristics of China's feudal code. Over nearly 100 years from the second year of Shunzhi to the fifth year of Qianlong, the Qing Dynasty has revised the law and compiled the *Ta Tsing Leu Lee*, which accumulated rich experience and assessed the gains and losses of the past dynasties, so the content of the law is quite detailed. Where the law does not apply, cases can be referred to determine the severity of the penalty. This combination shows both the stability and flexibility of its legal characteristics and was called the peak of the ancient Chinese legal system by Western legal researchers.

Secondly, the stable *Lü* part and the relatively flexible *Li* part. The *Ta Tsing Leu Lee* is a mixture with multiple branches of laws and dimensions, which follows the edict of the Ming Dynasty and the practice of the legislative system since the Ming Dynasty. Once the law is established, in addition to the official provision of "one minor revision in five years, and one major overhaul in ten years", others are strictly prohibited to change without authorization. The *Lü* part with 436 articles are actually the unchanged mode of legal moralization and legislative idealization, while the *Li* part with cases and examples are growing with the times. In other words, the contradiction between the stability of *Lü* and the variability of real life can be solved by increasing the number of *Li*.

Third, take the criminal law as the mainstay, and the criminal law is more important than the civil law. The number of clauses in the criminal law accounts for nearly half of the total provisions of the *Ta Tsing Leu Lee*, according to which civil cases are usually decided by means of punishment. From the distribution of the number of volumes, there are 15 volumes related to criminal punishment in the total 39 volumes. If adding the other volumes of the criminal punishment provisions belong to civil legal cases, the total number of criminal provisions in the *Ta Tsing Leu Lee* is conservatively estimated to account for more than 70% of the total law. Therefore, the *Ta Tsing Leu Lee* is not so much a combination of all laws as a legal text, rather it is one with penalty as the main and civil as the supplement. And in the specific judicial process, the judgment mode of most civil cases is always the same as that of criminal cases. In addition, from the point of view of the style arrangement form of legal texts, the *Ta Tsing Leu Lee* basically follow the form of Ming laws, and its overall framework consists of two parts: "*Ming Li Lü*(General Law)" and "(*Liu Lü*)(six kinds of laws, including the Fiscal Law, Civil Law, Ritual Law, Military Law, Criminal Law, Law relative to Public Work)". The first part is "General Law", a total of 46 articles, which provides for the principle of the composition of crimes and is equivalent to the "general principles" of modern law. Also, it makes general provisions on the application of law in terms of criminal names, scale of punishment, pardons, accomplices, and voluntary surrender and gives corresponding legislative interpretations.

Fourth, the practical function of *Li*(cases) is above the *Lü*(law). Since the issuance of the *Great Qing Law Collection* in the Qing Dynasty, the law text has been recognized as the written law observed by the descendants. Then, its revision was only according to the conditions of the time, so cases can be compiled at any time to supplement and modify the deficiencies of the law text. From more than 400 articles of the *Great Qing Law Collection and Appending* in the early years of Kangxi, to 824 of the *Great Qing Law Collection* in the third year of Yongzheng (1725 AD), 1,049 of the *Ta Tsing Leu Lee* in the fifth year of Qianlong (1740 AD), 1,456 in the 33th year of Qianlong (1768 AD), and 1,766 in the fifth year of Daoguang (1825 AD), the number of cases had been constantly increasing. By the ninth year of Tongzhi (1870), the number had increased to 1892. The rapid growth of the number of cases, on the one hand, reflects that the Qing rulers had to resort to new cases in order to prevent the traitors who slipped through the law and improper offense. On the other hand, it is because that the form of *Li* is relatively flexible and easy to elevate the ruler's will to *Lü* at any time. Therefore the *Li* were valued by the ruler, and their role and effect are above the *Lü*, in fact, which finally formed a situation that in judicial practice, if there are precedent, precedents are preferred over legal provisions; the new precedents take precedence over the old ones.

5.1.1 As the Channel for the West to Understand the Ancient Chinese Law

Westerners have long paid attention to Chinese law. *The Travels of Marco Polo*, written by Marco Polo in the Yuan Dynasty, already has a lot of descriptions about the legal situation in China. In the seventeenth and eighteenth centuries, Jesuits came to China and compiled their experiences in China into books, some of which dealt with the Chinese judicial system, such as *Mathew Ricci's Notes on China* and Tseng Dezhao's *Chronicles of the Great Empire of China.* Enlightenment thinkers such as Montesquieu, Quesnay, and Voltaire all learned about Chinese law by reading the works of Jesuits. However, the Jesuits' writings have certain defects, and the Jesuits' statements are sometimes inaccurate or even fallacious, either because of their lack of understanding of the Chinese legal system, or because of their personal understanding. In 1810, Thomas Staunton translated the *Ta Tsing Leu Lee* into English and published it in London, which was the first time for Westerners to see the complete Chinese code and have an intuitive understanding of the specific legal provisions of China. Since then, the study of Chinese law by Westerners has entered a new stage.

In 1792, the British government sent the Macartney Mission to China, and Sir George Leonard Staunton (father of Thomas Staunton) was appointed secretary of the delegation, and Thomas Staunton went to China as a page boy at the age of 11. Thomas Staunton, who already spoke four languages, learned Chinese on the ship to Beijing. In 1797, he entered Trinity College, Cambridge, where his father withdrew him due to the unfair distribution of freshman awards. In 1798, he was offered the post of Chinese clerk at the British Mercantile House in Guangzhou by the East India Company, and in 1808 he became its translator. In 1800, shortly after Thomas Stanton's arrival in Guangzhou, the "Providence" incident occurred, when a British sailor shot at a Chinese fisherman, wounding one man and killing another by falling into the water. The Qing government demanded that the British side thoroughly investigate this incident and hand over the murderer. The British, for their part, requested that British officials attend the trial. This event was later seen as the beginning of an issue of consular jurisdiction that would shape the next century of modern Chinese history. In the process of handling the case, Hall, chairman of the East India Company's commercial office in Guangzhou, found that the Chinese government dealt with the case according to the *Ta Tsing Leu Lee*, so he hoped that the British could also obtain a copy of the legal provisions printed in China at that time, but Ji Qing, the Viceroy of Liangguang,[1] was unwilling to give the relevant provisions to the British, only extracted 6 articles from it and printed 100 copies. Hall then asked Thomas Staunton to translate the six articles into English. These six articles are:

(1) Suspected theft and murder are tantamount to fighting and killing, shall be hanged.
(2) Killing with a shotgun is equivalent to intentional homicide, shall be beheading; those who kill (or injure) people shall be sent to the army.
(3) If the sinner was arrested and did not resist arrest, but the law enforcer killed him, then he shall be considered a crime of fighting and killing, and hanged.
(4) If falsely accusing good people of being thieves, in addition to the actual capital crime, the rest of criminals, no matter the principal offenders or accessory offenders shall be sent to the army.
(5) Accidental injury to people shall be considered as fight injury, and the punishment should be based on the severity of the injury.
(6) Those who drink heavily and make trouble and should be exiled, shall be sent to the southwestern remote areas as slaves.

Perhaps it was such a translation task that aroused Thomas Staunton's interest in studying Chinese law and translating the *Ta Tsing Leu Lee*. He believed that the main reason why the British encountered some problems in the process of commercial trade with the Qing Dynasty was that there was a wrong or imperfect understanding of the spirit of Chinese law. In order to have a comprehensive understanding of Chinese law so as to better protect his country's interests in the event of a conflict between China and Britain, Thomas Staunton managed to find two different versions of the *Ta Tsing Leu Lee*, and after comparing them, he began to translate the whole version of the *Ta Tsing Leu Lee*. In 1808, he completed the translation of the code on a ship returning to England. Back in England, booksellers Cadell and Davis bought the rights to the book for £500. After that, Thomas Staunton spent a lot of time on the translator's preface and appendix to the *Ta Tsing Leu Lee*, and it was not until March 1810 that *Ta Tsing Leu Lee* was officially published in London. This is an important event in the history of Sino-Western legal culture exchange, marking that

[1] The Viceroy of Liangguang, also known as the Governor of Guangdong and Guangxi; it was the highest official in charge of Guangdong and Guangxi during the Ming and Qing Dynasties, responsible for military and civil affairs and military food and pay.

China's legal image in the West has entered a new stage, and Westerners can finally read Chinese legal provisions directly through translation.

The original version of the *Ta Tsing Leu Lee* used in Thomas Staunton's English translation was issued in the fifth year of Qianlong. He translated all 436 articles of the *Ta Tsing Leu Lee* as the main text, and the appendix of the English translation contains a few translated cases and some relevant decrees. The book is divided into six parts: preface, table of contents, pretext citation, main body, errata, and bibliography. In the main body, Thomas Staunton divides it into seven parts, corresponding to the structure of the *Ta Tsing Leu Lee*, which are General Law*(Ming Li Lü)*, Fiscal Law*(Lì Lü)*、Civil Law*(Hu Lü)*、Ritual Law*(Lǐ Lü)*、Military Law*(Bing Lü)*、Criminal Law*(Xing Lü)*、Law relative to Public Work*(Gong Lü)*.

It should be noted that Thomas Staunton's translation of the *Ta Tsing Leu Lee* only translated 436 articles of *Lü* in the five-year edition of the Qianlong period, while the other 1042 cases in *Li* part were not translated comprehensively. In response, he explained that please allow the translator the freedom to cut the original, while striving for a more systematic arrangement, a more pleasant style, and a more harmonious wording. Thomas Staunton believes that this deletion is necessary, if the whole content of the *Ta Tsing Leu Lee* is translated, it will appear that Chinese law is too complicated and disorderly, and after deletion readers can easily understand the basic content of Chinese law.

It is worth noting that Thomas Staunton arranged the translation of the cases of *Li* very cleverly, and these cases are not codified in the articles of *Lü* as in the original, but are concentrated in the appendix. It is particularly notable because of its small quantity. In addition, some emperor's edicts and the capital city newspaper were added independently. As for the imperial edicts of the Qing Dynasty, Thomas Staunton believed that although their contents were not included in the *Ta Tsing Leu Lee*, they had the same effect as the code. In order to avoid the possible understanding deviation in the translation between Chinese and English, Thomas Staunton also added small notes in the English translation of the *Ta Tsing Leu Lee*, which mainly played the role of dredging and clarifying, and were mostly sandwiched between the corresponding articles or cases. Finally, he added Roman ordinals to the front of all the articles for numbering and marked the number of articles attached to the original law in the *Ta Tsing Leu Lee* after the law. "This detail makes up for the shortcoming of traditional Chinese codification techniques, which do not pay attention to the serial numbers of articles". It can be said that Thomas Staunton's practice harmonized the reading habits of China and the West and facilitated the Spreading of the *Ta Tsing Leu Lee* in the West. However, the main purpose of Thomas Staunton was to enable the English people in China to quickly master the law of the Qing Dynasty, to safeguard their interests in China, and to deepen Europe's understanding of the law and society of the Qing Dynasty. Due to such translation purpose and strategy, the translated version is indeed easy to be accepted by Western readers, but it cannot accurately restore the meaning of the text, resulting in a lot of distortions and misrepresentations, and thus the treaty between the two different legal systems cannot be realized in this sense.

5.1.2 The Value and Influence of Ta Tsing Leu Lee

Thomas Staunton believes that *Ta Tsing Leu Lee* is the first class book in China, but Western missionaries did not pay enough attention to the translation of legal works, and the English translation of the *Ta Tsing Leu Lee* can be regarded as a remedy for the deficiencies of legal translation.

After the English translation of the *Ta Tsing Leu Lee* was published, it received high attention in the British society. Many important British media, such as *Edinburgh review, Monthly review*, and *Chinese repository*, have reported on Jr. Staunton's translation of the *Ta Tsing Leu Lee*, and some have made relevant comments. The *Edinburgh Review* commented that, although great trade relations between Britain and China have been established for more than a hundred years, this is the first time that this work has been translated directly into our language. There is certainly no document which now enables us to know so reliably the condition and character of a country as the laws themselves. In addition, the French and Italian editions of the book were translated from English two years later (1812). The fact that all countries were translating the *Ta Tsing Leu Lee* proved that the laws of the Qing Dynasty had become a universal demand in Europe at that time. Later, a Spanish version of the *Ta Tsing Leu Lee* (1862) was published. In 1876 and 1924, the French have produced new French translations.

Notably, after the publication of the *Ta Tsing Leu Lee*, Thomas Staunton became a recognized "expert on the Chinese spirit" in Britain at that time, because of his knowledge of Chinese law, and had influence in Parliament. In 1833, Thomas Staunton, then a member of the British Parliament, proposed a bill to Parliament calling on the British government to establish a court in China to hear the cases of British people in China, citing the alleged backwardness of Chinese law. The motion was passed. Accordingly, the British Parliament enacted an act unilaterally giving the British Consul in China the right to hear cases involving British subjects. After the First Opium War, the British occupied Hong Kong, and the British authorities realized that taking the *Ta Tsing Leu Lee* as the basis of judicial judgment was conducive to their stable colonial rule in Hong Kong. At that time, the *Ta Tsing Leu Lee* used by the British was the English version translated by Thomas Staunton.

After the English translation of the *Ta Tsing Leu Lee* was published in 1810, European and American scholars conducted a century-long study on Chinese laws, which roughly presents two characteristics. One is the changes of attention from criminal provisions to civil provisions. Before the First Opium War, there were conflicts between foreign sailors, merchants and Chinese people in China's coastal areas, and criminal cases involving foreigners mainly occurred during this period, so Europeans and Americans mainly focused on the criminal provisions of the *Ta Tsing Leu Lee*. After the First Opium War, with the signing of a series of unequal treaties, the West not only gained the right of consular adjudication in China, but also was allowed to set up factories and churches in China to preach, and civil disputes between Chinese and foreigners also increased. During this period, Europeans and Americans began to pay attention to the provisions on civil relations in the *Ta Tsing Leu Lee*.

The other characteristic is the change of attitude toward the code. Before the First Opium War, the attitude of European and American people toward the *Ta Tsing Leu Lee* was mainly critical. For example, in May 1834, the *Chinese repository* (Volume 3) published an article by Morrison specifically discussing the crime of homicide in China, which was representative among Westerners in China at that time. After the First Opium War, Western scholars gradually bid farewell to the concentrated criticism of the *Ta Tsing Leu Lee* and began to pay attention to civil relations and introduce some principled systems. In the early twentieth century, some scholars interpreted the Chinese legal system from a cultural perspective and explained the rationality of Chinese civilization.

Viewed from the perspective of later generations, the translation of the *Ta Tsing Leu Lee* at that time was very important and valuable for Western understanding of Chinese law, since then Westerners can find reliable evidence through their laws, and these laws are not the biased empty rhetoric of China's admirers or haters, but the rich and original written laws of the country. On the one hand, it clarified the debate about China's legal image in the West before the nineteenth century, especially in the age of Enlightenment. The translation of the *Ta Tsing Leu Lee* in 1810 made the West analyze China's legal image for the first time from the perspective of the empirical text of Chinese law and tried to find a balance between praise and criticism. However, we must also realize that, on the other hand, the image of ancient Chinese law went through historical ups and downs of praise and criticism in the West and became stable after the translation of the *Ta Tsing Leu Lee*. On the other hand, behind this so-called stability was also the rejection of China's legal image in the West at that time and the conviction of its own legal legitimacy. In the early nineteenth century, under the influence of the review of the English translation of the China's legal image, Western legal centralism began to take shape. In the eyes of Western scholars at that time, the backward and closed image of ancient Chinese law gradually became a new "other" in the West, which was completely different from the Enlightenment era.

5.2 Cultural Misreading and Image Construction in Its First English Translation

From the micro level of translation strategies and methods, there are a lot of "faithlessness" and even a "misreading" of Chinese traditional legal culture in the first English translation of the *Ta Tsing Leu Lee*. Cultural misreading can be divided into unintentional misreading and intentional misreading, and the translation purpose directly determines translation strategies and methods. Based on Lefevere's translation manipulation theory, the misreading in Jr. Staunton's translation of the *Ta Tsing Leu Lee* is a kind of intentional misreading. The fundamental purpose is to serve Britain's political ideology of controlling China and cater to the ideology of cultural hegemony of the Western legal civilization centralism. Therefore, the translation of the *Ta Tsing Leu Lee* by Jr. Staunton needs to be reevaluated and repositioned. No matter the translation strategy featuring faithfulness, simplification, or rewriting, this deliberate cultural misreading is just a kind of cultural hegemony and power manipulation carried out by ideology on translation under the guise of cultural exchange.

In recent years, the first English translation of the *Ta Tsing Leu Lee* has been widely valued by the academic community, and there have been much research on this translation in the fields of translation, legal history, and history of international relations. Some articles discuss the influence of the translation in the Western world from the perspective of translation value, mainly from the macro level, or reveal the translator Jr. Staunton's motivation to translate the *Ta Tsing Leu Lee*, or sort out the historical background and process, or call for criticism and research on the translation of legal classics (Wang, 2001; Hou, 2009; Zhang, 2011; Xiong, 2019; Qu, 2019). At the micro level, these articles also occasionally mention translation strategies and methods, but the content is less, and most of them are passing by Scholar Zhao Changjiang's research pays more attention on the translation strategy, but mostly positive comments, such as being faithful to the original text, cutting the text to a certain extent, not joining the translator's thoughts, respecting the author and the original work. In addition, he defines the value of the translation as the cultural exchange between China and Britain, marking the beginning of direct cultural dialogue and exchange between China and Britain (Zhao, 2012a, 2012b). However, we find that there is much faithlessness in the translation strategies and methods of Jr. Staunton's translation, and even misreading of the traditional Chinese legal culture, which has a profound negative impact in the historical context. If the translation marks the cultural exchange and dialogue between China and Britain, the translator should be faithful to the original of the *Ta Tsing Leu Lee*, convey the true nature of Chinese culture as much as possible, and increase the understanding of each other, rather than produce much misunderstanding. Therefore, this study is to analyze the root cause of translator Jr. Staunton's misunderstanding of Chinese legal culture in translation, so as to reevaluate and position the first English translation of the *Ta Tsing Leu Lee.* This chapter adopts the method of case demonstration to go beyond the surface appearance to recognize its nature, first enumerates the specific misreading phenomenon in translation, and then, from the micro level to the macro level, with the help of Lefevere's translation manipulation theory, reveals the fundamental purpose of Jr. Staunton's cultural misreading in his translation. In this way, we can correctly and objectively view China's image and its historical value in the first English translation of the *Ta Tsing Leu Lee*, so as to get some reflection and inspiration for the foreign exchange of today's traditional Chinese legal culture.

5.2.1 *Cultural Misreading and Its Performance*

Le (1994) points out that due to cultural differences, when two cultures come into contact, there will inevitably be misreading. The so-called misreading is to interpret another culture according to one's own literary tradition, way of thinking, and everything one is familiar with. From the perspective of world history, the traditional Chinese legal culture belongs to the category of the Chinese legal system, which is different from the Anglo-American legal system and the continental legal system in terms of legal terms and concepts as well as traditional cultural heritage. This difference and uniqueness of the legal culture means that it is not easy to translate the *Ta Tsing Leu Lee* into English. Translators are required to have a more profound understanding of Chinese traditional legal culture. Traditional culture is the soil that nourishes the formation of the concepts and terms of the Chinese legal system, while the terms are the direct representation of the inner spirit and cultural values of the Chinese legal system, so the two are in a relationship that merges with each other. We find that Jr. Staunton's misreading in the English translation of the *Ta Tsing Leu Lee* exists in two levels. First of all, there is a phenomenon of avoidance and simplification in the translation and transmission of some Chinese cultural information; secondly, some Chinese legal terms were completely interpreted and replaced by Western legal terms.

5.2.1.1 The Avoidance of Some Traditional Chinese Cultural Information

This section explores the limitations of George Thomas Staunton's translation of the *Ta Tsing Leu Lee*, the Qing Dynasty legal code. While acknowledging Staunton's significant contributions to introducing Chinese law to the West, the analysis highlights his tendency to simplify or omit cultural nuances present in the original text. This approach, while making the code more accessible to Western audiences, inadvertently erodes the rich cultural context and unique characteristics of Chinese legal terminology and concepts. This is primarily manifested in three areas:

Hidden Legal Terms with Numbers In the ancient Chinese code, there are many terms beginning with numbers, such as ***Wu*** *Xing (**five** forms of punishment)*, ***Ba*** *Yi (adjudication on crimes against **eight** types of people)*, ***Shi*** *E (**ten** major crimes)*. Wang Donghai (2007) summarized them as "terms with numbers", but Jr. Staunton translated them as description of the ordinary punishments, the privileged classes, offenses of a treasonable nature. In fact, The *Bible* also contains The Ten Commandments, but in his translation of some of the Chinese terms with numbers, Jr. Staunton deliberately avoided the appearance of numbers, undoubtedly eroding the numerical character of terms in Chinese legal culture.

The Simplification of Traditional Cultural Information Jr. Staunton simply translated the term "化外人(*Hua Wai Ren*)" as "foreigners". This term appeared in the Tang Dynasty and was followed by successive generations. *Tang Code* in the commentary said, "*Hua Wai Ren*", are from countries of "蕃夷(*Fan Yi*)(an old general term for foreigners)", which are governed by other emperors. During the Tang Dynasty, the national power reached its peak, but except for the Huaxia, the predecessor of Han nationality, the etiquette system of some other tribes could not be compared with the Chinese civilization and even belonged to the barbarian states. Therefore, the "*Hua Wai Ren*" related to the adjustment of foreign legal relations, and foreigners and natives were treated equally, which directly reflected the political Enlightenment and economic prosperity of the Tang Dynasty. For example, *Tang Code* stipulates, "If *Hua Wai Ren* of the same country commits a crime in China, he or she shall be punished according to the laws of his or her own country; if *Hua Wai Ren* of different countries committed crimes against each other or the Tang people committed crimes against *Hua Wai Ren*, they were dealt with according to the *Tang Code*". The *Ta Tsing Leu Lee* stipulates, "Once a *Hua Wai Ren* commits a crime, he or she shall be judged by the government in accordance with the *Tang Code*, while if he or she is under the jurisdiction of the *Li Fan Yuan* (the ethnic minorities and diplomatic organ governing the outer regions), then he or she shall still be dealt with in accordance with Mongolian rules, which is the most core tool in the process of border criminal management in Qing Dynasty". Therefore, Jr. Staunton's simplified translation of "foreigners" certainly did not convey the cultural confidence of the Tang Dynasty.

For another example, "蛊毒(*Gu Du*)", according to the ancient legends, means to put a lot of poisonous insects in a vessel to made them eat each other, and the last remaining undead insect called *Gu*, is used to put in food to poison people (Lü & Ding, 2016). But Jr. Staunton translated it as "rearing venomous animals and preparing poisons". On the one hand, the unique and overall exotic taste of traditional Chinese culture in "*Gu Du*" disappears. On the other hand, it is easy to cause misreading by translating the two characters apart, because the two characters "*Gu Du*" together is one kind of poisonous animals, rather than understanding them as two things "animals and poisons".

What's more, "五服(*Wu Fu*)" refers to when mourning for relatives in the ancient times, mourning apparel is divided into five levels to distinguish between intimate and estranged relatives, according to the mourning period and its different materials and sewing methods (Gao & Ma, 1985). The *Wu Fu* system conveys complex information as seen in eight graphs in the original code of the *Ta Tsing Leu Lee*, but Jr. Staunton only takes up half a page translating it. Moreover, he uses the four levels of kinship in Europe—the first-degree, the second-degree, the third-degree, and the fourth-degree—to correspond to the five levels in China (Chen Li, 2015), which are, "斩衰(*Zhan Cui*)", "齐衰(*Zi Cui*)", "大功(*Da Gong*)", "小功(*Xiao Gong*)", "緦麻(*Si Ma*)". All the five levels of *Wu Fu* contain four meanings: the mourning period, the materials of the mourning apparel, sewing methods, and the proximity of kinship with the deceased. In order to translate the cultural implications behind this, we must appropriately increase some information and give a detailed explanation, for example, *Zhan Cui* is "the heaviest grade, and it applies to the sons and unmarried daughters mourning their parents, the great-grandsons mourning their grandparents, and the wives mourning their husbands. The mourning apparel is used the coarse raw linen, the edge is not sewn, and the service period is three years" (Gao & Ma, 1985). *Zi Cui* is "lower than *Zhan Cui*. The mourning apparel is made of burlap and edged. The service period depends on the relationship with the deceased. The one-year service period applies to grandsons mourning grandparents, husbands mourning wives, and married daughters mourning parents; The five-month service period applies to the mourning of great-grandparents; Three months applies to the mourning of high grandparents" (Gao & Ma, 1985). Using four levels to define the difference between *Wu Fu* is definitely a simplification and distortion of the original text, what's more, anyone who violates the "*Wu Fu* system" needs to use this as a standard to determine the severity of the crime, which is more necessary to make some distinctions in the translation of *Wu Fu*. However, simply replacing the terms in Chinese laws with those of the Western legal system will erase the cultural differences between different legal systems, resulting in the distortion of cross-cultural interaction between legal systems (Qu, 2019).

The Simplification of the Translation of Charges In the *Ta Tsing Leu Lee*, many charges appear in the form of small sentences, for example, "官司出入人罪(*Guan Si Chu Ru Ren Zui*)(regarding the guilty person as innocent and the innocent person as guilty)", which is an abbreviated expression of "出人罪(*Chu Ren Zui*)" and "入人罪(*Ru Ren Zui*)". The conviction of a felony as a misdemeanor or the acquittal of a guilty is called "出罪(*Chu Zui*)"; to make a felony out of a misdemeanor or to make a guilty out of an innocent is called "入罪(*Ru Zui*)" (Gao & Ma, 1985). Nevertheless, Jr. Staunton translated it as pronouncing and executing an unjust sentence. "Unjust" here means unfair, so naturally it did not fully convey the double connotation of the original charge.

Another example, "应捕人追捕罪人(*Ying Bu Ren Zhui Bu Zui Ren*)", refers to the crime that committed by ancient criminal and public security law enforcement personnel who did not fulfill their responsibility to hunt, while Jr. Staunton directly translated it into "the duty of police officers". It seems to cover more than the sole responsibility of "hunting down criminals", which is both a misreading of connotation and meaning and a simplified translation of it with Western legal terms.

In traditional Chinese legal culture, many words serve as culture-loaded words. In the historical context, these words do not exist in isolation, but are bred in rich cultural soil, with rich connotations and meanings. However, the simplified translation will certainly erode the artistic conception and color of this culture. In the cultural environment of the target language, it will become a common word, losing the same associative meaning and cultural value as in the original text, and "transmitting multiple sources with limited channels easily leads to the inaccuracy of the information transmission of the source and the uncertainty of the reception effect of the host" (Pan & Dong, 2020).

5.2.1.2 The Replacement of Chinese Legal Terms with Concepts in Western Law

Traditional translation study focuses on the equivalence of vocabulary, syntax, and even discourse, which seems to reflect the equal relationship between the two languages and the texts. However, the purpose of translation is far from this, and the translator will inevitably create new words, produce new meanings and even creative discourse in the process of translation, and even standardize it, bringing about some possible changes. Many cross-lingual political acts can be seen in Jr. Staunton's translation of the *Ta Tsing Leu Lee*. He not only conveyed a great deal of information about traditional Chinese legal culture for the target language culture, but also introduced many new definitions, phrases, and conceptual categories for the rewriting of the original text, which are still used today to compare and characterize Chinese legal traditions (Chen, 2015).

The Misreading of the Title Jr. Staunton translated the title "大清律例 (Da Qing Lü Li)" as *Ta Tsing Leu Lee: Being the Fundamental Laws, and a Selection from the Supplementary Statues, of the Penal Code of China.* In the common law system, Penal Code refers to the criminal code, which inevitably equates the *Ta Tsing Leu Lee* with a criminal law, leading Western readers to believe that civil law does not exist in China, which also caused misreading in a certain historical period. In fact, the *Ta Tsing Leu Lee* is a collection of various departmental laws, including regulations on government officials, taxation, markets, household registration, marriage, family, litigation, personal injury, etc. The compilation method of the ancient Chinese code has always been taking the criminal legal norms as the main body and covering civil law, administration, economy, and other department laws. In fact, the codification method of combination of laws was not unique to ancient China, but existed in many countries in the world before modern times, as seen in the ancient Oriental countries' *Code of Hammurabi* and *Manava Dharma Shastras*, the ancient Roman *Law of the Twelve Tables,* and the "barbarian code" of Germanic tribes (Zhang, 2014).

The Adjustment of the Codification Structure According to the Western Law Jr. Staunton also reorganized and rewrote the structure of the *Ta Tsing Leu Lee*. The codification style of the ancient Chinese code is completely different from that of the common law system and the civil law system. Before the spread of Western law to the east, the feudal code of China was not influenced by foreign legal culture, and the communication with the legal culture of the world was almost interrupted and isolated. It was not until 100 years ago that the *Draft of Qing Civil Code* and later the *Law of the Republic of China* began to adopt the codification style of the civil law system (Zhang, 2014), and it was this historical closure that also led to the uniqueness, locality, and nationality of the Chinese feudal codification style. The structure of the *Ta Tsing Leu Lee* is composed of the general part of "*Ming Li Lü*"and the other **six** sections of "***Liu** Lü*", a total of seven, and there is no subdivision between the specific provisions, which often are directly mixed together. This was common to Chinese readers at the time, but somewhat ambiguous to Western readers. In order to make the translation clearer for readers, Jr. Staunton adopted a multi-level division mode, that is, to reconstruct the original text in the form of division, book, chapter, and section.

Moreover, Jr. Staunton refined the terms of the original text and divided them into 436 articles. This stylistic arrangement is to adjust the structure of the Chinese code by borrowing the codification style of the civil law system, which is easy to give the reader the impression that the codification style of the Chinese code is no different from that of the civil law system.

The Replacement of Chinese Legal Terms with Western Legal Terms Specifically, in the translation of some professional terms in the Codex, Jr. Staunton also used existing Western legal terms to replace concepts unique to Chinese legal culture. For example, "吏律(*Lì Lü*)" concerned with the selection of officials and the punishment for breach of duty, which was translated as "civil laws", which seems to be a far cry from administrative institutions, because "civil laws" has multiple meanings in civil law systems, such as Civilian law, Roman law, civil law, private law (Xue, 2013). One more example, "户律(*Hu Lü*)" covers multiple contents such as household officials, fields and houses, marriage, warehouse, monetary debts. However, Jr. Staunton translated it as "fiscal law", obviously ignoring such diverse and rich connotation (Qu, 2019). For another example, in the criminal law section, the word "应捕人 (*Ying Bu Ren*)" refers to the ancient criminal and public security law enforcement personnel, which Jr. Staunton directly translated as "police officers". However, there is no concept of "police" in ancient Chinese law.

This "misreading" of Chinese legal culture with Western legal terms will naturally cause negative effects in the cultural environment of the target language. In the case of the title of the *Ta Tsing Leu Lee*, the simple use of a Western legal concept "criminal law" in translation cannot summarize such a complex and different legal system, which brings more problems to readers' understanding than Jr. Staunton can convey (Chen, 2015). As Jr. Staunton was the first translator of the *Ta Tsing Leu Lee*, it had an irreversible impact on the later translations of other languages based on this. In 1899, Ernest Alabaster published *Notes and Commentaries on Chinese Criminal Law and Cognate Topics, with Special Relation to Ruling Cases*, which translated both the *Lü* part and the *Li* part of the *Ta Tsing Leu Lee*, and also introduced Chinese family law, civil law, and custom law. He argued that it was necessary to "distinguish between the *Ta Tsing Leu Lee* and the 'criminal law'. In the past, the understanding that Chinese criminal law exists in the *Ta Tsing Leu Lee* is narrow. In fact, the contents of Chinese criminal law are very comprehensive and complex, and Chinese criminal law is of all-encompassing importance" (Zhang, 2011). Although Alabaster recognized this distinction, due to the influence of preconceived tradition and custom, he still adopted *Notes and Commentaries on Chinese Criminal Law and Cognate Topics, with Special Relation to Ruling Cases* as its title (Qu, 2019). Namely, he still subconsciously thought that the *Ta Tsing Leu Lee* is a "criminal" code. No matter what translation intention of Jr. Staunton is, the accuracy of the translation will affect the reader's judgment and have a profound and lasting impact. Until the twenty-first century, some scholars have been calling that traditional Chinese law should be examined in its original terms (Chen, 2015).

5.2.2 Analysis on the Causes of Cultural Misreading

Misreading is the variation of understanding in cultural communication. According to Wu Junchao (2006), focusing on the translator's subjectivity, cultural misreading in translation can be roughly divided into two forms: unintentional misreading and intentional misreading. Unintentional cultural misreading is usually caused by factors such as the translator's weak linguistic and cultural skills or irresponsible translation attitude, while intentional cultural misreading is caused by the translator's subjective motivation. It is a deliberate transformation or distortion of the source language cultural information and a deliberate betrayal of the source language culture. While Pan Wenjiao and Dong Xiaobo (2020) believe that cultural misreading is divided into reasonable misreading and unreasonable misreading. Reasonable cultural misreading makes culture to maintain a dynamic and balanced tension, thus forming the driver of cultural development, while unreasonable cultural misreading often leads to cultural misdirection and deepens the estrangement between cultures. It is indeed not easy to accurately translate and convey the information of traditional Chinese legal culture. In the preface to the English translation of the *Ta Tsing Leu Lee*, Jr. Staunton (2015) bluntly stated that the translation "encountered many difficulties" and "it might inevitably be a little unsatisfactory". Even today, accurate translation is difficult for contemporary American sinologists. American scholars D. Budi and C. Morris (1995) pointed out in the preface of the book *The Law of the Chinese Empire* that the ancient Chinese used in legal texts and cases is difficult to understand, which makes the translation work very difficult, especially the translator we invited lacks both an understanding of the *Ta Tsing Leu Lee* and basic knowledge of Chinese legal history.

We believe that the unintentional cultural misreading is value-free, but the intentional cultural misreading is value-related, encompassing the translator's value judgment, ideology, cultural psychology, and other ethical factors. According to the German functional school translation theory, translation is a purposeful act, and the purpose of translation determines the strategies and methods adopted in translation. In order to interpret the cultural "misreading" in the translation strategies and methods adopted by Jr. Staunton, we have to trace the fundamental purpose of his translation. Translation is a complex social practice, which is influenced by many factors. Guided by the theory of translation manipulation school, we will try to explore the real reasons behind it.

5.2.2.1 The Manipulation of Translation

Theo Hermans (1985), a representative of the translation manipulation school, proposed in his book *Literary Manipulation* that, from the perspective of target language literature, all translations manipulate the original text to some extent for some specific purpose. In Hermans' view, translation is not only a tool to manipulate the social system, but also the purpose of constructing social culture and literature.

Manipulation may be due to different motives, and the translator's conscious manipulation may be due to various pressures generated by language, culture, and literary norms (Liu, 2009). André Lefevere (1992) made "manipulation" a central lexical term in his treatise *Translation, Rewriting, and the Manipulation of Literary Fame*, which he mentions in the foreword that translation is, of course, a rewriting of the source text; rewriting, whatever its intent, reflects a particular ideology and poetics as a manipulation of literature, functioning in a particular way under a particular social context. As a form of manipulation in the service of power, rewriting has both positive and negative aspects and can have an impact on a culture, and even distort and contain a culture. In his view, all translation is a form of rewriting, and even the most faithful translation is a form of rewriting. The purpose of rewriting is either to cater to the mainstream ideology or to resist it. Rewriting can play a positive role in introducing new concepts, new styles, and new methods, but also has a negative effect of suppressing, distorting, and controlling. Translation is more of a means of text manipulation. Lefevere (1992) elaborates the concept of manipulation in a systematic way and combines translation with power, ideology, patronage, and poetics.

Translation is affected by social conditions, cultural environment, and other factors. The study of translation should not only consider the intention of the original text, the context of the original text, and the characteristics of the original text, but also take into account a series of factors related to the culture of the target language, such as the purpose of translation, the function of the target language text, the expectation and reaction of readers, the requirements of the client and the sponsor, and the review of the work by the publishing agency. The basic characteristic of the translation manipulation school is that it takes the manipulation of translation as the leading ideology, adopts the target language-oriented empirical method, emphasizes description in methodology, pays attention to system in case analysis, and obtains the recognition of the social culture of the target language in effect (Liu, 2009).

5.2.2.2 To Serve the British Political Ideology

In his memoirs, Jr. Staunton (2015) stated that he began translating the Codex that summer while on holiday in Macao, completed the translation on his return voyage to England, and then sold the copyright to Cadell and a Davies for five hundred pounds when he arrived in London. In other words, the translation was completed before the sale of the copyright, so the patrons and publishers did not give much influence in the process of translation. The reason why he chose to translate the *Ta Tsing Leu Lee* was more influenced by the political ideology at that time.

The main purpose of Westerners coming to China from the seventeenth to the nineteenth century was to conduct commercial trade. With the increasing number of Westerners coming to China, this also posed a challenge to the Qing government's management of Westerners in China. At that time, the Qing government implemented the "tributary system" for foreigners, which was a set of norms for foreigners based on the superiority of Chinese civilization and culture. Westerners who came to China had their own cultural background, but the Qing government controlled foreigners almost as much as it managed and controlled Chinese people, and only when the case involved the killing of Chinese people did it impose criminal jurisdiction on foreigners (Edwards, 2004). Westerners in China were so disgusted that they wanted extraterritorial rights in China to handle cases involving foreigners on their own.

In 1815, Jr. Staunton was elected chairman of the Select Committee of the East India Company's commercial office in Guangzhou and was in charge of the Company's trade with China (Hou, 2006). From the initial clerk to the chairman, he was also involved in many judicial disputes between China and Britain during his stay in China, such as the Neptune Affair (1807) and the Emily (1821) Affair (Li, 2015). This also forced Jr. Staunton to act in the British position and perspective, hiding some kind of motive. After the English translation of the *Ta Tsing Leu Lee* was published, Jr. Staunton also became famous in the British Parliament. In 1833, he proposed a motion to the British Parliament to set up a court in China to hear the cases of British people in China on the basis of the backwardness of Chinese law. This bill was also approved, and the United Kingdom unilaterally formulated rules and regulations for the trial of British cases in China based on the proposal of Jr. Staunton, which is also the earliest known case in which the British established consular jurisdiction in China (Hou, 2009). In a British parliamentary debate in 1840, he also said that it is clear that expulsion from China is the only remedy provided by Chinese law. Our high profile throughout the East is based primarily on the moral power of public opinion. If we submit to this kind of brutality and commercial deterioration perpetrated by China without any attempt at clarification, it is not long before the day arrives in India (Zhang, 2011). The expression of these words fully exposed that Jr. Staunton's translation of the *Ta Tsing Leu Lee* was shrouded by the British political circles and the ideology of the East India Company at that time. It is not purely out of interest in and research on Chinese law, but aiming to better control China by understanding Chinese law, thus opening the door to Chinese trade and safeguarding British business interests in China.

5.2.2.3 Intentional Misreading or Rewriting to Cater to the Ideology of the Western Legal Civilization Hegemony

Britain defeated the Netherlands and France in the process of the Industrial Revolution and thus became the first colonial country. The purpose of Britain sending the Macartney Mission to China may be to verify its superior position in the world with practical actions. The library on Macartney's ship was full of books and materials about China published over the past century. However, after they arrived in China, they found that all the praise and boasting of China by those travelers, missionaries, and historians was nothing but visionary hope. Britain's visit to China was to uncover the true veil of China. Thus, the development degree of Chinese civilization was judged and adjusted, and the attitude and policy toward China were changed (Wang, 2001). The word "civilization" appeared in the French and English world as early as the beginning of the Enlightenment, which was constructed by the Western world in the process of colonization and expansion, both as an examination of its own development and as a belief in human progress. After experiencing two Opium Wars and signing a series of unequal treaties, China finally became one of the "international members". Although China did not take the initiative, at least on the surface, it gave up its arrogant attitude, began to accept more Westerners into China, and gradually opened its door. At this time, what is the relationship between China and the rest of the world? And whether China is a member of the main body of state law constructed by the major Western countries? Lai (2012) believes that the answer lies in an emerging core clue that is the "civilization"; it delineates a movable line between itself and the "uncivilized" or "barbaric". This dividing line of "civilization" can play the role of distinction and exclusion.

A review of the writings of European international jurists in the second half of the nineteenth century shows that the concepts of "civilization", "civilized state", and "international community" are used quite frequently (Liu, 2014). In the nineteenth century, European intellectuals established a set of "civilized" discourse system, thus establishing a measurement standard and scope to distinguish Western countries from non-Western countries. Barbarism is a concept opposed to civilization. In their eyes, Western countries show the superiority of civilization, while non-Western countries are the symbol of barbarism and backwardness. Thus, a civilized "international community" can be formed, and those who share the characteristics of civilization become members of the international law community, while those who do not have the standards of civilization and its obvious signs are ringed outside the family, thus building an unequal international law order.

When Jr. Staunton translated the *Ta Tsing Leu Lee*, he not only served the political interests of the British ideology, but also represented an unconscious comparison and demarcation of the development degree between the East and Western civilization in the course of history. Although Jr. Staunton gave a lot of praise to the *Ta Tsing Leu Lee* in the translation preface, fundamentally speaking, he still believed that the level of civilization of the Chinese people was very low in the scope of civilized countries in the world, because Chinese laws greatly restricted the personal life of individuals, and citizens enjoyed too little freedom and rights, which was not conducive to the development of society (Hou, 2009). In the case of the relatively mature development of the Western legal system at that time, the view of the traditional Chinese legal system according to Western standards would naturally produce a backward cognition, and a gap between the advanced and backward laws between the East and the West would naturally form, which would not exist equal normative understanding in the ethics of cultural exchanges, let alone respect for other cultures.

The original text-oriented translation will inevitably apply the principle of "faithfulness", while the rewriting of translation is always oriented to target language, to cater to the mainstream ideology of the target language environment. Under the restriction of the historical context in the nineteenth century and the influence of the progress of Western social civilization, the translation and introduction of the code of Chinese legal system into the Western legal culture will inevitably be affected by the specific social and historical situation. In the face of the "exotic" style of traditional Chinese legal culture, Jr. Staunton used Western legal concepts to replace Chinese legal terms in his translation, which is actually a conscious rewriting. Of course, the translation strategy, whether it is rewriting, simplifying, or even cultural filtering, is influenced by the translation purpose and mainstream ideology. On the one hand, in order to facilitate the understanding of Western readers and conform to their reading habits, some existing Western legal styles, concepts, and terms are borrowed to translate Chinese legal terms, at the expense of the accuracy and authenticity of some concepts and terms. Qu (2019) holds that the purpose is to make Chinese laws seem more in line with the logic and visual senses of Westerners, and to avoid the natural barrier caused by cultural differences so as to be easy for British people to read and understand, and to take the initiative in the future conflicts involving law between Britain and China. On the other hand, influenced by the whole process of Western legal civilization at that time, Jr. Staunton actually stood on the Western standpoint, centered on the Western legal system and took Western legal civilization as the reference standard, and exerted power manipulation on the original text on the premise and basis that Chinese and Western legal civilization were superior to each other and that there was inequality between different national cultures. In order to better grasp China's legal system and realize its interests in China, it fundamentally reflects the cultural hegemonic thinking of "Western legal civilization centralism". It cannot be denied that just for the purpose of serving political ideology, this deliberate cultural misreading of Jr. Staunton's translation of the *Ta Tsing Leu Lee* will inevitably have a negative impact on the cultural environment of the target language.

5.3 Summary

Frankly speaking, the publication of the English translation of the *Ta Tsing Leu Lee* is not accidental, but the product of The Times. On the positive side, the English translation of the *Ta Tsing Leu Lee* is a dialogue in the history of legal culture exchange between China and foreign countries, which promotes the spread of Chinese legal culture to the outside world. However, from the perspective of the historical era in which it is located, objectively, it also means the leakage of "a large number of precious legal materials" in the feudal dynasty of China at that time, which were indeed used by the British colonialist aggressors later on, causing a lot of harm such as the interference of China's judicial trial and the judicial system. The *British Critic* said, "We heartily congratulate Sir Jr. Staunton on his success, and he is entitled to the best thanks from the public, for his translation contains a wealth of valuable information which we have not had before. The documents in the appendix come directly from Chinese and are the most interesting part of the translation, making the material clear". This passage in the *British Critic* elevates the translation of the *Ta Tsing Leu Lee* to a political height with obvious practical purposes.

From the late eighteenth century to the early nineteenth century, Britain established its maritime colonial hegemony and constantly sought to expand its colonies overseas. The rich ancient China was an important target for its expansion, and the British government sent envoys to China several times, to study China's political and legal system and foreign relations has become the need of British government. After the completion of the English translation of the *Ta Tsing Leu Lee*, it became the most indispensable script for the Western countries to decode the laws and society of the Qing Dynasty, and to some extent adapted to the overseas expansion and colonial needs of the British at that time.

Legal culture is always compatible with social and economic development. There is no superior distinction between different cultures and civilizations. Different legal cultures should communicate with each other on an equal footing, respect each other, and learn from each other. Legal terms are the formal characteristics and core content of legal system, and legal terms are produced in a certain legal culture. In the process of translation, how to deal with the terminology and legal culture in different legal systems reveals a kind of translation politics, reflecting the color of power and ideology. For the purpose of cultural equal communication, we should respect and preserve the heterogeneity of the original text culture and strengthen mutual understanding and knowledge, rather than subjectively transforming it to present more cultural characteristics of the target language. Of course, from a positive point of view, there is no doubt that Jr. Staunton's translation of some concepts and terms in the *Ta Tsing Leu Lee* is faithful, because he also adopts some strategies of "thick translation" for the differentiation caused by cultural differences. We can see that translators add a lot of notes in many parts of the text. It is easy for readers to understand and accept, for example, he translated a form of torture "*Ling Chi*" as "a slow and painful execution", and added notes as long as nine lines (Staunton, 1810), which is a little too "faithful". However, under the view of the ideological manipulation school theory and limited by the historical context, the translation strategies adopted by Jr. Staunton, whether literal translation, simplification or rewriting, was only under the guise of "cultural exchange", and its real purpose was to serve the British national political ideology and cater to the mainstream ideology of Western legal civilization at that time. The essence of this deliberate cultural misreading is a kind of cultural hegemony and power manipulation carried out by Western ideology on the translation of the *Ta Tsing Leu Lee.*

References

Chen, L. (2015). *Chinese law in imperial eyes: Sovereignty, justice, and transcultural politics.* Columbia University Press.

Edwards, R. R. (2004). *Jurisdiction over foreigners in the Qing Dynasty.* Tsinghua University Publishing House Co., Ltd.

Gao, C., & Ma, J. (1985). *Dictionary of ancient Chinese law.* Nankai University Press.

Hermans, T. (1985). *The manipulation of literature: Studies in literary translation.* Croom Helm.

Hou, Y. (2006). The *Ta Tsing Leu Lee* in the eyes of George Thomas Staunton. *State and Society in Late Qing.*

Hou, Y. (2009). The first attempt by Europeans to fully translate Chinese legal classics: Staunton and his translation of the *Ta Tsing Leu Lee.* Historical Archives 4.

Lai, J. (2012). The *Ta Tsing Leu Lee* in the eyes of George Thomas Staunton. *State and Society in Late Qing* 5.

Le, D. (1994). Cultural differences and cultural misreading. *Chinese Culture Research* 4.
Li, Y. (2015). Westerner's view of Chinese law in the 19th century under the influence of Staunton (*Ta Tsing Leu Lee*). https://d.wanfangdata.com.cn/thesis/ChJUaGVzaXNOZXdTMjAyMzA5MDESCUQwMTE2NTMwMhoIOTJvdnJzdmk=.
Liu, J. (2009). *A general history of western translation theory*. Wuhan University Press.
Lü, S., & Ding, S. (2016). *The contemporary Chinese dictionary*. The Commercial Press.
Pan, W., & Dong, X. (2020). To confront the cross-cultural misreading in the process of translation to foreign countries. *Social Sciences in China.*
Qu, W. (2019). A Study on the English translation of Chinese feudal codes and the motivation for English translation. *Chinese Translators Journal* 1.
Staunton, G. T. (1810). *Ta Tsing Leu Lee*. T. Cadell and W. Davies.
Wang, D. (2007). *A study of the semantic system of ancient legal vocabulary—Take the Tang code as an example.* China Social Sciences Press.
Wang, J. (2001). The introduction of western laws to China: Investigation on the early history of correspondence between Chinese and western legal concepts. *Tsinghua Journal of Rule of Law* 2.
Wu, J. (2006). Cultural misreading and translation. *Journal of Zhongzhou University* 4.
Xiong, D. (2019). The practical significance of the critical study of the translation of legal classics: The English translation of the *Ta Tsing Leu Lee. Social Sciences in China.*
Xue, B. (2013). *The compact English–Chinese dictionary of Anglo-American Law.* Peking University Press.
Zhang, Z. (2011). The study of laws of great Qing in Britain and America in late Qing dynasty. *Journal of Beijing Institute of Technology* (Social Sciences Edition) 3.
Zhang, Y. (2014). The compilation format of the civil code of China. *Legal System and Society* 11.
Zhao, C. (2012). The duality of the translation of legal texts: Cultural exchange and information leakage—Take the English translation of the *Ta Tsing Leu Lee* (1810) as an example. *Minority Translators Journal* 3.
Zhao, C. (2012). The English translation of the *Ta Tsing Leu Lee*: The first direct dialogue in the history of cultural exchanges between China and Britain. *Journal of Xi'an International Studies University* 3.

Chapter 6
Image Construction Through the Paratext of Chinese Legal Classics

Abstract The translations of Chinese legal classics in the English-speaking world have focused on three legal classics: *The Great Qing Code* (another translated version by Jr Staunton named *Ta Tsing Leu Lee), The T'ang Code, and The Great Ming Code* (Qu and Wan, Chinese Translators Journal 01:51–59, 2019). The English translation of all three legal classics has been published overseas. Several translators have expressed the purposes and strategies of the English translation in the form of subtexts such as preface, acknowledgment, and introduction, revealing a strong willingness to communicate with the readers of the translated texts. It also supplements and expands important information for the readers to read the English translations of the Chinese legal classics from different levels. The paratext enriches, explains, refines, and verifies the main text of the translation, and it, to a large extent, stimulates the readers' strong interest in reading (Pellatt, Text, Extratext, Metatext and Paratext in Translation, 2013). However, as the essence of traditional Chinese legal thought and culture, the paratexts in English translations of Chinese legal classics have received very little attention. Given this, according to the Paratext Theory, this chapter takes the English translations of *The Great Qing Code*, *The T'ang Code*, and *The Great Ming Code* as the research objects. It utilizes the methods of close reading and comparison and contrast to decipher the rich meaning contained in the paratexts, to understand the translator's purpose and strategy of the English translation of the Chinese legal classics, and to find out the functions of the paratexts with different characteristics in the construction of the relationship between the translator and the readers.

6.1 A Paratextual Perspective

The concept of "paratext" was originally introduced by the French literary theorist Gérard Genette. In 1979, "paratextuality" appeared in his book *Theory of Generalized Textual Instruction.* In 1982, Genette proposed five types of intertextual relationships, one of which pertains to the relationship between the main text and its paratexts (Genette, 2001). Expanding on this in 1987, Genette further categorized paratexts into thirteen types, including publisher's in-texts, author's name, headings, inserts,

X. Dong and Y. Luo, *The Legal Image of China in Chinese Legal Tradition*,
https://doi.org/10.1007/978-981-96-5797-1_6

dedications and inscriptions, prefatory exchange scenarios, original prefaces, other prefaces, in-text titles, hints, public out-texts, and private in-texts. Paratexts primarily consist of peritext, tangible forms attached to the text, and epitext, intangible forms detached from the text (Batchelor, 2018). The aesthetic intention behind paratexts is to ensure the coherence between the destiny of the text and the author's intent, that is, to obtain ideal readers and enable them to approach the textual purpose and meaning to the fullest extent based on the prompt information (Zhu, 2009).

The translator, through paratexts, establishes their existence within the objective material space of the text (Yusten, 2012). Consequently, the paratext is the translator's additional discourse beyond the translation of the original work and possesses several distinct characteristics. Firstly, it serves a communicative function. Within this communicative realm, the translator can communicate with the original author, readers, editors, and publishers. They can present translation purposes, record the translation process, elucidate translation principles, clarify terminologies, express personal evaluations, connect with other texts, or provide paths of interpretation. These interactions forge connections among the translator, the original author, authors of intertexts, readers, publishers, and editors. Secondly, it demonstrates extensionality. The translated text organically comprises both the main text and the paratext, with the paratext serving the main text while maintaining its own independence. Though subordinate in status, the paratext is an indispensable component of the translated text, generating the meaning of the main text. In reality, the paratext envelops and extends the text and functions as a structural element that elucidates, illustrates, and evaluates the text (Zhu, 2009), thus extending the meaning of the translated text and adding value to its content. Lastly, paratext exhibits an orientation function. Virtually all considerations about translation are appended to specific texts in the form of translator's prefaces (Xu, 2001). If the translator's paratext includes understanding the original text, certain viewpoints or theories that may imply reading routes and interpretative logic, the reader's reception of the text can be significantly impacted.

6.2 Overview of Chinese Legal Classics Translation and Relevant Research

In a narrow sense, legal classics refer to ancient legal classics and laws stipulated or recognized by the country and enforced with the state's coercive power, including formal legal classics and various supplementary forms. According to incomplete statistics in the literature, there are as many as 160 legal classics, ranging from *The Jiu-Zhang Law* to *The Great Qing Code* (Dong, 2021). However, the number of translated legal classics available for research is limited. Table 6.1 provides a basic situation of the complete English translations of the three legal classics.

Currently, the research on the translation of legal classics in China primarily focuses on four main themes: (1) the purpose of translation. Qu Wensheng and Wan

Table 6.1 The Basic Situation of Full Translations of Legal Texts

Legal Classics	Translator	Identities	Name of Translation	Publication Date	Works Evaluation
大清律例	George Thomas Staunton	tea merchants, emissaries, old China hand, diplomats and parliamentarians	*Ta Tsing Leu Lee; Being the Fundamental Laws, and a Selection from the Supplementary Statutes of the Penal Code of China*	1810	The first book in the West to provide a more complete and accurate understanding of the traditional Chinese legal system[6.1]
	William C. Jones	Chinese Law Scholars at the University of Washington	*The Great Qing Code*	1994	The closest English translation of *The Great Qing Code* to the original to date[6.2]
唐律疏议	Wallace Johnson	American Sinologist	*The T'ang Code*	1979 (Volume 1); 1997 (Volume 2)	Translations that have aroused the strong research interests of Chinese experts and cross-cultural researchers[6.3]
大明律	Jiang Yonglin	Ethnic Chinese scholar, former president of Society for Ming Studies	*The Great Ming Code*	2005	Provides the possibility for Western scholars to study the legal system of China during the period from the 14th to the seventeenth century[6.4]

[6.1] Wang, Jian. 2001. *Legal Significance of Communicating Two Worlds: Introduction to the Input of Western Legal Methods and Exploration of New Legal Terms in Late Qing Dynasty*. Beijing: China University of Political Science and Law Press

[6.2] Su, Yigong. 1996. Contemporary Chinese Law Studies in the United States. *Chinese and Foreign Law* 05: 69–73

[6.3] Bodde, and Morris. 1995. *Law in Imperial China*. Trans. Zhu Yong. Nanjing: Jiangsu People's Publishing House

[6.4] Qu, Wensheng, and Wan, Li. 2019. What Has Motivated English Translation of the Codes of Pre-modern Chinese Dynasties. *Chinese Translators Journal* 01:51–59

Li identified four translators' motivations when translating these three legal classics: George Thomas Staunton translated *Ta Tsing Leu Lee* to gain the initiative in Sino-British trade and interactions, and William C. Jones's retranslation *The Great Qing Legal Code* aimed to correct and present the original text accurately. Wallace Jiang Yonglin translated *The T'ang Code* to study Chinese law, while Jiang Yonglin translated *The Great Ming Code* to fill the gap in English translations of Chinese legal classics (Qu & Wan, 2019). (2) the translation strategies and techniques for legal terminology and cultural-loaded words. Hu Bo and Dong Xiaobo explored the untranslatability of legal terms in legal classics and proposed compensation principles, strategies of equivalent literal translation, and descriptive compensation translation (Hu & Dong, 2020). (3) research on translation and Spreading. Dong Xiaobo and Zhang Yafang pointed out that Western sinologists firmly seized the initiative to translate traditional Chinese legal classics and shaped rigid images of the Chinese legal system in the international community. Thus, it is necessary to reclaim the initiative in the output translation of Chinese legal classics and to restore the original appearance of legal classics (Dong & Zhang, 2021). (4) comparative study of translation. Xiong Demei analyzed the "adjacency" relationship between law and culture and the commonality and individuality of English and Chinese legal language and culture, and he also called for experts and scholars to critically supervise the quality of existing translations, enhancing the effectiveness of legal classics in international communication (Xiong, 2018).

6.3 Commentary on the Paratext of Chinese Legal Classics

6.3.1 Paratext Commentary on the Great Qing Code *and* Ta Tsing Leu Lee

According to the perspective of philosophical interpretation, translation is based on understanding, which involves the continuous integration of the translator's view with that of the original text. In this process, factors such as the translator's background, identity, and experiences wield considerable influence over the translation's presentation. Therefore, the paratext provided by the translator is crucial; it serves as a significant carrier of the translator's "presence".

6.3.1.1 Paratext Commentary on *Ta Tsing Leu Lee* Translated by George Thomas Staunton

George Thomas Staunton is a prominent figure in the modern history of Sino-British relations. His English translation represents the first English version of *Ta Tsing Leu Lee*. The paratext of the translation encapsulates the title, subtitles, publication information, and a 34-page translator's preface. In the translator's preface, Staunton offers a personal perspective on his understanding of the Chinese language, history, and law.

Multivocality Voice is defined as "the composite of thoughts, viewpoints, and attitudes expressed through language" (Bakhtin, 1998). In the translator's preface, Staunton uses concessive and adversative expressions, presenting a characteristic of multivocality. Regarding the original work, Staunton considers its language obscure and structure complex yet acknowledges its intrinsic value, authentic, authoritative materials, and significant and innovative themes. Concerning missionaries, Staunton appreciates their diligent labor in recording and translating works but criticizes their lack of fairness and discernment, expressing concern about the reliability of many contents. Concerning Chinese law, Staunton's multivocality is particularly notable:

"While acknowledging the defects and intricacies in this legal code, the Chinese people still regards it with pride and appreciation. They seem to share a common expectation for this legal code: fair enforcement, stability, and protection against corruption. Unfortunately, reality stands in stark contrast, as the executors and makers of Chinese law often lead in violating the law. However, compared to laws in other countries, the severity of this situation in Chinese law can only be speculated at present. Nevertheless, we have reason to believe that regardless of the violator's status, blatant or consecutive violations will face retribution. At least, this aspect of the Chinese system deserves recognition" (Staunton, 1810).

Staunton, from the perspectives of different voices, uses connective expressions such as "While…still…Unfortunately…However… Nevertheless…at least…" to construct multiple meanings, creating relationships of resonance, support, and refutation among different voices. The expressions like "full of defects" and "lead in violating" form a responsive connection, while "fair enforcement" and "face retribution" establish a supportive relationship. Although Staunton "encourages readers to independently judge Chinese law according to the mentioned standards", seemingly leaving interpretive space for the readers. The subjective nature of these comments, including translators' comments on Chinese law, coupled with China's relative unfamiliarity with the Western world at the time, indicates Staunton's intent to guide readers through the translation.

The Invisibility of "I" Among all kinds of paratexts, the importance of the translator's preface should not be overlooked. "It is always strange if a translated book of much importance has no translator's preface in front of it", according to Yu Guangzhong (2002), a famous translator in China. This indicates that it is necessary for a translator to "appear" to provide background knowledge before presenting the translated work. In the "Translator's Preface" written by George Thomas Staunton for the English translation of *Ta Tsing Leu Lee*, the first-person singular pronoun is conspicuously absent throughout the text. Instead, the third-person pronoun "the translator" is used, creating a distance between the translator and himself. This strategy highlights the translator's identity and skillfully conceals the personal "I". On the one hand, George Thomas Staunton wants to articulate his viewpoints; on the other hand, he aims to make it quietly. Therefore, even though the preface is written by himself, he never used the word "I" but "the translator", which can lead readers to perceive the preface as an objectively written piece. The readers will be immersed in a scenario where they believe the scene is non-subjective, and they can sense the authentic context of the translation and the true atmosphere of its early Spreading. While "I" remains concealed, the "translator" exerts his subjectivity under in certain intentions: *Ta Tsing Leu Lee* was repeatedly described as *the Penal Code of China* or *the Imperial Code of Penal Laws, with* the additional subtitle "Being the Fundamental Laws, and a Selection from the Supplementary Statute of the Penal Code of China" on the cover. All these might help readers form a one-sided understanding that *Ta Tsing Leu Lee* was just a criminal code.

6.3.1.2 Paratext Commentary on the Great Qing Code Translated by William C. Jones

The paratext in William C. Jones's English translation includes the preface, introduction, annotations, appendix of terminology compilation, and index. William C. Jones is a translator and a scholar of Chinese law and comparative law. The paratext of his translation conveys not only his translation motivations, strategies, and thoughts, but also provides a profound analysis of the core concepts and structural principles of certain legal systems in *The Great Qing Code*, which has significant academic value. In contrast to George Thomas Staunton's strategy of actively guiding readers in the paratext, William C. Jones relies more on existing research findings and employs a writing style that closely aligns with the original text.

Narrative and Evaluation Integration The translator's preface of William C. Jones seamlessly blends narrative and critique: the narrative encompasses his own learning experiences and the process of translating *The Great Qing Code*, while the critique includes feedback on various translations of the code and a brief assessment of his translation. In the translator's preface, William C. Jones, in the first person "I", recounted his initiation into studying Qing Dynasty law in the 1970s. While reading *Contemporary Chinese Law*, a book containing numerous cases, he felt the need to delve into *The Great Qing Code itself*. But the problem he faced was that there were no people who understand Chinese around to discuss about *The Great Qing Code*. Instead he referred to numerous translations critically, but found George Thomas Staunton's English translation "almost useless, too flowing, and not precise enough"; P. Gui Boulais and Paul-Louis-Felix Philastre's French versions were of "low readability and substantial omissions of the original text"; Paul-Louis-Felix Philastre's translation of *the Annamite Code* was "first-rate, yet it does not encompass the entire legal text, and he tends to employ legal jargon in the translation but with numerous inadequacies…" (William, 1994). Under these circumstances, William C. Jones began to translate *The Great Qing Code*, aiming to address issues in previous translations and faithfully present the full essence of the legal code. With considerable effort, the translation was finally completed. William C. Jones evaluates his work by stating, "it is not perfect translation, despite efforts to avoid some errors" (William, 1994). This statement underscores the translator's dedication to preserving the original text's meaning and admission of potential imperfections in the translation.

Mutual Enhancement of Research and Translation William C. Jones believed there must be some way to study China's traditional legal system with legal codes as the core. As early as 1974, he published "Studies on Qing Dynasty Legal Codes—*The Great Qing Code*" in the *American Journal of Comparative Law*, providing a detailed exploration of *The Great Qing Code* (Staunton, 1810). His ongoing efforts to explore research approaches are reflected in the introduction of his translation. As a scholar of Chinese law and comparative law, William C. Jones emphasizes the importance of studying Chinese law, seeing it as an effective means for legal scholars to break free from Eurocentric thinking. Recognizing the differences between China's legal system and the United States, he advocates that researchers trained in one system must abandon familiar concepts when studying another system and attempt to understand the concepts in the new system. William C. Jones explores the feasibility of studying Chinese legal principles from a Chinese perspective, striving to present the original text. Meanwhile, he also incorporates existing research findings into his translation. For example, in the introduction, he integrates his translation insights into the comparison of Chinese and Western law: "In China, laws are enacted to ensure the state interests, and in this process, individual interests often receive protection as an indirect result"; "but in the west, laws develop outwardly, stemming from individual concerns... society indirectly receive benefits while individual interests are protected" (William, 1994). William C. Jones' translation of the *Great Qing Code* complements his research in Chinese law and comparative law, forming a significant characteristic of the paratext in his English translation.

6.3.2 *Paratext Commentary on the T'ang Code*

Wallace Johnson's English translation of The *T'ang Code*, based on the Chinese original *Lv Shu* by Ch'ang-sun Wu-chi (c. 594–659, a politician and historian of the early Tang Dynasty) and others, was published in two volumes. The first volume was published in 1979, providing a clear exposition of the fundamental principles and application standards of Tang law. The second volume, published in 1997, described behaviors subject to legal punishment and the corresponding punitive measures. The paratext of both volumes includes prefaces, introductions, annotations, appendixes of terminology compilations, bibliography, indexes, and an appended list of corrections.

6.3.2.1 Perspectives of Legal Philosophy

The title page of the second volume of the English translation of the *Code* states boldly, "... *The T'ang Code* is not just a legal document; studying these 445 articles is quite enlightening for learning Chinese culture..." (Johnson, 1979). Before translating, Wallace Johnson extensively researched the original work and its philosophical meaning and cultural significance. He also recommended that readers review the introduction before delving into the main text. The introduction covers the historical background of the Tang Dynasty (A.D. 619–906), legislative intentions, the structure of *The T'ang Code*, an overview of research, the textual content, and the implied philosophical views. He believes that the primary purpose of the law is to "maintain the balance of society and harmony between man and nature" and discusses the philosophical idea of "unity of heaven and man" in the "Chinese legal system" from Dong Zhongshu's theory of yin-yang and five elements (Johnson, 1979). In the chapter "General Principles" of *The T'ang Code*, Wallace Johnson, under the title of "Harmony of Law and Nature", thoroughly explored the connection between the *Code* and the Yin-yang and five elements. The code represents Yin, the dark side of social control, while ritual, morality, and education represents Yang. Based on William C. Jones' work, Wallace Johnson focused on the dialectical unity of the translation form and its legal connotation. He also started from the primacy and fundamentality of language in shaping thought and delved into the important spirit of the Chinese legal system—the unity of heaven and man. Moreover, he conducted semantic analyses of crucial legal concepts such as "五刑*(Wu Xing)* (five punishments)" from a philosophical perspective, enhancing readers' understanding of Chinese traditional legal culture, social background, and historical context.

6.3.2.2 Annotation Strategy

In the preface, Wallace Johnson explicitly stated that the target readers of the translation "include not only sinologists but also those interested in legal history and comparative law, such as historians, anthropologists, and sociologists" (Johnson, 1979). Therefore, before commencing the translation, Wallace Johnson consulted a plethora of research literature on *The T'ang Code* and provided extensive annotations in the main texts and paratexts, aiming to place the translation within a rich linguistic and cultural context and to make it accessible to those without sinological education. These endeavors effectively addressed the challenges of balancing the readability of the translation, constructing context, and bridging the gap in legal and cultural communication. The code was written in concise and profound classical Chinese, posing significant difficulties for people without specialized training. To assist readers to the maximum extent, Wallace Johnson adhered to comprehensive annotation, accuracy, and uniform style principles. Two hundred eight annotations were provided in "Part Two, The T'ang Code: General Principles Chapters I-VI" in the second volume. These annotations gave readers a rich source context, immersing them in the corresponding historical environment. For instance, when translating the phrase "皇帝彝宪在怀，纳隍兴轸" (in modern Chinese means the emperor prioritizes the implementation of common law, feeling sorrow when seeing people unjustly treated, akin to personally pushing people into a ditch) (Cao, 1989), Wallace Johnson added the annotation: "This has reference to a story in the Mentius about Yi Yin, who was one of the advisors of the legendary emperor T'ang, the supposed founder of the Shang dynasty (1600–1046 B.C.). He thought that among all the people of the kingdom, even the private men and women if there were any who did not enjoy such benefits as Yao and Shun conferred, it was as if he pushed them into a ditch - Legge, *The Chinese Classics*, ii, 364–365" (Johnson, 1979). It is evident that Wallace Johnson consulted a substantial amount of literature and historical materials. His paratext demonstrates his academic attitude as a translator and researcher, balancing in-depth legal research with the readability of the translation. This meticulous, authoritative, considerate, and practical translation ensures an effective understanding of the *Code* for readers, further stimulating their interests in Chinese culture and philosophy.

6.3.3 *Paratext Commentary on the Great Ming Code*

In 2005, Jiang Yonglin, a renowned scholar in the Department of East Asia at Bryn Mawr College, published the English translation of *The Great Ming Code*. This translation is based on the text of *The Great Ming Code* contained in Gao Ju, ed., *Da Minglü jijie fuli* (*The great Ming code* with commentaries attached by regulations), originally published during the Wanli reign (15,731,619) and reprinted in five volumes by Taiwan Xuesheng Shuju in 1970. Jiang Yonglin's paratext in the translation includes acknowledgments, annotations, an introduction, an appendix with a glossary of terms, and a bibliography.

6.3.3.1 Continuity and Transformation

In the acknowledgments, Jiang Yonglin reflected on his learning and research experiences. In the 1980s, he was recommended by Wallace Johnson, the translator of *The T'ang Code*, to study East Asian law at Harvard Law School. In 1990, Jiang Yonglin assisted William C. Jones in translating *The Great Qing Code*. He believed that these experiences improved his language skills and provided a new perspective on researching Chinese legal history (Jiang, 2005). From the standpoint of academic genealogy, he is connected to two significant English translators of Chinese legal classics. In the "Note on the Translation" section, Jiang Yonglin (2005) mentioned that he referred to works like Wallace Johnson's *The T'ang Code* and William Jones's *The Great Qing Code* when translating Chinese legal and social terms into English. From the titles of the translation, it can be seen that Jiang Yonglin's work was influenced by William Jones: while William translated "大清律例*(Da Qing Lü Li)*" as "The Great Qing Code", Jiang Yonglin translated "大明律*(Da Ming Lü)*" as "The Great Ming Code" and added the corresponding Chinese pinyin "Da Ming Lü" as supplementary. He maintained this strategy of transliteration throughout the legal code translation. In terms of annotations, Jiang Yonglin's work was influenced by Wallace Johnson's translation, providing extensive annotations in both the main texts and paratexts. However, a difference is seen in the use of parentheses and square brackets to distinguish between the original legal text and his added explanations. "The text that appears in parentheses () refers to the interlinear legal notes, which are an integral part of the Code. The text that appears in square brackets [] and chapter, section, and article numbers were not originally part of the Code but are my explanatory material" (Jiang, 2005). Besides textual annotations, he also provided a table of Ming units of measure and money to help readers understand the conversion method of the length units such as cun, chi, zhang, and li, weight units like qian, liang (tael), jin, capacity units like sheng, dou, shi, dan, and area units like mu (mou) and qing. Jiang Yonglin stood on the shoulders of predecessors, inheriting certain translation principles of William C. Jones and Wallace Johnson. Simultaneously, he positioned himself on the historical heights of the new era, gave full play to the advantages of his profound understanding of Chinese culture as a Chinese-American scholar, and developed the essence of codex translation in the academic era of cross-cultural communication.

6.3.3.2 Cross-Cultural Dialogue

In the introduction, Jiang Yonglin introduces the founding of the Ming Dynasty, the codification process of *The Great Ming Code*, and its major content. The *Code* starts with "Laws on Punishments and General Principles"*(Ming Li Lü)* as the first part, and the second part was arranged in accordance with six major categories of government functions: Personnel, Revenue, Rites, Wars, Justice, and Public works, namely, "Laws on Personnel"*(Lì Lü)*, "Laws on Revenue"*(Hu Lü)*, "Laws on Rituals"*(Lǐ Lü)*, "Laws on Military Affairs"*(Bing Lü)*, "Laws on Penal Affairs"*(Xing Lü)*, and "Laws on Public Works"*(Gong Lü)*. From a historical perspective, this arrangement is derived from the *Institutes of the Yuan Dynasty (Yuan Dian Zhang)*. From a cultural perspective, Jiang Yonglin offers his speculation: "...the early Ming ruling elite restructured the Code because they believed that the Six Ministries symbolized the comprehensiveness of the social relations regulated by the imperial government...According to this Confucian classic, *The Institutes of Zhou (Zhouli)*, all government personnel are grouped under the six ministers of Heaven, Earth, Spring, Summer, Autumn, and Winter... 'six ministries' follow the ancient system of 'six ministers'... gather all government affairs into the hands of the six ministers and symbolize the comprehensiveness of cosmic space (Heaven and Earth) and cosmic time (four seasons)" (Jiang, 2005). This paratext that narrates history and presents cultural highlights Jiang Yonglin's effort to convey the cultural nuances of traditional Chinese law, allowing readers to connect with the underlying Chinese culture behind the translation. At the end of the translation, Jiang provides a glossary of key legal terms in *The Great Ming Code* in the form of "Hanyu Pinyin, Chinese characters, and English translation". This form of blending of both English and Chinese languages represents that the translator gives equal importance to both the source and target languages and cultures. Habermas (1989) views translation as a communicative activity, where different subjects use language as a medium to achieve mutual understanding through dialogue, and the translator plays a crucial connecting role in this process. In the "dialogue" with the author of the original legal code, Jiang Yonglin demonstrates a full understanding of the original text and engages in a "dialogue" with readers in the paratext. He supplements cultural insights of the legal code according to the reader's needs to allow the readers to perceive the visage of the "other" in the target language, further promoting cultural prosperity and development.

6.4 Summary

The paratext and main text are interdependent, forming the semantic interpretation field and playing an important role in the Spreading and reception process of translations. Introducing paratext theory into the study of English translations of Chinese legal classics goes beyond treating paratext as mere evidence of translators' purposes, theories, and strategies. Instead, it systematically interprets paratext as an independent literary form, offering a new perspective to deepen the translation of Chinese legal classics and assisting Chinese legal culture in "going out". In the preface to the English translation of *Ta Tsing Leu Lee*, George Thomas Staunton adopts the perspective of "the translator" to give out "multiple voices" of Chinese law and history. These "voices" encompass the active role of the translator under certain guiding intentions, subtly influenced by "unseen hands" such as societal ideologies and positions. James Feinerman commends the translations of *The Great Qing Code* by William C. Jones, *The T'ang Code* by Wallace Johnson, and *The Great Ming Code* by Jiang Yonglin as fundamental materials for studying ancient Chinese legal systems in Western academia (Su, 2007)). The paratexts of these three essential materials, either assimilate existing research on Chinese legal classics, provide annotations that balance accessibility and scholarly depth, or recreate the contextualization for the global Spreading of traditional Chinese culture. From the viewpoint of the paratext, Chinese legal classics have transitioned from cross-cultural manipulation to dialogue.

References

Bakhtin. (1998). *Complete works of Bakhtin* (Translated by Qian Zhongwen, et al.). Hebei Education Press.
Batchelor, K. (2018). *Translation and paratexts*. Routledge.
Bodde, D., & Morris, C. (1995). *Law in imperial China*. Z. Yong, Trans. JIANGSU People's Publishing House.
Cao, M. (1989). *Translation and annotation of the T'ang code*. Jilin People's Publishing House.
Dong, X., & Zhang, Y. (2021). Translation and research of traditional Chinese legal classics. *Chinese Law Review (English Edition), 03*, 23–58.
Dong, X. (2021). The translation and spreading of ancient Chinese legal classics. *Guangming Daily*, May 22.
Genette, G. (2001). *The collected essays of Genette* (Translated by Shi Zhongyi). Baihua Literature and Art Publishing House.
George, S. (1810). *Ta Tsing Leu Lee*. T. Cadell and W. Davies.
Gérard, G. (2013). *Genette's Essays*. Z. Shi, Trans. Baihua Wenyi Press.
Habermas. (1989). *Interaction and social evolution* (Kommunikation und soziale Entwicklung) (Translated by Z. Boshu). Chongqing Publishing House.
Hu, B., & Dong, X. (2020). On the untranslatability of the legal terminology in ancient Chinese legal texts from Chinese to English and its compensation strategies. *Chinese Cultural Studies, 04*, 140–149.
Johnson, W. (1979). *The T'ang code*. Princeton University Press.
Jiang, Y. (2005). *The Great Ming Code/Da Ming Lü*.
Jürgen, H. (1989). *Kommunikation und soziale Entwicklung*. Zhang, B., Trans. Chongqing Press.

Kathryn, B. (2018). *Translation and paratexts*. Routledge.

Mikhail Mikhailovich, B. (1998). *Complete works of Bakhtin*. Qian, Z., et al., Trans. Hebei Education Press.

Pellatt, V. (2013). *Text, extratext, metatext and paratext in translation*. Cambridge Scholar Publishing.

Qu, W., & Wan, L. (2019). What Has motivated English translation of the codes of pre-modern Chinese dynasties. *Chinese Translators Journal, 01*, 51–59.

Staunton, G. (1810). *Ta Tsing Leu Lee*. T. Cadell and W. Davies.

Su, Y. (1996). Contemporary Chinese law studies in the United States. *Chinese and Foreign Law, 05*, 69–73.

Su, Y. (2007). In memory of Professor William C. Jones and his contributions to the study of Chinese Law. In China Institute of Legal History (ed.) *Proceedings of the Journal of Legal History (Vol. 1)*. Social Sciences Academic Press.

Valerie, P. (2013). *Text, extratext, metatext and paratext in translation*. Cambridge Scholar Publishing.

Wallace, J. (1979). *The T'ang code*. Princeton University Press.

Wang, J. (2001). *Legal significance of communicating two worlds: Introduction to the input of western legal methods and exploration of new legal terms in Late Qing Dynasty*. China University of Political Science and Law Press.

William, J. (1994). *The Great Qing Code*. Clarendon Press.

Xiong, D. (2018). An interpretive approach to Degal culture from ancient China. *Journal of Southwest University of Political Science and Law, 05*, 13–21.

Xu, B., & Yuan, W. (2001). *Language and politics of translation*. Central Compilation and Translation Press.

Yu, G. (2002). *Discussions on translation by Yu Guangzhong*. China Translation & Publishing Corporation.

Yuste Frias, J. (2012). *Paratextual elements in translation: Paratranslating titles in children's literature* (pp. 117–134). Peter Lang.

Zhu, T. (2009). The narrative poetics value of subtext in interpreting complex texts. *Jiangxi Social Sciences, 04*, 39–46.

Chapter 7
Image Construction Through Ancient Chinese Legal Words and Terms

Abstract *A Dictionary of the Chinese Language* is the world's first English-Chinese and Chinese-English dictionary, containing a relatively comprehensive collection of various Chinese terms and their translations related to early Chinese law. The presentation and interpretation of Chinese legal vocabulary and concepts in *A Dictionary of the Chinese Language* provided a necessary environment for mutual recognition and interaction between early Chinese and Western legal cultures. However, there are also many misinterpretations and misunderstandings of Chinese law in the dictionary. On the one hand, the distortion and misrepresentation of Chinese legal culture in the dictionary stem from the objective limitations of the compiler's Chinese language abilities, constituting unintentional misreadings. On the other hand, it results from the translators being influenced and manipulated by Western ideologies, which is a deliberate rewriting. Both contribute to the inaccurate transmission of legal cultural information and are detrimental to the "going out" of Chinese legal culture. Therefore, while vigorously promoting the global Spreading of Chinese legal culture, it is essential to reevaluate and reposition the historical value of traditional Chinese legal cultural classics and related works introduced by Western translators.

7.1 Related Study of *A Dictionary of the Chinese Language*

Robert Morrison (1782–1834), the first Protestant missionary from the West to China, "had a profound impact on Western views and perceptions of China in the nineteenth century" (Morrison, 2008). He was acclaimed as the "founder of spreading Chinese culture" (Zhao, 2017) and "the first person to initiate a new wave of Western learning moving East" (Xiong, 2019). During his time in China, Morrison spent 13 years compiling the world's first Chinese-English dictionary, *A Dictionary of the Chinese Language*, significantly contributing to the early mutual recognition and interactive exchange between Chinese and Western civilizations. In recent years, academia has gradually recognized the unique value of *A Dictionary of the Chinese Language* in the fields of translation studies, communication studies, lexicography, and literature and has conducted specific research in these areas. However, it is noteworthy that the

X. Dong and Y. Luo, *The Legal Image of China in Chinese Legal Tradition*,
https://doi.org/10.1007/978-981-96-5797-1_7

translation of Chinese legal culture in *A Dictionary of the Chinese Language* has not received sufficient attention from the academic community. According to the author's search on CNKI (China National Knowledge Infrastructure), only two scholars, Qu Wensheng and Wang Jian, have attempted to explore the legal values in the dictionary (Qu, 2010; Wang, 2001). However, their studies focused on the second part of the dictionary, namely *Wu Che Yun Fu*, and did not include the first part with the richest citations and the most detailed interpretations. Additionally, their research prioritized static comparisons between Chinese and English legal terms, with limited attention given to the dynamic manifestation of the author's agency. Therefore, this chapter, from the perspective of legal linguistics, aims to review and investigate the bilingual expressions of early Chinese legal vocabulary in *A Dictionary of the Chinese Language*. It also seeks to reveal the author's unintentional misreadings and deliberate rewriting of Chinese legal culture during the dictionary compilation process. The goal is to contribute to the systematic improvement of research in this field and provide valuable experience for the overseas Spreading of traditional Chinese legal culture as well as the mutual exchange and learning between Chinese and Western legal civilizations.

7.2 Analysis on the Chinese Legal Words and Terms in *A Dictionary of the Chinese Language*

A Dictionary of the Chinese Language contains a comprehensive list of various commonly used legal terms and concepts in early China and direct references to the codes of the Tang, Song, Ming, and Qing Dynasties. It can be said that Morrison's translation of traditional Chinese legal culture in the dictionary can be described as a combination of point-face, which is comprehensive and systematic. To elucidate the internal logic of the English translation of legal words and terms in the dictionary, the follow will study the content of Chinese law translated in the dictionary from three aspects: criminal law vocabulary, civil law vocabulary, and procedural law vocabulary.

7.2.1 Criminal Law Vocabulary

It is well known that the feudal codes of Chinese Dynasties showed a basic feature of penalization, and the basic idea of Chinese feudal times is adjusting various legal relations in social life through unified criminal law means. This feature of pan-penalization is also reflected in the Chinese legal words recorded in *A Dictionary of the Chinese Language*. The following table categorizes some criminal law words, allowing for subsequent analysis.

By comparing the bilingual expressions in Table 1, several key features of Morrison's translation of the "五刑 *(Wu Xing)* (five forms of punishment)" system in China become apparent. Firstly, in the translation of "笞 *(Chi)*" and "杖 *(Zhang)*": the instruments used for both punishments are made of bamboo or thorny branches. The distinction between the two lies primarily in the specific specifications of the implements, the severity levels of the penalties, and the legally prescribed execution quantities. Chi punishment, the lightest among the five punishments, is typically defined in *The T'ang Code* as using a small bamboo or sticks "with a diameter of two *fen*[1] to one *fen* five *li*" to lash the offender between ten to fifty times. Zhang punishment, slightly more severe than chi, employs a bludgeon or great bamboo "with the big end of a diameter of two *fen* seven *li* to three *fen* two *li* and the small end of one *fen* seven *li* to two *fen* two *li*" to administer fifty to one hundred blows to the offender (Niida Noboru 1989). These are just the rules of the Tang Dynasty, and different dynasties might have variations in materials, specifications, and types of the two implements. Elaborating extensively on these differences might introduce unnecessary complexities for foreign readers. Therefore, when compiling the dictionary, Morrison did not mechanically opt for a "word-for-word translation" but employed the approach of domestication, using the contrasting English terms "small bamboo" and "great bamboo", as well as "stick" and "bludgeon" to underscore the different severity levels of the two punishments. He pointed out that, compared to zhang punishment, chi punishment is considered a "petty punishment of China". This approach ensures a clear and concise translation, minimizing potential misunderstandings and difficulties while maximally preserving the original meaning for readers.

Then, in the translation of "徒 *(Tu)*" and "流*(Liu)*": they are often collectively referred to as "徒流 *(Tu Liu)*" due to their common in their institutional regulations. However, this does not imply an absence of differences between the two. "徒 *(Tu)*" originated from the Zhou Dynasty (1045–221 B.C.), signifying the deprivation of personal freedom for criminals who were then dispatched to remote areas within the country, accompanied by one to three years of mandatory labor. "流*(Liu)*", an expression of Confucian benevolent governance, means "the reluctant avoidance of capital punishment by sending the offender to a remote district", specifically referring to sending the offender to a more remote region compared to "徒 *(Tu)*", about 2000 to 3000 li[2] away but within the confine of the empire. Notably, "流*(Liu)*" itself carries an additional year of mandatory labor. Meanwhile, "流*(Liu)*" is just one form of the punishment in the Chinese exile system, which include three other punishments of migration, military conscription, and external banishment. Reflecting on the English translation of *A Dictionary of the Chinese Language*, it is evident that Morrison demonstrates a strong awareness of both Chinese and Western cultures. For instance, when translating "流*(Liu)*", he uses the expression "the confine of the

---

[1] Units of length in ancient China, 1 *fen* = 10 *li* (厘), 1 *cun* = 10 *fen*, 1 *chi* = 10 *cun* = 12.3 inches (approx.) = 31.8.

[2] Units of length in ancient China, 1 *zhang* = 10 *chi*, 1 *li* (里) = 1/3 mile = 572.4 m (approx.) centimeters (approx.).

empire", specifying the execution range within the territory of the Chinese Empire. Though in the eighteenth century, England also had the exile system, the locations for exile were more extensive, primarily including countries such as North America, the West Indies, and Australia. In other words, British exile destinations were outside their national borders, significantly different from the corresponding Chinese system. Therefore, Morrison's translation shows his valuable awareness of effectively highlighting the differences between China and England in the exile system. On the other hand, as a foreigner, Morrison's proficiency in Chinese is limited, so many aspects of his translation are to be debated. For example, in *Wu Che Yun Fu*, Morrison inaccurately translated the prescribed execution periods for "徒 *(Tu)*"as "three years" and "流*(Liu)*" for "three thousand li". According to Chinese legal codes stating "徒刑五 *(Tu Xing Wu)* (five levels of *Tu*)" and "流刑三 *(Liu Xing San)* (three levels of *Liu*)", which means each punishment has different severity levels and classification grades, but Morrison's translation corresponds precisely to the most severe punishment for each, potentially exaggerating the intensity of Chinese legal penalties. Additionally, Morrison uses both "crime" and "offence" to describe the types of crime applicable to 流*(Liu)*, where "crime" generally denotes a convicted crime, while "offence" implies a violation or less severe crime, which shows Morrison's translation had a normative problem of violating the principle of term consistency in legal translation. Finally, Morrison simply translated "笞杖徒流 *(Chi Zhang Tu Liu)*" as "to bastinade and transport", which involves obvious information omission. Moreover, the repeated use of the common word "transport" in the dictionary fails to convey the punitive connotation of "徒流刑 *(Tu Liu Xing)*". Such translation might not be the optimal choice for Chinese learners.

Finally, in the translation of "死 *(Si)* (death)". The death penalty, also known as the ultimate punishment, execution, or the penalty of life, is one of the world's oldest forms of punishment. As the most severe penalty among the "五刑 *(Wu Xing)* (five forms of punishment)", the death penalty is generally reserved for heinous criminal acts that pose a threat to the order of governance. In practice, the execution methods for the death penalty varied, including 斩 *(Zhan)*, 戮 *(Lu)*, 绞 *(Jiao)*, 焚烧 *(Fen Shao)*, 枭首 *(Xiao Shou)*, 弃市 *(Qi Shi)*, 考竟 *(Kao Jing)*, 坑杀 *(Keng Sha)*, 炮烙 *(Pao Luo)* and 凌迟 *(Ling Chi)*. However, since the Sui and Tang Dynasties, many cruel forms of corporal punishment have been abolished, and the legal code stipulates that "beheading" and "strangulation" are the primary methods of execution. From the table, we find that Morrison adopts three categories of translation for "死 *(Si)*" in the infinitive form: one category encompasses the act of depriving a criminal of their right to life in a broad sense, expressed as "to put to death". The other two categories are specific: "斩 *(Zhan)* (to behead)" and "绞 *(Jiao)* (to strangle)". Overall, Morrison successfully comprehensively conveys the fundamental meaning of "死 *(Si)*" into the target language. Simultaneously, we understand that "斩 *(Zhan)*" and "绞 *(Jiao)*" each have their subdivisions, namely "立决 *(Li Jue)* (immediate execution)" and "监候 *(Jian Hou)* (pending review)". The latter undergoes successive reviews by local authorities, provincial officials, and central authorities, and the actual disposition of the death penalty criminals can involve various scenarios, such as 情实*(Qing Shi)* (immediate execution), 缓决 *(Huan Jue)* (delayed execution), 可矜 *(Ke*

Jin) (leniency), or 留养承祀 *(Liu Yang Cheng Si)* (retention for ancestral rites). Thus, this type of death penalty is similar to today's death with reprieve, not necessarily characterized by the definite termination of the criminal's life. In light of this, the author believes that if Morrison could include translations for "立决 *(Li Jue)*" and "监候 *(Jian Hou)*" in the dictionary, it would have positive implications for the comprehensive and nuanced representation of traditional Chinese legal culture in overseas Spreading.

7.2.2 Civil Law Vocabulary

The impact of the assertion that the Chinese legal system was "a integrated system of all law, with no distinction between civil law and criminal law" has persisted for half a century (Jiang, 2020). The existence of civil law in ancient Chinese legal systems has been a much-debated issue. However, according to the research of Mr. Yang, "examining the codes from the Ming and Qing dynasties, the vast majority of laws is related to governing administration, economy, military, and rituals, with hundreds of specific laws" (Yang, 2002). This indicates that traditional Chinese law indeed includes a substantial number of legal norms for regulating civil relations. Table 2 contains some civil law vocabularies and their English translations in *A Dictionary of the Chinese Language.*

Morrison, in his dictionary, has repeatedly translated and introduced the phenomenon of renting out wives and divorcing a wife in ancient China. "出妻 *(Chu Qi)* (to repudiate a wife)" essentially means "休妻*(Xiu Qi)* (to divorce a wife)", and the two terms have virtually the same meaning. When translating these two concepts, Morrison uses "repudiate" and "divorce", respectively. Although these two words have similar meanings, there are subtle differences. "Divorce" refers to "the legal ending of a marriage and separating", which underscores "to legally end one's marriage with one's spouse and to dissolve the marriage contract, typically initiated by either party". However, according to the English definition of "repudiate" as "to refuse to accept; to reject as untrue or unjust; to refuse to have anything to do with; to divorce or separate formally from a woman to whom one is betrothed or married", the most common means of "repudiate" is "to deny; to refuse (to acknowledge)". When used to denote "divorce", it emphasizes the delicate situation where the man initiates the divorce and the woman is forced to accept. As mentioned earlier, "divorce" indicates the end of a marriage due to a breakdown in mutual affection, while "repudiate" emphasizes the unilateral (by the man) denial and dissolution of the marital relationship. As the primary method of divorce in ancient Chinese society, "出妻 *(Chu Qi)*" was a system granting the man exclusive rights within the context of the context of "rituals" and "law". In this system, a man could forcibly divorce the woman, but the reverse was not permissible. Therefore, the author believes that if the English translation for both "休妻*(Xiu Qi)*" and "出妻 *(Chu Qi)*" in the dictionary could be unified as "to repudiate a wife" or "repudiation", it would better capture the legal and cultural context of that time. When translating "典妻 *(Dian Qi)*", Morrison seems to confuse it with "租妻 *(Zu Qi)*". The character "典 *(Dian)*" in "典妻*(Dian Qi)*" comes from the term "典质 *(Dian Zhi)*" and gradually gained the meaning of "pledging for redemption" from the Sui and Tang periods onward. Taking the Qing Dynasty as an example, "典妻*(Dian Qi)*" formed three common forms: "典 *(Dian)*", "卖 *(Mai)*", and "租*(Zu)*", with no significant difference in customs. Both the person pledging and the recipient must sign a contract in the presence of a "go-between". However, regarding the specific terms of the contract, "generally, the lease term for '租妻 *(Zu Qi)*' is relatively short, and the rent fee is low, while the pledge term for '典妻 *(Dian Qi)*' is longer, and the corresponding fee is higher" (Lv, 2012). The former is typically 1–3 years, and the latter usually extends beyond 3 years. Therefore, Morrison's translation "to rent out their wives" is more in line with the meaning of "租妻 *(Zu Qi)*". To express "典妻 *(Dian Qi)*", it would be better to add the corresponding duration afterward.

For crimes involving illegal possession of property, infringement of citizens' property rights and interests, and personal rights, *A Dictionary of the Chinese Language* also provides relevant introductions, with "强劫 *(Qiang Jie)*" and "强盗*(Qiang Dao)*" being the most representative. For the former, *The Great Qing Code* stipulates, "few people with no weapons, it is snatch; many people with weapons, it is armed robbery", meaning that the number of offenders and the presence of weapons determine the classification. However, Morrison's translation does not mention these two points, potentially causing readers to confuse "强劫 *(Qiang Jie)*" with "抢夺 *(Qiang Duo)*". Additionally, when translating "强劫 *(Qiang Jie)*", Morrison uses the term "rob", which in the English context means "to take something away from by force; to take personal property from by violence or threat". In other words, "rob" implies "by force/violence". Therefore, Morrison's translation may seem a bit redundant. Similarly, the translation of "强盗*(Qiang Dao)*" requires careful consideration. Morrison has realized that "强盗*(Qiang Dao)*" can be both a noun and a verb, which is commendable. However, the author thinks "plunder" is not an optimal choice. This word does have the meaning of "stealing goods from a place or person". However, in English, it emphasizes large-scale looting that typically occurs during war or civil disorder. In ancient texts, the criminal subject of "强盗*(Qiang Dao)*" is usually in a general circumstance rather than wartime. Therefore, the author believes that translating "强盗*(Qiang Dao)*" as "to rob" or "robbing" is sufficient to convey the original meaning.

7.2.3 Procedural Law Vocabulary

Ancient Chinese law adopted a legislative approach of "integration of substantive law and procedural law", which means there was no independent procedural law. However, it is evident that many procedural rules were intricately woven into written substantive law, playing the social functions of "regulating social order, pursuing limited justice, upholding imperial autocracy, and embodying Confucian ethics"

(Chen & Li, 2012). The following table includes some representative vocabularies related to procedural law selected from the dictionary.

Taking *The T'ang Code* as an example, the chapter on "Sentencing and Review of Cases *(Duan Yu)*" contains substantial content related to procedural law. According to scholars' rough estimates, the regulations on procedural law in *The T'ang Code* can be broadly categorized into two types: measures to control criminals and constraints on judicial officials, with the latter constituting as much as 70% (Chen & Li, 2012). This characteristic is reflected in the codes of later dynasties. In *A Dictionary of the Chinese Language*, Morrison provides targeted translations of judicial procedures based on the different subjects of interrogation, including specific sentencing and execution regulations for females. After listing the common words and phrases of the word "妇 *(Fu)* (women)", Morrison specifically points out that Chinese law made special provisions for "crimes committed by women". On the one hand, ancient Chinese lawmakers believed that it was inappropriate to torture and imprison a pregnant woman for "fear of injuring her fetus"; on the other hand, "a postpartum woman is not yet able to bear the punishment because of the deficiency of Qi and blood within one hundred days after childbirth". So, if the pregnant woman is to be punished, it is necessary to carry out the punishment after the hundredth day after delivery (Shen, 2000). In this regard, Morrison translated the stipulations in *Laws on Penal Affairs* in *The Great Ming Code*: "In all cases where women commit crimes, for fornication and capital crimes they shall be imprisoned; for all other miscellaneous crimes they shall be put in charge of their husband for supervision. If they have no husband, they shall be put in charge of their relatives within the degrees of mourning or the neighborhood for supervision. They shall be held at the disposition of the yamen to be called [to appear]. They shall not be imprisoned generally", and "if pregnant women commit crimes and should be judicially tortured or beaten [with the light or heavy stick], they shall all be judicially tortured or beaten 100 days after the delivery. If they are judicially tortured or beaten before the delivery and, as a result, they abort, officials or functionaries shall be punished for injury in ordinary affairs reduced by three degrees. If, as a result, death occurs, the penalty shall be 100 strokes of beating with a heavy stick and penal servitude for three years", presenting a full presentation and explanation of the strict judicial procedures in ancient Chinese law. It is easy to see that Morrison focuses on explaining Chinese words and concepts. It also takes the words and concepts as the center and emanates them to the surrounding system, encompassing a more specific and comprehensive Chinese culture. Instead of explaining Chinese terms, *A Dictionary of the Chinese Language* writes and presents Chinese culture. This way of translating and introducing the way words and sentences maximize the information of the source language and culture in the smallest space, thus creating a legal language and cultural environment where foreign audiences can experience the "discourse system in which the Chinese people are immersed" (Yu, 2008)).

"In procedural law, there are also vocabularies related to the litigation system, such as "越诉 *(Yue Su)*". It is a legal term under the Qing Dynasty's judicial system known as the "examination, transfer, and review system", referring to the act of bypassing lower-level judicial authorities to file a lawsuit. According to *The Great*

Qing Code: "All lawsuits brought by military personnel or civilians must begin at the lowest authorities and move to the higher authorities. For those who bypass their own superior offices and who, without authorization, bring the suits directly to the higher authorities, they shall be punished by 50 strokes of beating with the light stick (only if the person in charge of the case does not accept it or accepts it but is wronged can he/she appeal to higher courts)". In other words, litigation should be conducted "bottom-up" from districts and counties to Fu, Nie si, and then the provincial-level authorities charged by Zongdu or Xunfu.[3] If the litigation does not follow the prescribed legal procedures, regardless of the truth or falsehood of the allegations, the litigant will be charged with the offence of "越诉 *(Yue Su)*" and subjected to punishment. During the Jingtai period of the Ming Dynasty, the severity of the punishment reached the extent of being sentenced to remote military service. Morrison adopts an explanatory translation strategy, rendering it "to appeal to higher courts by passing over the inferior ones", which means "bypassing lower-level courts and appealing to higher-level courts" when translated back into Chinese. Although this translation conveys the meaning of "appealing to higher level courts", it does not highlight the "illegality" of "越诉 *(Yue Su)*". Therefore, it is difficult for readers to discern the implied message that arbitrary litigation bypassing appropriate jurisdiction will be subject to punishment while they are reading the translation. In this context, the author believes the translation by the American scholar William C. Jones, "a complaint that does not follow the proper order", is preferable and worth considering.

In ancient times, in addition to "the prohibition of bypassing the proper jurisdiction", another restriction on "告诉 *(Gao Su)* (litigation)" was "crackdown on false accusations". In the later periods of many feudal dynasties, due to the intensification of social class contradictions, false accusations gradually became a rampant social malpractice. To prevent the chaos in social order and political instability caused by a large number of false accusations and to maintain the stability of feudal legal systems and national governance, rulers in the legal system made clear provisions on the definition and punishment of the act of "false accusations". The general comment on the false accusations in the Laws on Penal Affairs of *The Great Qing Code* states: "Fabricating baseless facts and accusing others of crimes is called false accusation". The term "诬告 *(Wu Gao)*" refers to the fabrication of facts and the falsification of evidence to implicate others falsely. It is a criminal act characterized by creating something out of nothing, with the intention of leveraging the judicial system to achieve the malicious goal of falsely accusing the innocent. The subjective intention is obvious. Morrison translates "诬 *(Wu)*" as "false", which, when translated back into Chinese, expresses more about the meaning of "incorrect accusations" and does

[3] Districts and counties are responsible for the initial hearing of various cases; *Fu*, as upper administrative unit, mainly reviews the relevant judicial documents of the transferred cases in writing; *Nie si* is the institution in charge of judicature in the provincial organs of Qing Dynasty; Zongdu or Xunfu, as the highest provincial administrator in the Qing Dynasty, has the power to make the final judgment on the imprisonment cases that did not involve human life, and the imprisonment cases involving human life and the cases of soldiers and refugees had to be reported to *Xing Bu* (the Ministry of Punishment) for review after the review of the governor.

not reflect the subjective motives of the accuser. Therefore, the author believes the phrase "false and malicious accusations" is more accurate. Similarly, using the back-translation method, we find that "to conduct a lawsuit" is translated as "提起诉讼", which is far from the meaning of "包揽词讼" in Chinese. The term "包揽词讼 *(Bao Lan Ci Song)*" originates from the *Dream of Red Mansions*, where it refers to the act of soliciting and undertaking other people's lawsuits for personal gain. In other words, "包揽词讼 *(Bao Lan Ci Song)*" has two characteristics: firstly, it involves taking on the affairs of others, often unrelated to the parties involved; secondly, the person involved seeks personal gain from it. In the ideological background of "suppressing lawsuits and discouraging troublemakers from maintaining peace and goodness", taking on and inciting lawsuits were considered crimes that disrupted social order and stability. In Chinese feudal law, harsh legal measures were taken to convict and punish the legal pettifoggers. Given the English word "champerty", defined as "an illegal bargain between a party to litigation and an outsider whereby the latter agrees to pay for the action and thereby share in any proceeds recovered" in English, aligns closely with the meaning of "包揽诉讼; 帮诉罪" in Chinese, it realizes functional equivalent with the word in the source language. Thus, the author holds the view that translating "包揽词讼 *(Bao Lan Ci Song)*" as "to practice champerty" is a concise, accurate translation.

7.3 The Performance of Rewriting Legal Words and Terms and Possible Reasons

For a long time, translation was understood as a procedural and mechanized transformation of encoding and decoding language symbols within a closed and self-sufficient system. However, with the advent of the "cultural turn" in translation studies, researchers shifted their focus from meaning factors within the text to social factors outside it. The understanding of translation also changed accordingly. "Translation is no longer viewed as a copy attached to principles in the traditional sense; instead, it is seen as a creative act, involving the creation of a new original in another language" (Bassnett & Trivedi, 1999). The translated work, as a "new original", implies that the "lossless" flow of information between different languages is an ideal state. At the same time, addition, reduction, distortion, and transformation are the norm in translation. Regarding information distortion, Andre Lefevere, the representative of the School of Manipulation in translation, argues that translation is not a purely word game conducted in society. It is a rewriting of the original text constrained by history, culture, value, aesthetics, and societal norms. Lefevere emphasizes that "all rewritings, whatever their motivation, reflect a certain ideology and poetics, thus manipulating literature to function in a certain way in a particular society" (Bassnett & Lefevere, 1990). Furthermore, "every aspect of the translation process demonstrates that if there is a conflict between language and ideology or poetic, the latter always prevails" (Lefevere, 1992). In other words, translation activity is always a purposeful act manipulated and controlled by power discourse. It is "a form of (re)production that highlights the necessity of seeking ownership and control" (Sun, 2014)). Translators, living in specific times and societal-cultural contexts, are not merely transformers of language symbols; they are "endowed with a certain power to construct a literary image for readers and share some power with literary historians and critics" (Xu, 2014)).

The significance of the Manipulation School's theory lies in dissecting how translators, under ideological manipulation, rewrite the language of the original text. This analysis unveils the translator's attitudes toward both cultures, bringing to light their underlying "cultural agenda" reflecting the translator's purposes to demonstrate the purposefulness, complexity, and intervention nature of translation activity. In *A Dictionary of the Chinese Language,* the manipulation of translator on rewriting the Chinese legal words and terms can be concluded in three aspects.

7.3.1 Overinterpretation

The term "interpretation" involves both "determining the precise meaning of words, phrases, and passages" and "revealing implicit meanings, making unclear things clear" (Wang, 1999). "All translators are interpreters" (Gadamer, 1999), "so all translation is already an interpretation where translators interpret the words given to them" (Gadamer, 1999). It can be said that "interpretation" is not only the essence of translation but is also integrated into translation activities as translation methods and strategies. However, excessive interpretation often reflects the translator's agency and introduces a distinct subjective color to the interpreted object.

On page 208 of the *Dictionary*, Morrison introduces the ancient punishment of " 凌迟/陵迟 *(Ling Chi)*". The term originally referred to the slow ascent of a hill but later symbolized "a gradual and deliberate approach to sentence to death" (Shen, 2011). "Lingchi" is a culture-loaded term in ancient Chinese law and should not be translated literally but rather through interpretive. For instance, in the dictionary, Morrison translates it as a form of death that is "lingering" and "ignominious", often referred to as "cutting into ten thousand pieces". This translation effectively conveys the core meaning of the original text. However, Morrison goes beyond this. Although he acknowledges that the definition of "lingchi" in modern times and the period of slavery differs, he still provides an extensive subjective interpretation starting with "it is said…", including cutting flesh, removing sexual organs, dissecting, breaking bones, and shattering joints, filling almost half a page. Therefore, Morrison's translation of this punishment exhibits clear signs of overinterpretation, with language infused with his personal emotions, such as describing it as "the most disgusting" form of punishment. Chinese legal codes also provide explanations for "lingchi", as seen in the *History of the Song Dynasty · Criminal Law Volume 1*, where it is described as "an extreme punishment of that time which first severs the limbs and then cuts the trachea". However, in comparison, Morrison's subjective interpretation reveals a strong condemnation and criticism of ancient Chinese law, and to some extent, overly emphasizes the terror and brutality of Chinese law.

7.3.2 Subjective Commentary

Take the Chinese term "妻妾殴夫*(Qi Qie Ou Fu)*" (Morrison 1815: 618) for example. "Chinese was shaped in the philosophy of domestic governance" (Montesquieu, 2009), and it can be said that the concept of "家 *(Jia)* (family)" has been an unchanging "constant" throughout Chinese history. The ancient feudal laws in China also emphasized maintaining the ethical order and harmony of the "family"—considered the fundamental unit of society—serving as the foundational logic for governing the nation. Consequently, legal codes contained numerous specific provisions to prevent violence among relatives within the family and offenses committed by subordinates against their superiors. To some extent, the detailed and explicit delineation of violent behavior among relatives and its penalties in ancient China reflects the legislative emphasis on harmonious family relationships, a concrete manifestation of the comprehensive legal system at that time. However, in the *Dictionary*, Morrison "preemptively" characterizes the political system in China as tyranny and despotism before introducing such laws and speculates at the end, "From these laws, we can speculate that domestic violence frequently occurs in China". Regardless of the authenticity of these comments, from the perspective of the principles of dictionary compilation, the compiler should adhere to an objective and neutral stance in arranging and explaining words and phrases rather than injecting subjective inferences into the dictionary. Therefore, Morrison's translation lacks professionalism and could negatively impact the Spreading of Chinese law.

Another term is "功过格 *(Gong Guo Ge)*" (Morrison 1815: 619). The delineation of "功 *(Gong)* (merit)" and "过*(Guo)* (demerit)" in "功过格 *(Gong Guo Ge)*" highlights traditional Chinese ethical and moral values, such as benevolence toward people and things, loyalty to the ruler, filial piety, and the reverence of the Three Treasures (Tao, scriptures, and teacher). While not explicitly codified as official laws, "功过格 *(Gong Guo Ge)*" played a role similar to legal norms during the Ming and Qing Dynasties and exerted a widespread influence on the general populace and even elite groups (Lin & Zhu, 2022). Morrison introduces the concept and practical application of "功过格*(Gong Guo Ge)*" many times in the dictionary, including examples of its actual application in maintaining relationships between husbands and wives. Morrison translated the sentence "嫌夫貌丑千过。" which ended with a period in the original text, as "Disdaining one's husband unattractive is a fault of *one thousand*!", emphasizing the number by marking it in italics and changed the period in the end to an exclamation mark to make it visually more striking. As a devout Christian, Morrison firmly believed in everyone's right to live in an environment of universal love and equality. Hence, although these translations may seem like subtle changes to the original text, they effectively reflect Morrison's dissatisfaction and irony toward the gender system in traditional Chinese feudal society.

The translation of Chinese term "酒诰 *(Jiu Gao)*" (Morrison 1815: 625) presents the same problem. *Jiu Gao* is the earliest prohibition on alcohol in China. At that time, alcohol was considered the root cause of great disorder, moral decay, and the downfall of the country. According to the law, people were not allowed to drink alcohol except during sacrificial ceremonies, and violating this rule could result in the death penalty. Morrison found it difficult to accept such a law and commented: "(We) find it hard to imagine why being drunk could be sentenced to death. In fact, it's almost inconceivable for us to even think of such an idea. The rulers of China fantasize that those who gather to drink at night are all rebellious, disloyal troublemakers disrupting public order. Similar laws exist in the current legal system, stating that those who gather at night and disperse at dawn are all subject to the death penalty". In reality, from the Song Dynasty (960–1279) to the Qing Dynasty (1644–1911), there were strict measures controlling the masses' religious nighttime gatherings, especially for foreign religions such as Christianity. "Gathering at night and dispersing at dawn" (Ge, 2003) became synonymous with inciting the masses and engaging in immoral and rebellious activities. When the authorities and scholars enumerate the charges against heretical religions, the often-used accusation is "gathering at night and dispersing at dawn". Morrison was likely somewhat familiar with this. Since Morrison's main purpose in coming to China was to spread Christianity, his comments on the prohibition of alcohol and the deliberate introduction of the law, "those who gather at night and disperse at dawn are all subject to the death penalty", indicating his intention to criticize the Qing court's strict restrictions and suppression of missionary activities.

7.3.3 Replacing Chinese Legal Concepts with Western Legal Terms

In ancient Chinese, "差役*(Chai Yi)*" primarily referred to "those who were assigned duties in the yamen (government office)", while "捕执 *(Bu Zhi)*" means the act of arresting by law enforcement officers in criminal or public order matters. Morrison translated these two legal terms as "a police runner" and "to apprehend as by the officers of the police", both using the term "police (警察)". It's recorded that Liang Qichao used words like "警察官 *(Jing Cha Guan)*", "警察权 *(Jing Cha Quan)*", and "警官 *(Jing Guan)*" in his translation of *Theory of State* in 1899 (Su & Zhang, 2021). This is considered the earliest usage of "警察*(Jing Cha)*" to refer to China's national public security agencies and personnel. Before this, there was no specific concept of "police" in ancient Chinese law. Therefore, it appears that Morrison substitutes Chinese cultural-loaded terms with existing Western concepts.

For another example, Morrison translated "刑部 *(Xing Bu)*" as "the tribunal of punishments". "刑部 *(Xing Bu)*" was primarily responsible for reviewing various laws and reexamining criminal cases nationwide, embodying a strong traditional Chinese legal and cultural concept under the central administrative system of "三

省六部制*(San Sheng Liu Bu Zhi)* (three departments and six ministries)". However, "tribunal" means "court" and is widely used in Western countries like Britain, the United States, Australia, Canada, and New Zealand, rather than China. Therefore, Morrison's "Westernized" translation somewhat diminishes the cultural characteristics of ancient Chinese law, hindering the audience's understanding and digestion of Chinese law.

What's more, "保甲制 *(Bao Jia Zhi)*" was an important legal system for grassroots control, and Morrison translated it as "tything act". The English term "Tything", which equals in Chinese as "太兴制 *(Tai Xing Zhi)*", refers to "a communal policing system aimed at preventing crime and maintaining public order, with members jointly sharing responsibility" (Hu, 2012). It is characterized by the control of society by the units of "太兴 *(Tai Xing)* (tything)", "百户*(Bai Hu)* (company commander)", and "郡 *(Jun)* (county)". It is clear that Morrison referred to the Western legal concept of "Tything" in introducing the "保甲制 *(Bao Jia Zhi)*". Similarly, when translating "五服 *(Wu Fu)*", Morrison rendered it as "four kinds of mourning", aligning the Chinese five-degree system with the European four-degree relationship structure, which means using first-degree, second-degree, third-degree, fourth-degree to correspond to "斩衰*(Zhan Cui)* (unhemmed sackcloth)", "齐衰 *(Zi Cui)* (hemmed sackcloth)", "大功 *(Da Gong)* (greater coarseness)", "小功*(Xiao Gong)* (lesser coarseness)", and "缌麻 *(Si Ma)* (coarse hemp)". This interpretation based on Western law is a misinterpretation and misunderstanding of the original text, leading to a distortion in cross-cultural interactions between Chinese and Western legal systems (Qu & Wan, 2019).

The translation of "酒 *(Jiu)*" is also a typical example. Morrison translated the ancient Chinese concept of "禁酒" as "forbidding wine", demonstrating the manipulation by Western cultural perspectives. The alcoholic beverages consumed in ancient China were typically grain-based and more akin to what is referred to as liquor today, so "liquor" would be a more appropriate translation. Morrison's use of "wine" specifically refers to grape wine, significantly different from ancient Chinese alcoholic beverages. It is known that the West has a long tradition of grape wine production, and the consumption of wine is a distinctive feature of Western society. Therefore, Morrison's translation is an example of the distortion and transformation of Chinese legal culture under Western thought patterns.

7.4 Summary

Based on existing research, this section provides a categorization analysis of the legal vocabulary translations in *A Dictionary of the Chinese Language*. Through this, it guides the academia in reevaluating and repositioning the legal significance of this dictionary. Undoubtedly, even with unintentional misreadings caused by his proficiency in Chinese, *A Dictionary of the Chinese Language*, as the world's first Chinese-English dictionary, played an indelible role in the process of "Chinese learning spreading to the West" in the background of "Western learning spreading to the East".

The compilation and publication of *A Dictionary of the Chinese Language* opened a window for the Western world to systematically understand and study early Chinese law at the linguistic level. This also presented a valuable opportunity for promoting the cross-cultural Spreading of traditional Chinese legal culture and early exchanges between Chinese and Western legal civilizations. At the same time, Morrison was the first person to translate the entire Bible into Chinese and the founder of the first church school—Anglo-Chinese College, with the primary purpose of missionary work, aiming to bring more Chinese people to embrace Christianity (Gong, 2011). Therefore, the overall conceptual structure of his dictionary compilation is rooted in the Christian faith (Gong, 2011). "Being a translator means being called or shaped into a translator by ideology" (Lefevere, 1992), so *A Dictionary of the Chinese Language* is also the translator's intentional rewriting of Chinese law and culture under the manipulation of Western ideologies. Different legal civilizations should engage in interactive communication and mutual learning on the basis of equality, cooperation, and mutual benefit. Therefore, in the process of promoting the "going global" of Chinese legal classics and traditional legal culture, the translation community should, on the one hand, rectify from the source and maintain a critical attitude toward foreign translations. On the other hand, it should firmly uphold cultural confidence, ensuring the comprehensiveness and authenticity of the global Spreading of Chinese legal culture, thus serving as the "gatekeeper" for exchanges and mutual learning between Chinese and Western legal civilizations.

Table 7.1 Examples of translations of criminal law terms in *A Dictionary of the Chinese Language*

Chinese Legal Glossary	Source	English Translation
笞 *(Chi)*、杖 *(Zhang)*、徒 *(Tu)*、流 *(Liu)*、死 *(Si)*	*Dictionary*, p. 224	to beat with the small bamboo; to beat with the great bamboo; to transport to another district, and subject to hard labour for a term of years; to banish perpetually to the confine of the empire; to put to death
流三千里 *(Liu San Qian Li)*	*Dictionary*, p. 634	be transported to 3000 le's distance
徒三年 *(Tu San Nian)*	*Dictionary*, p. 663	transported three years
笞 *(Tai)*	*Wu Che Yun Fu*, p 40	to beat with the bamboo or stick; to flog; one of the petty punishments of China
杖 *(Zhang)*	*Wu Che Yun Fu*, p 22	to beat with the stick or bludgeon; To beat with the bamboo; Chinese punishments
笞杖徒流 *(Chi Zhang Tu Liu)*	*Wu Che Yun Fu*, p 40	to bastinade and transport; the two first and two last express different degrees
流徒绞斩 *(Liu Tu Jiao Zhan)*	*Wu Che Yun Fu*, p 545	to transport three thousand le, to transport three years, to strangle, to behand, four punishments
流罪 *(Liu Zui)*	*Wu Che Yun Fu*, p 545	a crime which is punished with transportation three thousand le
犯流罪 *(Fan Liu Zui)*	*Wu Che Yun Fu*, p 150	to commit an offence which subjects one to be transported three thousand le

Table 7.2 Examples of Translations of Civil Law Terms in *A Dictionary of the Chinese Language*

Chinese Legal Glossary	Source	English Translation
出妻 *(Chu Qi)*	*Wu Che Yun Fu*, p 103	to repudiate a wife
休妻 *(Xiu Qi)*	*Wu Che Yun Fu*, p 271	to divorce a wife
典妻 *(Dian Qi)*	*Dictionary*, p 621	rent out their wives
强劫 *(Qiang Jie)*	*Wu Che Yun Fu*, p 394	to rob openly by an act of violence
强盗*(Qiang Dao)*	*Dictionary*, p 228	a robber, or to plunder

Table 7.3 Examples of Translations of Procedural Law Terms in *A Dictionary of the Chinese Language*

Chinese Legal Glossary	Source	English Translation
妇人犯罪 *(Fu Ren Fan Zui)*	*Dictionary*, p 663	women who commit crimes
越诉 *(Yue Su)*	*Wu Che Yun Fu*, p 1045	to appeal to higher courts by passing over the inferior ones
诬告*(Wu Gao)*	*Dictionary*, p 489; *Wu Che Yun Fu*, p 987	the false accuser; a false accusation
包揽词讼 *(Bao Lan Ci Song)*	*Wu Che Yun Fu*, p 640	to conduct a law suit

References

Andre, L. (1992). *Translation, rewriting, and the manipulation of literary fame, 39.* Routledge.
Bassnett, S., & Trivedi, H. (Eds.). (1999). *Post-Colonial Translation: Theory and Practice*, 1. London: Routledge.
Gadamer. (1999). *Truth and Method* (Vol. 2, p. 494) (Translated by Hong Handing, Shanghai Translation Publishing House).
Chen, J., & Li, F. (2012). On the special functions of ancient Chinese procedural legal system. *Historical Teaching Issues* 02.
Ge, Z. (2003). An historical analysis of ancient Chinese thought on the concepts of day and night. *NTU Historical Journal* 32.
Gong, D. (2011). Interpreting culture from the translation of *Morrison: Pioneer Missionary in China. Literary Education* 12.
Hu, J. (2012). A study on the interrogating system in England. *Journal of Jishou University (Social Sciences Edition)* 03.
Jiang, H. (2020). Reflection on stereotyped narratives of Chinese traditional law based on the investigation of legal orientalism. *Journal of Lanzhou University (Social Sciences Edition)* 04.
Lin Z., & Zhu, Y. (2022). A moral book: *Liao Fan's records of merits and demerits. Guoxue Lunheng* 01.
Lv, L. (2012). A historical exploration of the legal aspects of ancient Chinese contractual marriages. Fudan University.
Montesquieu. (2009). *The spirit of the laws*, 327. M. Xu, Trans. The Commercial Press.
Morrison, R. (2008). *Selected works of Robert Morrison (14 volumes).* Translated by Zhengzhou. China: Elephant Press.
Niida, N. (1989). *Collection of Tang code supplementary regulations*, 727. J. Li, Trans., et al. Published by Changchun Press.
Qu, W., & Wan, L. (2019). What has motivated English translation of the codes of pre-modern Chinese dynasties. *Chinese Translators Journal* 01.
Qu, W. (2010). A study on the early English translation of Chinese legal terms—Taking Morrison's *a dictionary of the Chinese language* as an investigation object. *Historical Research* 05.
Robert, M. (1815). *A dictionary of the Chinese language (PART I— VOL. I)*, 618. East India Company's Press.
Robert, M. (1815). *A dictionary of the Chinese language (PART I— VOL. I)*, 619. East India Company's Press.
Robert, M. (1815). *A dictionary of the Chinese language (PART I— VOL. I)*, 625. East India Company's Press.
Robert, M. (1815). *A dictionary of the Chinese language (PART I— VOL. I)*, 88. East India Company's Press.
Robert, M. (1815). *A dictionary of the Chinese language (PART I— VOL. I)*, 59. East India Company's Press.
Robert, M. (1815). *A dictionary of the Chinese language (PART I— VOL. I)*, 224. East India Company's Press.
Robert, M. (1815). *A dictionary of the Chinese language (PART I— VOL. I)*, 636. East India Company's Press.
Robert, M. (1815). *A dictionary of the Chinese language (PART I— VOL. I)*, 177. East India Company's Press.
Shen, J. (2011). *A study on historical criminal laws (Volume I)*, 99. The Commercial Press.
Shen, Z. (2000). *Annotations on the Grand Qing Code*, 1047. In X. Huai, & J. Li (Eds.). Law Press.
Su, Y., & Zhang, Y. (2021). From "truth" to "custom": A study on the conceptual history of "police". *World Religious Cultures* 06.
Sun, Y. (2014). On the violence of translation. *Chinese Translators Journal* 06.
Susan, B., & Harish, T. (1999). *Post-colonial translation: Theory and practice, 1.* Routledge.
Susan, B., & Lefevere. (1990). *Translation, history and culture*, ix. Cassell.

Wang, J. (2001). *Legal significance of communicating two worlds: Introduction to the input of western legal methods and exploration of new legal terms in Late Qing Dynasty*, 50–56. China University of Political Science and Law Press.
Wang, Y. (1999). *Phenomenology and hermeneutics literary theory*, 169. Shandong Education Press.
Xiong, Y. (2019). *The west wind rising in the East and modern society*, 69. Renmin University of China Press.
Yang, Y. (2002). An important area of misunderstanding in the study of the genealogy of Chinese law—Doubts about "all laws were incorporated into one and there was no difference between civil and criminal laws". *China Social Sciences* 06.
Yu, J. (2008). *Law and scholarship in modern China*, 16. Peking University Press.
Zhao, C. (2017). *A study of English translation of Chinese cultural classics in the 19th century*, 88. Shanghai Foreign Language Education Press.

Chapter 8
Image Construction Through the Traditional Culture

Abstract Culture, due to its holistic, practical, structural, intermediary, and political nature, has become the theme, method, and goal of contemporary philosophy, so contemporary philosophy is basically a cultural philosophy (Ouyang, Q. (2015). The "cultural turn" in contemporary philosophy. Frontiers of Social Science 01.). To a certain extent, philosophy can be regarded as the result of culture, and culture will certainly give birth to its corresponding philosophy, which is the generalization, inheritance, development, and transcendence of its "mother" culture. *A Dictionary of Chinese Language* is a cultural encyclopedia covering Chinese literature, history, geography, religion, philosophy, science and technology, and local customs. Chinese culture spread to the Western world through *A Dictionary of the Chinese Language*. The examination of the translation of Chinese culture in *A Dictionary of the Chinese Language* provides insights into Chinese philosophical thoughts introduced in the dictionary. While compiling the dictionary, Morrison extensively referenced and incorporated Chinese classics, particularly internalizing the dominant Confucian philosophical thinking in Chinese history, which became the source of his citations and explanations. Translating traditional Chinese into foreign languages is an inevitable path for Chinese culture to go global. In the process of compiling *A Dictionary of the Chinese Language*, the mutual understanding, integration, mutual aggression, and rejection between Chinese and Western cultures reveal the significant roles played by the translator's language perspective, cultural perspective, translation perspective, and ideology in the translation process. This chapter explores the complex translation activity of Chinese culture in Morrison's compilation of *A Dictionary of the Chinese Language* from three aspects: the selection of materials for translation, the background of translation, and the motivations behind translation. It looks at the translation of traditional Chinese culture from the perspective of a foreign translator, aiming to provide intellectual support for the cross-cultural Spreading of Chinese civilization in the context of the new era.

X. Dong and Y. Luo, *The Legal Image of China in Chinese Legal Tradition*,
https://doi.org/10.1007/978-981-96-5797-1_8

8.1 Chinese Culture in the Eye of Morrison

The author of *A Dictionary of the Chinese Language*, Robert Morrison, was the first Protestant missionary to set foot on the Chinese mainland during the late Qing Dynasty, making him the "Father of Protestant Missions in China". Due to his unique period and significant achievements, Morrison has become a central figure in the history of Sin-Western cultural exchange. Chinese scholar Tan Shulin (2004) regards Morrison as the "trailblazer of the second wave of Sino-Western cultural exchange", and Zhao Changjiang (2017) refers to him as "the founder of spreading Chinese culture". Professor Christopher Hancock (2008) of Oxford University even commented, "We may not like him, but it is difficult not to admire him".

"It is difficult to categorize Morrison's works because he has accomplished many different types of work (Barton, 1998)". However, if it is necessary to organize Morrison's works, "we must consider his dictionary as the starting point for appreciating his legacy… because on his tombstone, the description of this work in Macau predates any mention of his translation of the Bible" (Barrett, 2015). Throughout history, *A Dictionary of the Chinese Language* has been a major starting point for scholars researching Sino-Western cultural exchange. A search on the China National Knowledge Infrastructure (CNKI) using keywords "Morrison" and "A Dictionary of the Chinese Language" reveals that existing academic research mainly focuses on the following aspects: macro introductions to the main content of *A Dictionary of the Chinese Language* by scholars such as Tan Shulin (2003) and Luo Mengyang (2020); discussions on the insights from the compilation of the dictionary to modern outward-looking dictionaries and Chinese language teaching by scholars such as Yang Huilin (2016)and You Mengyu (2012); and explorations of the translation strategies involved in *A Dictionary of the Chinese Language* by scholars like Xia Chen (2019), Wang Xiuwen and Ruan Yuyu (2019). However, the review of the above studies shows that existing research on cultural translation-related issues tends to be limited to the linguistic level, analyzing the conversion rules between source and target languages without delving into the cultural translation behavior from the perspectives of ideology and power relations. Additionally, the paratext in *A Dictionary of the Chinese Language* has not been systematically studied, so that the subtle relationships among the translator, the text, the readers, and the translation sponsors are overlooked.

In translating *A Dictionary of the Chinese Language*, either the mutual understanding and integration, or the attack and rejection of Chinese and Western culture revealed the influence of translator's language views, cultural views, translation views, and ideology in the translation process.

"Faced with difficult-to-translate sentences, I spare no effort to quote extensively, aiming to achieve a meaning that does not deviate from the original" (Mrs Morrison, 2004). Morrison's extensive quoting during the dictionary compilation is mostly reflected in the internalization and absorption of Chinese classics. Wang Weiqi (2019) conducted a statistical analysis of the distribution of literature in the first three volumes of *A Dictionary of the Chinese Language* and found that the recognizable classical literature quoted in the dictionary totaled 52, covering various classics of Confucianism, Taoism, Legalism, as well as Tang and Song poetry, historical records, and biographies. Among them, the most quoted literature was *The Book of Songs*, with 220 examples, accounting for 23.23% of the total. Confucius once commented on *The Book of Songs*, saying, "The Odes can exhilarate, give awareness, teach dissociation and cause resentment. Bring you near to being useful to your father and mother, and go on to serving your sovran" (*Confucian Analects · Yang Ho*). It can be seen that *The Book of Songs*, as the first collection of poetry in China, played a positive role in constructing the Confucian philosophical system. "The quoting of *The Book of Songs*" in the translation and introduction of *A Dictionary of the Chinese Language* appropriately reflects that Morrison regarded Confucianism, historically dominated Chinese philosophy, as the source and foundation for his quoting classics and explaining words. Through the induction of the quoted classics in *A Dictionary of the Chinese Language*, Morrison applied three Confucian perspectives to condense and introduce Chinese culture.

8.1.1 The System of Virtuous Conduct Centered Around "Ren (Benevolence)"

Mencius once said, "Benevolence is the distinguishing characteristic of man. As embodied in man's conduct, it is called the path of duty" (*Mencius · TSIN SIN. PART II.*). Huang Xianfan (2004), a Chinese historian, interpreted the meaning of "仁 *(Ren)*" in Confucianism as synonymous with "人*(Ren)*". *The Analects*, stating "Man is benevolent" and "Benevolent men love humanity", encapsulates that benevolence and humanity share the same origin and have a close relationship. The essence of Confucian philosophy is a human-centric philosophy, with "benevolence" and " 人*(Ren)*" being interrelated and mutually supportive. Everything is born and utilized for humanity. Since the concepts of "人 *(Ren)*" and "仁 *(Ren)*" are inseparable and closely related, the statement "The benevolent is humanity" can be understood as all virtues belonging to humanity fall under benevolence, signifying that benevolence covers the extension of virtues. At the same time, "Humanity is benevolent" also indicates that "benevolence" belongs to the category of "humanity" (An, 2005). To a certain extent, "仁*(Ren)*" governs various moral qualities such as 孝 *(Xiao)* (filial piety), 悌 *(Ti)* (brotherly love), 忠 *(Zhong)* (loyalty), 真 *(Zhen)* (sincerity), 善 *(Shan)* (kindness), 恕 *(Shu)* (forgiveness), and 礼 *(Li)* (ritual). They support and complement each other, collectively defining the "humanity". In *A Dictionary of the Chinese Language*, Morrison, on page 181 under the character "克 *(Ke)*", discusses "To overcome one's self and return to propriety, constitutes goodness" (*Confucian Analects · Yan Yuan*). On page 59, under the character "仁 *(Ren)*", he quotes Liu Xi, a Confucian in the Han Dynasty (206 B.C.-A.D. 9), saying, "Man, i. e. benevolence; benevolence to animated nature" (*Shi Ming*). On pages 63 and 795, he respectively cites, "Jin, is the foundation of righteous conduct; it is peaceful concord embodied: he who obtains it, is honourable" and "the virtuous have perfect complacency in virtue; the wise consider it the greatest gain". Furthermore, Morrison provides comprehensive explanations of various virtues under the category of "仁 *(Ren)*", such as filial piety and brotherly love (page 216, "He who is a brother and son, without doors exercises filial piety performs the duties of a brother") and loyalty (page 46, "He who, in serving his Prince, can sacrifice his person"). In summary, in Morrison's logic of "establishing, discussing, learning, contemplating, aspiring to, advocating, and practising benevolence", the Chinese culture in *A Dictionary of the Chinese Language* demonstrates greater vitality.

8.1.2 The View of Chinese Civilization as Expressed in the Integration of Rituals and Music

Confucius advocated, "Find inspiration in the Odes, take your place through ritual, and achieve perfection with music" (*Confucian Analects · Tai Bo*). In all matters, nothing can be set without "礼*(Li)* (ritual)", and "乐 *(Yue)* (music)" in contemporary society can be seen as the internal integration and coordination of the differences of rituals based on the principle of "the human mind reacting to external influences and producing activity". This transforms the various positions from a qualitative change of "each in its own place" to a state of "each in its proper place". It can be aptly summarized as, "Music seeks unity, while ritual values diversity. Unity fosters love, and diversity promotes mutual respect" (*Records of the Grand Historian ·Yue Shu*). "礼*(Li)*" and "乐 *(Yue)*" play distinct roles—the former emphasizes constraint specifications, while the latter focuses on holistic harmony. Their combined effect enables the norms of rituals rooted in universal human emotions, so both sides can evoke common emotions, fostering consensus in communication and naturally conforming and maintaining order (Lv, 2021).

Although these two may seem distinct, they are born of the same origin, coexist dialectically, and form a harmonious unity. Regarding "礼*(Li)*", Morrison, in *A Dictionary of the Chinese Language* on page 723 under the character "孜 *(Zi)*", quotes, "in life they should be served with the decorum which good principles prescribe; when dead they should be interred with decorum, and sacrifices should afterwards be offered to their manes with decorum" (*Confucian Analects · Wei Zheng*) and "the rules of decorum (or the ritual of etiquette) are the means by which to determine the nearer and more distant seats; to decide jealous doubts and prevent dislikes; to separate persons and things that rank the same, from those that are ranked differently; and to distinguish clearly, right from wrong" on page 677 (*Book of Rites· Qu Li*). With regard to "乐 *(Yue)*", on page 475, he mentions, "Confucius being at the state Tse, listening to their music, was three months without ever perceiving the relish of food, and said, I did not conceive that music could attain such perfection as this". Additionally, on page 553, he presents the harmonious scene of "The elder brother sounds the heucn, and the younger brother sounds the Che to accord with it" (*Book of Songs · Xiao Ya · Who's He*). In conclusion, "Music is what moves internally, and rituals are what move externally" (*Book of Rites*). "礼*(Li)*" act upon the external demeanor of individuals, diminishing their desires and regulating their actions. On the other hand, "乐 *(Yue)*" takes root in the internal nature of individuals, filling their emotions and harmonizing their differences. With both coexisting, they are enough to observe the sentiments of heaven and earth and comprehend the virtues of the divine.

8.1.3 Chinese Cultural Philosophy with the Aim of "Educating People"

Confucius is the mainstream school of thought in East Asia, placing the utmost importance on education (Huang, 2016). The Confucian sages deeply understood the pivotal role education plays in a nation's existence, renewal, and continuity. The English term "education" is derived from the Latin word "educare", where the prefix "e" means "to draw out", and the suffix "ducare" means "to lead". Together, they convey the idea of bringing forth something latent in certain ways. Similarly, Mencius expressed, "Benevolence, righteousness, propriety, and knowledge are not infused into us from outside. We are certainly furnished with them. And a different view is simply owing to want of reflection" (*Mencius · Kao Tsze I*), illustrating that various virtues already exist in the "heart" of a person. To discover them, one only needs to reflect and comprehend, and the condition for this reflection and understanding is the proper guidance of education.

During the process of dictionary compilation, Robert Morrison provided meticulous explanations of how China educates its people. Regarding the purpose of education, on page 747, he quoted "In ancient limes the Seaou-heo taught children to sprinkle, and to sweep; to cry, 'here', and to answer; to enter and to retire; and such like forms; —also to love parents; to respect superiors; to honor teachers; to associate with good friends; —and such like principles, all of which are fundamental things in teaching personal virtue; in regulating families; in governing a country; and in tranquilizing the world" (*Xiaoxue·Lijiao*) and "The principles of learning proper for grown persons, consist in a right understanding of illustrious virtue; it consists in acting so as to reform other people—it consists in permanently remaining in the practice of the highest goodness" (*The Great Learning*), so as to distinguish between the categories of "大学 *(Da Xue)*" and "小学 *(Xiao Xue)*". Concerning the content of study, he cited on page 747, "a posthumous work of Confucius and to the beginner or young student of moral science is the gate of virtue" (*The Great Learning*). Regarding the methods of learning, on page 737 and page 400, he respectively quoted "to study alone and without a friend, makes a man an orphan rustic, and one who has heard little" (*Book of Rites · Xueji*) and "To investigate deeply, and think closely" (*Confucian Analects · Zi Zhang*). Concerning the attitude toward learning, he respectively cited Zhu Xi's advices on page 753 and page 756, "the first thing required of us scholars, in our reading, is to form a resolution" and "do not say 'If I don't learn today, tomorrow is coming; if I don't learn this year, another year is coming" (*Quotations from Zhu Zi*). These exemplary sentences in *A Dictionary of the Chinese Language* are abundant, reflecting China's significant allure to scholar Robert Morrison as an ancient and modern educational powerhouse.

8.2 Factors Affecting the Formation of Morrison's Cultural Views

Time and space serve as powerful clues to trace the roots of translation activities. Therefore, the following discussion will, taking this clue as a logical starting point, reconstruct the context of the compilation of *A Dictionary of the Chinese Language* and comprehensively reveal the causes and the author's thought course of this translation activity.

8.2.1 The Historical Background

Engels once emphasized that the theoretical thinking of each era is a product of history. Different ages shape different forms and endow them with significantly different contents (Bureau of Compilation and Translation of the Works of Marx, Engels, Lenin and Stalin of the Central Committee of the CPC 1972). To uncover the reasons behind Robert Morrison's translational behavior in *A Dictionary of the Chinese Language*, it is essential to examine him and his work in the context of the time. The background at that time is a history of encounters, conflicts, exchanges, and developments between the Eastern and Western civilizations exemplified by Confucianism and Christianity, respectively.

Taking Robert Morrison's formal entry into China in 1807 as a historical reference point, it can be observed that the contemporary context was vastly different from the environment of earlier Christian missionaries represented by Matteo Ricci in the late Ming and early Qing Dynasties. During the tumultuous late Ming period, many intellectuals recognized that the Song-Ming Neo-Confucianism, with its ontology of "unity", the epistemology of "gradual unity", and the teleology of "returning to the original", had gradually degenerated into a form of empty talk, insufficient to meet the needs of stabilizing the country and governing society. Therefore, in this context, Matteo Ricci, with profound knowledge, brought advanced Western sciences such as astronomy, geometry, and geography and simultaneously gained a favorable reputation among the literati by introducing practical Western understanding. In the early Qing Dynasty, Emperor Kangxi decreed that the Catholic Church should preach in China and lifted the ban on religious practice among Chinese, creating favorable conditions for the spread of Christianity in China. However, the rites controversy led to the ruler's outrage and doubts, "China has its religion, so does the West; the Western religion does not need to be practiced in China, just as Chinese religion cannot be practiced in the West". Subsequently, a century of religious suppression began, which is also the background when Morrison entered China for missionary work. Thus, the ideological and theological forms between Chinese and Western thought were already sharply opposed. The ultimate reasons stem from the evident differences in the modes of thinking between Chinese and Western civilizations and the significant disparities in their future development.

Zhang and Cheng (1991) pointed out that traditional Chinese thinking tends to be holistic, comprehensive, intuitive, and imagistic, which sharply contrasts with the Western mode of thinking characterized by partiality, analysis, and reasoning. The Chinese traditional culture, exemplified by Confucian thoughts, is a philosophy of holism that adheres to a worldview of "the unity of heaven and humanity", which comprehensively reflects the subtle relationships of the origin, coexistence, and mutual transformation of all things. Thus, it can be seen as a philosophy of "the unity of heaven, man, and harmony, coexisting with a shared heart". In this philosophical thinking activity, individuals employ all their senses, passion, and wisdom, completely immersing themselves in the object of thought to achieve a state of selflessness. Therefore, in Confucian thoughts, there is no distinction between the other shore and this shore, substance and phenomena, reality and transcendence; they are all united (Ren, 2004). As a representative of Western civilization, Christianity holds a thinking mode that highlights a "dichotomy between human and the world" in epistemology. Under this dualistic thinking, the development of Western civilization can be understood as the process of artificially separating individuals from nature and continually deepening the understanding and knowledge of research objects through abstract speculation and logical reasoning. This "dualism" imparts strong exclusivity to Christianity, elevating God to a supreme authoritative position. It is evident that Confucian culture in China and Christian culture in the West are two highly heterogeneous cultures. Therefore, conflicts between Confucianism and Christianity are inevitable. The urgent challenges Robert Morrison faced were how to appropriately reconcile the relationship between these two modes of cultural thinking and how to organically integrate Christianity with Confucian culture to achieve the localization of Christianity in China.

8.2.2 The Sino-Western Collaboration

In recent years, the perspective of paratext in translation studies has gradually developed into a new and cutting-edge trend in translation studies. The concept of paratext was introduced by the renowned French narrative theorist Gerard Genette in 1979, and he continuously constructed, perfected, and developed this concept in his various works. He once said, "A text without paratext has never existed, and such a text will never exist" (Genette 1997). Paratext refers to "all verbal and non-verbal materials that coordinate the relationship between the main text and the reader and are used to display the work" (as mentioned above). It includes titles, prefaces, postscripts, illustrations, notes, and appendices, playing a role in providing various clues for translation activities and supplementing the main text, thereby revealing the translator's translation ideas, uncovering translation motivations, interpreting the generation mechanism of translation, and restoring the role of the translation scene (Feng, 2019). Chinese scholar Chen (2020) also pointed out that sometimes, paratext may impact the reader's reception more than the text itself. Therefore, the study of the paratext of *A Dictionary of the Chinese Language* helps us clarify how Morrison transitioned the relationship between Christianity and Confucianism from a history of conflict and confrontation to a history of mutual understanding and development.

Morrison first keenly perceived the imprint of a cultural way of thinking, most concentrated in the language and his writing. Therefore, coordinating Chinese and Western languages and writing was the first step Morrison took to lead Sino-Western relations toward harmony. China's unique history, culture, and ecological environment in the East created a language that emphasizes concrete ideograms and intuitive experiences, while the Western culture originating from the Greek maritime civilization nurtured a language that emphasizes abstract reasoning and rational speculation. Morrison was well aware of the significant differences between the source and target languages. In the preface of Volume 1 of *A Dictionary of the Chinese Language*, on page 9, he wrote, "a mere translation of *Kang-he's Dictionary*, would be far from answering the purposes of the European Student". On page 10, Morrison explained, "The Chinese Language originated in pictures of visible objects, and from thence by allusion, gradually extended from things visible and capable of being represented, to things immaterial and beyond the cognizance of the senses". He then expressed his opinion, "As sight is quicker than hearing, so ideas reaching the mind by the eye, are quicker, more striking, and vivid, than those which reach the mind by the slower progress of sound…The Chinese fine writing darts upon the mind with a vivid flash; a force and a beauty, of which Alphabetic Language is incapable". This indicates that Morrison recognized that Chinese characters' form, meaning, and sound interact and are interrelated, forming a unified whole. Among these three, form is of utmost importance, with an infinite charm of "taking the image to store the meaning, establishing the image to exhaust the meaning, and the meaning being self-evident" (Zhu, 2017). Under this view of the Chinese language, Morrison, in *A Dictionary of the Chinese Language*, particularly emphasized the deconstruction of Chinese characters from the perspective of "form" and then constructed their "meaning" based on this foundation. For example, under the character "孝 *(Xiao)* (filial piety)". On page 722 of the first volume, Morrison divided it into two parts, obtaining the characters " 老 *(Lao)* (old)" and "子 *(Zi)* (son)". Then, based on their spatial relationship, he deduced the conclusion that the elder issues orders from a higher position, and the younger obey the command from a lower place.

Secondly, Morrison actively drew lessons and accumulated experience from the Sino-Western Rites Controversy. This controversy made Morrison acutely aware that for Christianity to take root in China, it was necessary to address whether Chinese

Christian believers could "offer sacrifices to Confucius and ancestors" while "worshipping God". In this matter involving the fundamental interests of Confucianism and Christianity, Morrison chose a stance that downplayed or even denied the religious color of Chinese Confucius. On page 61 in Volume 1 of *A Dictionary of the Chinese Language*, he commented, "It is difficult, or perhaps impossible, to obtain for one's satisfaction, or to give to the captious Inquirer, such proof as curiosity and ingenuity may demand, as to the existence of spiritual Beings, the Soul of man, and the Deity, as well as our account, ableness to God". This viewpoint is further confirmed in the subsequent parts of the dictionary. In the annotation for the character "孔 *(Kong)*" on page 713, Morrison pointed out that Confucius did not believe in an afterlife: "To his mind 'life and immortality' do not seem to have been revealed. Nor does it appear that he prayed to Heaven or any God when death drew near". Later, Morrison recounted the story of Confucius' illness, where his disciple Zilu wanted to pray to various gods, and Confucius' response, "Ziqiu has been praying for a long time" clearly indicates that he didn't believe the efficacy of praying to heavenly gods and earth spirits for healing. This story provides evidence for later generations to determine that Confucius did not believe in ghosts and gods. In summary, Morrison denied the religious nature of Confucianism, following Matteo Ricci's tolerant stance toward Confucianism, regarding ancestor worship as a Chinese custom to maintain filial piety ethics. Therefore, offering sacrifices to Confucius was seen as an expression of gratitude from Confucian scholars to Confucius and his teachings. It was not idol worship and had no religious significance, so this foreign religious ritual did not necessarily need to be excluded (Liu, 2018).

Finally, Morrison moved from resolving the "differences" between Confucianism and Christianity to gradually seeking the "commonalities", demonstrating the integration of Eastern and Western thought. By comparing these two philosophies, it becomes evident that their overlapping convergence is permeated and occupied by the radiance of "love". In Christianity, this is embodied in a love that transcends from "loving God above all" to "loving one's neighbour as oneself", which is a kind of "universal love". In Confucianism, love originates in filial piety and family bonds, naturally manifesting in the mutual respect and love within the relationships of "parent and child, ruler and subject, husband and wife, elder and younger, friends with trust". Therefore, it is a kind of "benevolent love". The common pursuit of "love" reflects the mutual infiltration and integration of intrinsic values in Confucianism and Christianity. It is based on the inherent unity in love that one can extend to the unity in goodness, as love and goodness are expressions at different levels (Zhao, 2018). In other words, both Confucianism and Christianity harbor a compassionate concern for the country and the people. They advocate using love as a potent remedy to cure the stubborn ills of moral decay and societal corruption prevalent at that time, aiming to save the country and the world. In the preface of Volume 4 of *A Dictionary of the Chinese Language*, on page 10, Morrison points out that the truly good man occasionally goes beyond the individual and his family and makes decisions for the benefit of humanity in the long run. However, such decisions do not manifest effects in the short term or benefit him or his family. On page 11, Morrison's analysis of Confucian thought under Chinese culture also indicates that Chinese sages and moralists are quite in favor of peaceable endeavors to communicate the knowledge one man possesses to another. They traveled to instruct and civilize others while also blaming selfishness, which, under various plausible pretexts, would hide the light of truth. Their sentiments suggest that we should not perceive and understand the world solely from our perspective. In conclusion, Morrison states that this doctrine is perhaps universally acknowledged in respect of individuals and is equally true of large communities and nations. The more it is adopted and acted on by these, just in the same proportion will Peace and Order prevail throughout the world, and ultimate happiness, the wish of every heart, be generally diffused. It is easy to see that Morrison's interpretation of the essence of Confucianism also aligns with the core doctrines of Christianity. His portrayal of Chinese sages traveling to other nations parallels the actions of Christians spreading the gospel worldwide. Therefore, while maximizing the presentation of the harmonization of the two philosophical thoughts, Morrison, through his efforts, established a temporary Confucian-Christian community of knowledge and practice, which facilitated the integration of Eastern and Western thinking into a harmonious space, realizing a dialogue and development between two languages, thoughts, and civilizations.

8.2.3 The Motivation and Purpose

Translation activities are never conducted in a vacuum but within a specific cultural, economic, and political context. For the most active group of translators, as stated by Lefevere, their translation actions are deeply influenced by mainstream ideological and poetic factors (Lefevere 1992). While translators showcase their subjectivity in terms of "what to translate" and "how to translate", they cannot escape the influence of the zeitgeist and societal norms on the core question of "why translate". In other words, a translator's motivations and purposes are forever constrained by ideology and power relations. Thus, while translating *A Dictionary of the Chinese Language*, Morrison's earnest effort to integrate Chinese and Western cultures is inevitably subject to ideological manipulation and operates within the sphere of power relations.

As the first Protestant missionary coming to China, Morrison, like David Faure, Medhurst, and Legge, left a distinct missionary imprint on his words and deeds. Morrison was acutely aware that achieving the goal of "The Christian Occupation of China" required the localization of Christianity in China. This is necessitated a meticulous study of the Chinese language, history, culture, customs, political systems. This is because Confucianism held a dominant position in Chinese society, providing the spiritual impetus for Chinese morals, beliefs, and social and political life. Morrison's translation of *A Dictionary of the Chinese Language* can be seen both as an effort to fill the linguistic gaps in cultural exchange between China and the West and as a strategy to familiarize himself with Chinese thought so that he can "know oneself and the other" in his missionary career. Tong Qingbing (2005) also pointed out that the translation sponsor is a significant coordinating factor in translation activities. The East India Company, with its colonial undertones, served as Morrison's direct sponsor, generously funding the compilation of the dictionary. It reveals the intention of the Western world, under the guise of cultural exchange, to form a historical relationship with the indigenous social thought of China that is both mutually permeating and interdependent, yet simultaneously mutually rejecting and hostile. Such complex historical relationship is intertwined with the political situation, ethnic confrontation and integration, and societal changes in China at the time (Gu, 2010). Hence, the generous sponsorship of the East India Company for Morrison indicates a historical intention to lay the groundwork for later expansion and colonial plunder. Therefore, viewing Morrison's motivation and purpose for compiling *A Dictionary of the Chinese Language* from this perspective, we can find that this translation activity is manipulated by power relations and ideology, exhibiting a pronounced utilitarian hue and, consequently, possessing certain historical limitations.

Ji Guangmao (2005), a professor at Beijing Normal University, once pointed out that "ideology" is "one of the most extensive, ambiguous, elusive, and frequently used categories in the Western intellectual history of the twentieth century". German sociologist Karl Mannheim distinguished ideology into total ideology and particular ideology. The former refers to a historical-social group's thought structure and ideology in a certain era, representing the mainstream ideology existing universally in society. The latter refers to the ideas and thoughts manifested in the individual members of society, often "in disagreement with" and even in conflict with the mainstream ideology. The author argues that during the compilation of *A Dictionary of the Chinese Language*, Morrison demonstrated what Mannheim referred to as a particular ideology. When studying Morrison's motivation and purpose in translating the dictionary, we should consider not only the sponsor of the translation, the East India Company, but also the London Missionary Society to which he directly belonged. The London Missionary Society gave Morrison a written directive for his work in China: "First, you can compile a Chinese dictionary, surpassing any previous dictionaries of this kind; second, you can translate the Bible into Chinese so that one-third of the world's population can read the Chinese Bible directly" (Mrs. Morrison, 2004). It can be seen that the primary task assigned to Morrison by the London Missionary Society in China was to master the Chinese language rather than the missionary work itself. The London Missionary Society considered proficiency in the Chinese language a necessary prerequisite for missionary work, placing linguistic work before the religious mission. This added a touch of linguistic and literary vitality to Morrison's tasks and removed some of the rigidity of religious doctrine. It was in this spirit of instruction that Morrison developed his unique ideology, which unfolds in three main aspects.

Firstly, Morrison criticized the utilitarian tendencies the West displayed at the linguistic and cultural levels. German sociologist Habermas differentiated between two types of rationality: purpose-instrumental rationality and communicative rationality. In his universal pragmatics, the former focuses on how external resources are used in social behavior to satisfy the actor's purposes, while the latter refers to a reflective, critical, and argumentative ability based on equal dialogue between subjects (Hou, 2017). In the view of many Western scholars in the nineteenth century, language was considered a mere tool, helping the West exploit knowledge and wealth in other corners of the world. In such a context, Morrison called for a return to the essence of language learning, which means realizing communicative functions between different cultures. He pointed out that if the purpose of learning a language is unilaterally equated with promoting economic or technological development, this utilitarianism will inevitably backfire on the progress of science. This insight was undoubtedly valuable at that time. In *A Dictionary of the Chinese Language*, Morrison wrote, "The author's object has been, and the intention of the Dictionary ought to be, to communicate the Language to Europeans (Morrison 1819)". Here, Morrison avoids using words like "teach", perhaps because such words inherently view language as a teachable skill, which would make the dictionary a mere tool for language learners to search for a one-to-one correspondence between two languages and cultures rigidly. Instead, he deliberately chooses the verb form of "communication" to affirm his original intention. In English, this word has various meanings, such as correspondence, communication, interaction, exchange, and association, so it is a process of sharing experiences and knowledge, exchanging thoughts, and feelings through the transmission of information (Wang, 2020). Therefore, Morrison holds that learning a foreign language is never an authoritarian act of the powerful, imposing orders on the weak for a specific purpose. Instead, it is a process of equally communicating ideas, sharing results, and mutual learning and appreciation among subjects from different cultural backgrounds through language assistance.

Secondly, Morrison refuted the linguistic inferiority view of "useless Chinese" in Western thinking. Western scholars once debated the utility and importance of the Chinese language, with the conclusion that it is the responsibility of merchants and missionaries to navigate the chaotic, primitive Chinese world to find a desert belonging to Chinese literature (Morrison 1819). This conclusion conveys two underlying meanings. Firstly, Chinese is considered a primitive and backward language, where all words and phrases seem to lack order and rationality. Chinese literature in this ecological environment is bound to be an inherently barren and impoverished land. Secondly, the backwardness of Chinese discounts its value, relegating Chinese to a language of little interest that only missionaries and merchants approach for the needs of spreading the Gospel and exploiting resources. Morrison straightforwardly points out that this is a narrow and biased view of language which ignores the role of language users as subjects. Compared to perspectives that view humanity with freedom, progress, and Enlightenment, this can only be seen as a one-sided insight filled with nationalism or European sentiment (as above). According to Morrison, Chinese is one of the world's oldest and most profound languages, containing beautiful poetry, interesting and enlightening history or biographical narratives, and important moral thoughts. All of these aspects can provide significant insights into the West. For instance, Morrison explains on the same page that despite the Western Christian world advocating for individuals to cherish and practice the true spirit of altruism, it rarely, if ever, implements this concept at the level of academic or national organizations, as the Chinese sages did, so that people only consider the interests of others. Furthermore, Morrison highlights the contribution of the Chinese to national unity. Comparing Chinese with European languages, he writes that the spelling of words in the Western alphabet system changes with the pronunciation of different eras, while Chinese appears more stable and eternal. Therefore, it is perhaps this characteristic of Chinese writing that, to some extent, maintains the integrity of the Chinese nation. In summary, as Morrison firmly believes, over time, more people will understand Chinese, discover its value, and the strengths and weaknesses of Chinese will receive a fair and appropriate evaluation.

Finally, in view of the "West-centrism", which is reflected by "East for West", Morrison also put forth his own understanding. The internal changes in Western society require an ideological "other" for self-transcendence or self-confirmation, and the translation of Chinese culture to the West largely satisfies these demands (Zhu & Yuan, 2021). As one end of the history scale leaned toward the Western world in the nineteenth century, China at the other end naturally became the "other" in the eyes of the Western world. "The image of the 'other' is never a self-contained, objective product but an imaginative creation of the self about the other, a creative fiction made according to the self's needs, and a projection of the desires of the image-shaper" (Jiang, 2014). Therefore, Westerners always translated Chinese culture from their perspective, subjecting Chinese classics to politically unconscious manipulations, including arbitrary additions, deletions, or distortions, so as to realize the "self-oriented" and "East for West" while Westernizing Chinese culture. For example, in this mindset, the West tends to interweave stories and anecdotes from Greek and Roman history throughout the dictionaries they compile. Morrison criticizes this phenomenon: "China is a nation with originality; their modes of thought and reasoning are novel and creative, vastly different from Western thinking (Morrison 1918)". In the process of cultural exchange between Chinese and Western civilizations, Morrison suggests that Western exploration of Chinese requires joint efforts from both sides and more talents from different backgrounds and pursuits are needed in the process. Europe's efforts in this regard are currently insufficient (as above). Therefore, Morrison advocates a cultural view of diversity and equality, encouraging multi-dimensional exchanges, communication, and mutual learning between cultures based on full respect for the source culture. This stands in stark contrast to the prevailing "egotistical" culture in the West at that time, embodying its correctness, innovation, and progress.

8.3 Summary

The translation of Chinese culture is an inevitable path for Chinese culture to go global. This chapter explores the complex process of translating Chinese culture outward through three aspects: selection of translation materials, translation background, and translation motivations, providing theoretical and practical support for the further international recognition of China's material culture, spiritual culture, and institutional culture. In summary, at the level of self-awareness, successful translation of Chinese culture requires that participants in translation activities always keep in mind the original intention of cultural exchange and the purpose of language learning, discard zero-sum thinking of cultural superiority and linguistic hierarchy, and promote the civilization cooperation tradition of equal dialogue, mutual learning, and mutual respect between different language cultures. At the level of problem awareness, all participants should clarify that although there is no superior or inferior language culture, differences still exist in national characteristics. In the process of cultural translation, we need to constantly respect and preserve the heterogeneous characteristics of the source culture and respond to the needs and concerns of the target audience based on this foundation, thereby deepening mutual understanding and recognition between different cultures. At the level of practical reflection, we should actively carry out ideological criticism activities for cultural translation and closely follow the clues of time and space to explore and analyze the social and cultural factors that invisibly restrict translation activities, including power relations and ideologies. While exposing the manipulation of mainstream ideologies, we should affirm the revolutionary and progressive aspects presented by non-mainstream ideologies, enabling cultural exchange to achieve self-development and transcendence in practice continuously. Along the long road of translation, with the translators' hearts in contemplation, the translation of Chinese culture has opened up new theoretical perspectives and explanatory spaces for Chinese culture to go global, waiting for colleagues in the academic community to jointly explore and promote the healthy development of Sino-Western civilization exchanges.

References

An, D. (Ed.). (2005). *Of DeYi classics series readers: Interpretation of the deeds Volume, 106*. Wuhan Press.

André, L. (1992). *Translation, rewriting and the manipulation of literary fame, 14*. Routledge.

Barrett, T. H. (2015). A bicentenary in Robert Morrison's scholarship on China and his significance for today. *Journal of the Royal Asiatic Society, 04*, 707.

Chen, T. (2020). Explorers of the translation of classical Chinese poetry into English: The translation path and characteristics of Yuwen, Suoan's poetry. *Chinese Translators Journal* 03.

Christopher, H. (2008). *Robert Morrison and the birth of Chinese protestantism, 256*. Continuum Inter.

Feng, Z. (2019). Column on the study of "subtext in translation". *Journal of Tianjin Foreign Studies University* 03.

Gérard, G. (1997). *Paratexts: Thresholds of interpretation*, 1. J. E. Lewin, Trans. Cambridge University Press

Gu, W. (2010). *Christianity and modern Chinese society, 25*. Shanghai People's Publishing House.

Hou, J. (2017). *Course on western sociological theories, 347*. Nankai University Press.

Huang, J. (2016). Educational philosophy of East Asian confucianism: A new perspective. *Journal of East China Normal University (Philosophy and Social Sciences Edition)* 02.

Huang, X. (2004). *A preliminary exploration of ancient texts—Selected academic papers of Huang Xianfan, 464–465*. Guangxi Normal University Press.

Ji, G. (2005). *Ideology, 1*. Guangxi Normal University Press.

Jiang, Z. (2014). *Western mirror, Eastern Image*, 6. Central Compilation and Translation Press.

Liu, W. (2018). *A study on Morrison's communication activities to China*. Nanjing Normal University.

Luo, M. (2020). *A Case study on the translation and spreading of confucianism in Robert Morrison's A dictionary of the Chinese language*. North China University of Technology.

Lv, M. (2021). Returning to the "harmony" of ritual and music: The orderly unfolding of "harmony" from the perspective of confucianism. *Shandong Social Sciences* 02.
Morrison. (2004). *Memoirs of the life and labors of Robert* Morrison, 155. C. Gu, Trans. Guangxi Normal University Press.
Ouyang, Q. (2015). The "cultural turn" in contemporary philosophy. *Frontiers of Social Science* 01.
Ren, Q. (2004). The incarnation of the Tao and the unity of substance and function: A comparison of Christian and confucian ontology. *Journal of Sun Yat-sen University (Philosophy and Social Sciences Edition)* 03.
Robert, M. (1819). *A dictionary of the Chinese language (PART II — VOL. I)*, viii. East India Company's Press.
Robert, M. (1819). *A dictionary of the Chinese language (PART II — VOL. I)*, x. East India Company's Press.
Robert, M. (1819). *A dictionary of the Chinese language (PART II — VOL. I)*, vii. East India Company's Press.
Starr, J. B. (1998). The legacy of Robert Morrison. *International Bulletin of Mission Research, 02*, 73.
Tan, S. (2003). *A dictionary of the Chinese language* and Sino-Western cultural exchanges. *Chinese Cultural Forum* 01.
Tan, S. (2004). *Robert Morrison and Sino-Western cultural exchanges, 4*. China Academy of Art Press.
The Editorial Bureau of the Marx-Engels-Lenin-Stalin Works of the Central Committee of the Communist Party of China. (1972). *Selected works of Marx and Engels (Vol. 3)*, 465. People's Publishing House.
Tong, Q. (2005). The elements in construction of Literary Canon and their inter-relations. *Journal of Peking University (Philosophy and Social Sciences Edition)* 05.
Wang, W. (2019). A study on the book citations in *A dictionary of the Chinese language. Journal of Suihua University* 08.
Wang, X. (2020). Chinese culture going global: Connotation, aim and path. *Jianghuai Forum* 03.
Wang, X., & Ruan, Y. (2019). Studies on the dynamic role of translators in cultural spreading translation research on the confucian classics from Morrison's *A dictionary of Chinese language. Foreign Languages and Translation* 03.
Xia, C. (2019). Study on Robert Morrison and *A dictionary of the Chinese language* from the perspective of translation. *Journal of Tongling University* 01.
Yang, H. (2016). Reflective researches on Chinese–English learner's dictionaries seen from *A dictionary of the Chinese language* by Robert Morrison. *Foreign Language Education* 02.
You, M. (2012). *On the treatment of cultural information in foreigner-oriented Chinese-English dictionaries—A case study of Morrison's A dictionary of the Chinese language*. Nanjing University.
Zhang, D., Cheng, Z., et al. (1991). *Chinese mindset bias, 1*. China Social Sciences Press.
Zhao, C. (2017). *A history of English translations of Chinese classics in the 19th century, 88*. Shanghai Foreign Language Education Press.
Zhao, H. (2018). The comparison about Christian education and the traditional education of confucianism. *China Religion* 02.
Zhu, Q. (2017). A comparison of thinking mode between confucianism and Christianity. *Journal of Nanchang University (Social Sciences Edition)* 05.
Zhu, Z., & Yuan, J. (2021). How the cultural values guiding sinologists' English translation of Chinese classics affect China's image in the western countries. *Chinese Translators Journal* 02.

Chapter 9
Extraterritorial Spreading of the Source of Modern Legal System

Abstract From the viewpoint of history, there are changes of dynasties in ancient China, yet the main components of ancient national governance systems never disappear and have been continuously developed and improved in the long history. Throughout thousands of years of the development of civilization, the Chinese nation has accumulated rich experience in governance and management of the country, and many of its ideas and wisdom of which has integrated into the cultural blood, which emerged as the internal gene and bright sign of our national governance systems. They have been passed down from generation to generation and upgraded itself, displaying strong vitality. *Aphorisms from the Ancient Chinese* said that "It is better to use ancient ideas for today's reference, for without the past there is no present". *Guanzi* is a fundamental law for politicians in pre-Qin Era to maintain the state rightly and make all peaceful. As a pioneer of the Legalist School, Guan Zhong was the first to put forward the idea of run state affairs according to law. As the main representative of enlightened innovators in the Spring and Autumn Period, he advocated the combination of "Tian Dao" and law, the reform of old rituals and the creation of new laws, and the use of law to rule the government, applying both law and rituals, and using legal means to promote military, administrative, and commercial policies, so as to promote the enrichment of the country and the strengthening of the army. The Qin and Jin Legalists, represented by Han Fei and Shang Yang, have been regarded as the masters of Chinese Legalism, while the significance of Qi Legalism, represented by Guan Zhong, has been underestimated in the history of thought. The book *Guanzi*, on the other hand, focuses on the Qi Legalist thought represented by Guan Zhong. In the case of *Guanzi*, the ancient Chinese classic book, this chapter explores the ancient Chinese idea of the rule of law as presented in the book and the translation and Spreading of the *Guanzi*, so as to learn from the past and guide the present. In this way, on the one hand, it is conducive to inherit Chinese traditional legal thoughts and provide ideas for China's modern rule of law construction at the levels of legislation, law enforcement, justice, and law-abidance, and on the other hand, it promotes overseas Spreading of traditional Chinese rule of law ideas and facilitates the exchange of the rule of law between China and the West and contributes to the shaping of China's objective, true, and three-dimensional image of the rule of law in the international community.

X. Dong and Y. Luo, *The Legal Image of China in Chinese Legal Tradition*,
https://doi.org/10.1007/978-981-96-5797-1_9

9.1 Introduction

Legalism has a profound impact on China's modern legal system, especially the Qi legalist thought represented by Guan Zhong, whose political value in history has been seriously underestimated. Liang Qichao wrote in his *Commentary on Guanzi* (1909), "The rule of law is the highest norm of governance. However, through the five continents and thousands of years, who was the first person to invent the idea of 'rule by law' and to form his own school? It is Guanzi in China". He believed that the origin of ruling-by-law thought lied in the Chinese Legalists.

The source of Legalist thought can be traced back to the judge in the Xia and Shang Dynasties, as the *History of the Han Dynasty* said: "The school of Legalism probably originated from *Liguan (理官)*[1]". During the pre-Qin period, the states' administration was mainly based on rituals and regulations, and although there were some legal contents, it was still the rule of man in essence. In this process, the legalist thought represented by *Guanzi* came into being. Guanzi was the first to put forward the idea of rule by law and put into practice in Qi, Jin, Zheng, and other countries, and then Shang Yang, Han Fei, Li Si, and other scholars inherited and developed the legalist thought, which put the ruling-by-law thought to the country to a new climax.

Throughout the change of Chinese Dynasties and the governance philosophy of all ages, the rulers of Yin and Shang Dynasties lost the support of people due to the tyrannical system as shown in the popularity of killing innocent people as sacrifices; Zhou Dynasty replaced and advocated benevolence and righteousness while focusing on moral education and careful punishment. Yet a society simply relying on morality with the lack of legal constraints was destined to suffer the great destruction of rules and regulations of feudal ethics. As a result, there was a common rule of ritual and law in the Spring and Autumn period, and by the time of the Warring States period, the ruling-by-law thought was already highly regarded. In the turbulent times, the Qin Dynasty grew strong with the law and was quickly destroyed by a system of draconian law that lacked humanistic concern. Since then, from the Han Dynasty to the Qin Dynasty, most rulers of successive dynasties have promoted the strategy of governing the country that ostensibly advocates Confucianism but actually relies on the ideas of Legalism, and the situation of Confucianism and Legalism complementing each other has continued for more than 2,000 years.

The ninth volume of *History of the Han Dynasty, the record of Emperor Yuan of the Han dynasty*, records a remark by Emperor Xuan of the Han Dynasty: "The Han Dynasty had its own system, which used both the Kingly Way (Benevolent Governance) and the Despotic Governance, so how could it be like the Zhou Dynasty, which used the so-called 'rites and righteousness' purely for indoctrination?" It directly breaks the mystery of it. During the pre-Qin period, Confucianism and Legalism developed opposing political ideologies. Legalism advocates the Despotic Governance, which is a form of governance in which the monarch uses force, punishment, and power, and relies on a tight and reliable bureaucracy to carry out governmental

[1] In ancient China, *Liguan* refers to the official in charge of justice, whose specific duty is to hear cases.

affairs, emphasizing order and power; Confucianism advocates the Kingly Way, a political proposition in which the monarch governs the world with benevolence and righteousness, believing that the governance of the country should be left in the hands of a gentleman who scrupulously abides by virtue and morality, and emphasizing that governance should be based on virtue and that the people should be taught to be virtuous. During the Han Dynasty, the feudal legal system gradually matured. Most content of the Han Law was directly inherited from the Qin Law and the provisions were neat and strict characterized by legalism. In view of Qin's demise by ruling with legalistic ideas, Emperor Xuan of Han Dynasty said that he would take a mixed way of governance with both Kingly Way and the Despotic Governance, which was in fact a means of ruling the country with the Legalism as the bone and the Confucianism as the skin. Actually, such a system with those mixed thoughts was already established from the time of Emperor Wu of the Han Dynasty, and it was indeed an effective way of governing the country. Since "Dismissing the Hundred Schools and Respecting Only the Confucians", the rule of the country by Confucianism has been respected by the feudal rulers of all generations, and Confucianism has become the orthodoxy and mainstream of Chinese traditional culture for more than 2,000 years. However, Dong Zhongshu's Confucianism is no longer the original Confucianism of the Spring and Autumn and Warring States Period, which is mixed with the Taoism, Legalism, Yin-Yang and Five Agents Theory, and other schools of thought, and in the practice of ruling the country, it is indeed the use of Confucianism and Legalism.

In ancient China, there were many laws. As *The Book of History·Lü Xing* states: "When the Miao people did not comply with the order, they were subdued with punishments and five types of torture were enacted as a law". Ban Gu pointed out in *History of the Han Dynasty—Criminal Law Records* that in order to punish those who violated governmental orders, the Xia Dynasty made "Yu Xing (the general term of criminal law in Xia Dynasty)", the Shang Dynasty set "Tang Xing(the general term of criminal law in Shang Dynasty)", and the Zhou Dynasty used *Jiu Xing(Nine Punishments).* When it comes to the "law" of the pre-Qin Dynasty, many scholars have discussed it in terms of "Xing(punishment)". According to Liang Qichao, "The so-called law in ancient times had the same meaning as punishment" (Liang Qichao,1996,p.56). D. Bodde and C. Morris argued that, "The high frequency of the term 'Xing(punishment)' used in early legal literature, either independently or as a substitute word for 'law', demonstrates the ancient Chinese awareness of law that, law equals punishment and the original meaning of written law is criminal law" (Bodde & Morris, 2004, p.8). Legalism in the Spring and Autumn and the Warring States Periods was also known as the study of punishment, and its "law" tends to be "punishment", but it would be lop-sided to generalize the pre-Qin Legalist thought as "punishment". There is a clear difference between the Qi legalists represented by Guan Zhong and the Qin and Jin legalists represented by Han Fei and Shang Yang, although both of them are consistent in realizing the goal of "ruling by law". Guan Zhong's idea is different from Han Fei's and Shang Yang's belief of severe punishment that is "more penalties, fewer rewards". *Guanzi* not only practices the Despotic Governance and puts forward the specific plan of rule by law, but also pays tribute to the virtue of the Kingly Way and attaches importance to the fundamental role of moral education; it not only stresses the respect for the ruler and the inferiority of the ministers and promotes the political system with the monarch as the core, but also advocates the people as the basis, balancing the development of agriculture, industry, and commerce; it avoids the tendency of the Legalists to neglect the morals and the will of the people and supplements the inadequacy of Confucianism's lack of practical political experience, all of which shows its great importance in the history of ideas (Chi Wanxing, 2003, p. 8).

9.2 Guan Zhong and Guanzi

Confucius once commented Guan Zhong in *the Analects of Confucius—Xianwen*on Guan Zhong, "If it weren't for Guan Zhong, I'm afraid our hair would be hanging down and our lapel open to the left". Sima Qian, a famous historian of the Western Han Dynasty, also evaluated Guan in his *Records of the Grand Historian-Guan Zhong and Yan Ying*, "Duke Huan of Qi State called for the alliance of the lords many times, and thus gained the world, which was all due to the strategy of Guan Zhong".

Guan Zhong (723 BC-645 BC) was born in the 56th year of the reign of Duke Zhuang of Qi State. His personal name is Yiwu and his courtesy name is Zhong. It was said that Guan Zhong's ancestor was the descendant of Emperor Mu of the Zhou Dynasty, who shared a common ancestor with the royal family of Zhou. His father, Guan Zhuang, was an official of Qi, but his family's fortunes declined, causing Guan Zhong to live in poverty. To earn a living, he went into business with his friend Bao Shuya, but the business failed. Still trying to make a living, Guan Zhong worked as a merchant and traveled to many places, coming into contact with all kinds of people and seeing the world, thus accumulating a wealth of social experience. Guan Zhong experienced lots of setbacks: he was defeated in battle and fled, and he was dismissed from his official position several times. Later, when Duke Xi of Qi State died, the conflict between the successors broke out. His friend Bao served Jiang Xiaobai (the son of Duke Xi of Qi State), while Guan Zhong served Jiang Jiu (the son of Duke Xi of Qi State), and finally Jiang Xiaobai won and became Duke Huan of Qi State, while Jiang Jiu died and Guan Zhong was imprisoned. Then Bao recommended Guan and Guanzhong was employed as the officer of Qi State and assisted Duke Huan of Qi in achieving imperial supremacy. *Lie Zi-Li Ming records* that "When I was poor, I used to do business with Bao, and I used to take more when dividing the wealth, but Bao didn't regarded me as greedy, because he knew that I lived in poverty. I once worked for Bao and made him even poorer, but Bao didn't think I was stupid and knew that there were favorable and unfavorable times. I had been dismissed from the office by the ruler many times, but Bao does not think that I was incompetent and knew that I had not met with a good time. I had fought many battles and fled in defeat, but Bao didn't consider me timid, knowing that I need to support my old mother. When Jiang Jiu failed and Zhaohu died for me, I was imprisoned and humiliated, but Bao did not think me shameless, knowing that I would not be ashamed of a minor detail, but would be ashamed because my merits and fame had not been made known to the world. It is my parents who gave birth to me, but it is Bao Shuya who understands me". The deep friendship between Guan Zhong and Bao Shuya have become a long-lasting story in ancient China.

According to the research of scholars, *Guanzi* was not written by Guan Zhong himself, but is a compilation of the speech of various schools of thought in the pre-Qin period, and its content is very extensive. According to the traditional classification of schools of thought, it includes Confucianism, Daoism, School of Yin-Yang, Legalism, Logicians, Mohism, Agriculturalism, and so on. Classified by modern science, it includes various ideas such as politics, economics, philosophy, law, military science, agriculture, geography, calendar, education. Therefore, it is also regarded by successive generations as a treasure trove of ideas of the pre-Qin period. The ideas of *Guanzi* are the fundamental principles and laws of Chinese politicians in the pre-Qin period for ruling the country and conquering the world. It is also believed that some of its contents came from the Jixia school of thought. *Records of the Grand Historian—Tian Jing Zhong Wan Aristocratic Family* states that: "Emperor Xuan loved the learned and eloquent scholars, and gave all seventy-six mansions, such as Zou Yan, Chun Yu Kuan, Tian Pian, Jie Yu, Shen Zhi, and Huanyuan, a class of scholars, and made them officials, so that they could specialize in scholarly discussions instead of dealing with political affairs. As a result, the number of Jixia scholars in Qi State increased to nearly several thousand".

According to the research of scholars, *Guanzi* was roughly written like this: due to the important historical status and influence of Guan Zhong, scholars in the Warring States period and the subsequent period either recorded his words and deeds, or in the name of Guan Zhong, explained their own ideas. Through years of efforts, it finally compiled into *Guanzi*. Ye Shi of the Song Dynasty said, "*Guanzi* was not the work of a single person, nor was it completed in a short period of time". In the 1930s, Luo Genze, a renowned scholar, published a book *Guanzi Tan Yuan(《管子探源》)*, in which the age and author of each volume of *Guanzi* were examined one by one, and it was believed that these works were written in the middle of the Warring States period, at the end of the Warring States period, between the Qin and Han Dynasties, and up to the time of Emperor Wenjing and even Emperor Wuzhao of the Han Dynasty. The authors are either political thinkers, legalists, Taoists, Confucianists, Yin-Yangists, Syncretist (*za jia*), medical scholars, or militarists, but the mainstream of their thought is Legalism and Huang Lao Taoists, which is characterized by the organic combination of Taoist and Legalist thought, which not only finds a philosophical basis for the rule-by-law, but also practically implements the Taoist thought into the society. Sun Yat-sen regarded *Guanz*i as the "origin" of Chinese economics and pointed out that its economic theories mainly included the theory of enriching the country and the people, physiocracy, and the like. In a word, the title of *Guanzi* comes from Guan Zhong, and its contents are mainly related to Huang Lao Taoism. It not only puts forward the concrete plan of rule-by-law, but also attaches importance to the basic role of moral education; it stresses the political management system with the monarch as the core and advocates the people-oriented, promoting the balanced development of agriculture, industry, and commerce; it also advocates effective means to safeguard the interests and security of the nation while emphasizing the importance of morality and benevolence; it avoids the tendency of the Legalists of Han, Zhao, and Wei States to neglect the will of people and complements the lack of practical political experience of ideal Confucianism. Therefore, it has an important position in the history of ancient Chinese political thought, and to a certain extent, reflects the basic thought of Guan Zhong.

9.3 The Connotations of the Legal Thoughts in Guanzi

"No worries about food and clothing" can be said to be the most real and simple wish of the ancient laboring people, and as early as in the Spring and Autumn Period, the statesman Guan Zhong put forward the idea of strengthening the country and enriching the people and successfully practiced this idea in Qi for forty years, helping Duke Huan of Qi to "unite all the dukes and conquer the whole world", and becoming the head of the five overlords in the Spring and Autumn Period. The understanding and the practice of the law of *Guanzi* reflects the ideas of people-oriented thinking and the rule of law. The ideas of *Guanzi,* such as the rule of law, putting the people first and giving equal importance to both rituals and laws, are advanced beyond the times and are still of great significance for the construction of the rule of law until today.

9.3.1 A People-Oriented Principle in Governing the Country

Taking "people-oriented" as the foundation of the rule-by-law is a distinctive feature of the legal thought of *Guanzi.* The entire *Guanzi* is a persuasive statement, and the object of its "persuasion" is the monarch. In ancient Chinese society, the power of the monarch had supreme power, which would determine the rise and fall of the world. *Guanzi* realized that if Qi State was to stand out in the Spring and Autumn period, the supreme ruler of Qi had to fully understand the importance of being people-oriented; only when the monarch's view of "people-orientation" governance was established, would there be a basis for a strong and rich state. Therefore, when Duke Huan of Qi asked how to conquer the world, *Guanzi* put forward his viewpoint: "The people of Qi are the foundation". "What is the basis? What makes the monarch of a great nation high in status? The answer is: the number of people used by him". The authority of the monarch comes from the people who support him; "The reason why a decree can be implemented is that it complies with the people's wishes; the reason why a decree is abolished is that it goes against the people's wishes". The rise and fall of the regime all depends on the support of the people; "When the people engage in agriculture, they will be able to reclaim fields; when more fields are reclaimed, food production will surely increase; when food production increases, the country will become rich". Agriculture is the economic lifeline of the country, and the people are the bearers of agricultural production; "the army must rely on the support of the people to win the war, and only with the support of the people can the army win". The success or failure of the army lies in the people's obedience to the dispatch. Guanzi reminds the monarchs of the four aspects of the authority, power, economy, and military strength, and that they should always keep in mind the people as the source of their power.

Guanzi suggests that, with the principle of people-orientation, the monarch would have mastered the way of governing the country, and the art of carrying out this way is to use benefits to manage them. Guan Zhong believes that people are born to pursue what is good for them and avoid what is harmful. Therefore, one of the ways to win the people's hearts is to meet their desires. "If the people are averse to hardship and toil, I will make them comfortable and happy; if the people are averse to poverty and lowliness, I will make them rich and prominent; if the people are averse to danger and calamity, I will make them secure in their existence; if the people are averse to extinction and death, I will make them fruitful and multiply". It is only if one can relieve the people's worries, enrich the people's wealth, protect the people's security and nurture their livelihood, and link the interests of the state with those of the people, that the people will embrace the monarch to serve the state. In other words, whether the people live well or not fundamentally determines the stability of the state. "If the people are rich, they will be at ease in their native homes, and if they are at ease in their native homes, they will pay more attention to their families, and if they pay attention to their families, they will respect the emperor and fear to commit crimes, and if they respect the emperor and fear to commit crimes, they will be easy to be ruled". In addition, Guan Zhong also stressed that material satisfaction is the prerequisite for the pursuit of a spiritual realm, as the saying goes, "When the granary is solid, one knows the etiquette; when the clothes and food are sufficient, one knows the honour and disgrace", and that it is only when you are well fed and clothed that you can pursue a higher level of spiritual self-discipline.

9.3.2 A Balanced View of Governance: Taking and Giving in Moderation

"The Rule of the Golden Mean" is the essence of our ancient "harmony" culture, a balanced way of dynamic development. The ancients emphasized the "mean" and pursued balance, hoping that things could be in a state of "just right", where the part and the whole fit together as well as contradiction and unity coexisted, and where there was neither deficiency nor excess. Influenced by this, Guan Zhong put forward the policy of "taking and giving in moderation", advising monarchs to maintain a moderate attitude when dealing with things or getting along with others and to master the skill of balance in response to cope with complex situations and avoid going to extremes or losing control. If there are certain restrictions and norms on the acquisition and use of material things, then people will not have excessive greed and fantasies. *Guanzi·Quan Xiu* has the following words: "The land has a certain season for the production of goods, and the labor of the people has a certain limit, while the monarch's desire is endless. If the people, who are tired of producing goods and labor, are used to support the monarch, whose desire is endless, and there is no moderate standard in between to limit it, then it is going to lead to the people being dissatisfied with their superiors". The output of the land and the productivity of the people are limited, and if the monarch wants to win the hearts of the people, he should restrain his own desires and obtain in moderation, so as to stabilize the social order. Giving in moderation can bring people together. As the saying goes, "If you give great rewards, your country's wealth will be scarce; if you impose severe penalties, your country's decrees will seem tyrannical. If the state's wealth is scarce and its laws are tyrannical, and the people are treated in this way, they will not support the ruler". In dealing with rewards and punishments, the monarch should be careful and prudent, and pay attention to the balance between the two. If there is a mismatch between merits and demerits or rewards and punishments, in the long run, the people will be resentful and the prestige of the monarch will be damaged. Therefore, according to *Guanzi*, a wise ruler should make good use of the principle of balance in the process of governance and take and give in moderation.

In *Guanzi*'s view, the wealth of the state comes from the people, and the wealth of the people depends on the protection of the state, which are both interdependent and contradictory. How to regulate this contradiction was a major problem for the monarch to solve in governance. Through a series of policies and systems, *Guanzi* cleverly solved this problem by applying the art of balance to the fullest extent. Taking agricultural tax as an example, *Guanzi* proposed that "all types of land should be converted into standard cultivated land area according to actual output(*Di Jun Yi Shi Shu*)", which means barren mountains, swamps, hills, rivers, and so on should be converted into cultivated land area according to the actual production value, and different types of land should correspond to different conversion rates, so as to achieve the standardization of the land statistics; "Agricultural taxes shall be levied according to different conditions of land(*Xiang Di Er Cui Zheng*)". The quality of the land is taken as a consideration for taxation, and taxes are levied differently according to the grade of the land; and the taxes are flexibly reduced and exempted according to the annual success of the land to ensure that the taxes are reasonable and measured, and to achieve a dynamic balance between the land and the taxes, as stipulated that "in a good year, 30% of the land rent is levied, in a medium year, 20%, and in a bad year, 10%"; the people can pay taxes in physical form to save them from the pain of servitude, and at the same time proposing to levy land tax in units of "mu(亩)" and unify the unit of taxation. These moves, in the economic conditions at that time, stimulated the farmers' enthusiasm for production, which partially emancipated the productive forces.

9.3.3 A Systemic View of Building a Strong Nation of Rule-By-Law

If the monarch recognizes the importance of the people in his mind and knows how to use the art of balance in the process of governance, will he be able to achieve the wish of a strong state and a rich people? Guan Zhong's answer is still negative. In Guan Zhong's system of thought on governance, if the first two are "soft measures", then the system of "rule by law" is the "hard means" of governance. Guanzi has made many definitions of "law". In the chapter On Prohibition and Storage*(Jin Cang)* he pointed out, " The law is the measure of the world so that it is used to settle affairs that are in doubt and to tell right from wrong", The chapter "The Seven Standards*(Qi Fa)*" measures and weights such as *chi, cun,sheng, mo, gui, ju, heng, dan, du, hu, jiao, and liang* are addressed as law*(Fa)*. It can be seen that in Guanzi's view, "law" is a way to distinguish between right and wrong, and to measure merits and demerits, as well as rewards and punishments. According to Guanzi, the function of "law" is to "promote success and fear of violence", "to identify rights and obligations and stop disputes" and "to make people know what to do", which means that the ruler, ministers, and people should follow the law. Guanzi proposed to use the coercive power of law to ensure the orderly implementation of the initiatives to enrich the people and to lay a solid institutional foundation for a strong state and rich people.

The whole book of *Guanzi* contains 86 chapters, of which 76 are still in existence, almost one-fifth of them are related to law. The laws and regulations are related to civil affairs, administration, penalties, taxation, economy, military affairs, water conservancy, environmental protection, and other aspects, which can be regarded as the key texts of pre-Qin jurisprudence. Historical experience tells us that the economy and the rule of law are complementary. For one thing, economic development and resource allocation are becoming more and more refined and need laws to guide, regulate, and protect. Secondly, a stable environment is a necessary condition for economic development, and the law is needed to establish and maintain order. As the saying goes, "without rules, nothing can be done", and *Guanzi*, with its rich legal content, advocates internal restraints on members of society and external prevention of abuses of power, which provides rich ideological nourishment for the ancient judiciary.

In order to make good use of the "law" as the most important weapon of the state, Guanzi put the concept of "rule by law" into practice in the program, proposing that "Before any action is taken, an order must be issued first. That is to make clear the standards for awards and punishments when any action is taken. People in charge of it should stick to the order cautiously to dispense awards and punishments. They should also supervise it and report the progress to the government, and awards conferred and punishments executed should be reported too. If there are people not acting according to the provisions of the order, they will be regarded as 'Zhuan Zhi' even though they might have accomplished some outstanding achievements, and therefore they will be executed without pardon. After the ways of doing things are clarified, the action can be taken" ("On Establishing Right Policies*(Li Zheng)*"). Guanzi believed that there was a need to make it clear that the law should be strictly adhered to at all stages of the preparation, execution, inspection, and reporting of affairs. In this way, the people's every move in production and life is subject to rules and regulations; the country's governance of the people and implementation of policies has clear regulations. There is a law and an order to follow.

As an excellent national cultural heritage, *Guanzi* has extensive and profound connotation which adapts to the needs of the time and has a lot of inspirations for today's society.

9.4 The Overseas Spreading of the *Guanzi*

According to scholars, *Guanzi* had already been transmitted eastward to Japan by the early Nara period (710 AD-794 AD), i.e., in the early years of the Kaiyuan period of the reign of Emperor Xuanzong of the Tang Dynasty (713 AD-741 AD). After its introduction to Japan, *Guanzi* was included in the *Catalogue of Japanese Books*. The catalogue was compiled by Fujiwara Nosukeyo (847 AD-898 AD), a scholar of the Heian period, and is generally believed to have been written in the third year of Emperor Udo's reign (891 AD), while some scholars believe that it was compiled between the end of Emperor Yosei's reign (876 AD) and the end of Emperor Kei's reign (876 AD), and the end of Emperor Yosei's reign (876 AD). Some scholars believe that the book was compiled "between the last year of Emperor Yosei's reign (876 AD) and the first year of Keiyuan (884 AD)". The book contains more than 1,500 Chinese classics, with more than 17,000 volumes, which were handed down in Japan during the pre-Heian period. Almost all of these Chinese classics "were imported during the Tang dynasty". During the Asuka and Nara eras, Japan sent many envoys to the Tang Dynasty. When the envoys returned home, they often brought with them a large number of Chinese books, and "all the rewards received were used to buy in books and bring them home across the ocean (traveling around the country)" (*Old Book of Tang*). Against this background, *Guanzi* was brought to Japan along with other books and documents by the envoys. In the Edo period, with the development of Japan's commercial economy at that time, the previous monopoly of culture by aristocrats and monks was broken and gradually shifted to the common people. The expansion of the cultural class increased the demand for books, and a large number of Chinese books were imported into Japan with the commercial trade, including *Guanzi*. The large number of Chinese editions of the *Guanzi* and the large number of printed copies of *Guanzi* in Japan created a situation in which *Guanzi* was widely circulated in Japan during the Edo period.

China and the Korean Peninsula are connected by mountains and rivers, and *Guanzi* was introduced to the Korean Peninsula at a very early stage. Because ancient Korea is a traditional Confucian society and has a belief in the doctrine of Zhu Zi, and the Four Books and Five Classics were widely circulated, while *Guanzi*, which emphasized the benefits of knowledge on governance, was given a cold shoulder. Therefore, *Guanzi* has long been circulated as a Chinese text on the ancient Korean

Peninsula. In modern times, Korean society and academic thought have changed dramatically, and *Guanzi* has been emphasized along with *the Analects* and the *Mencius*, resulting in the appearance of Korean translations of *Guanzi*. The translation of *Guanzi* in Korea was first a selective translation and then a full translation. The earliest selected translation was the 1969 edition of the Korea Free Education Promotion Association, which was included in the World Classical Collection. It was followed by the 1972 Daeyang Book Publishing House book and the 1977 Hyunamsa book, also in the form of a series of books. It was not until 1985 that the first single-volume translation of *Guanzi* was published by Myungwondo, and after the establishment of diplomatic relations between China and South Korea in 1992, cultural exchanges between the two countries became more and more frequent, and *Guanzi* became a subject of increasing interest in South Korean society. Since the reform and opening up of China, China has made significant economic achievements. *Guanzi* advocates pragmatic change, which is in line with the spirit of China's reform and opening up, and this inadvertently promotes the study of *Guanzi* in Korea. From Korea's perspective, China is an important partnership country. Previously, Korea needed to study Confucius and Mencius to understand China, but now it is believed that China needs to be understood through *Guanzi*. Against this background, the first full Korean translation of *Guanzi*, the Pine Tree Edition, was published in 2006.

As early as the end of the nineteenth century, Western scholars began their attempts to study and translate *Guanzi*, although systematic translations of *Guanzi* did not become popular until around the middle of the twentieth century. From the end of the nineteenth century to the 1920s, German and French sinologists' overviews of *Guanzi* were mainly aimed at introducing the main ideas of *Guanzi* to the West, but there was a lack of systematic research, and the translations were very superficial and fragmentary. Gabelentz, a professor and sinologist at the University of Leipzig in Germany, published in French in 1886 "Philosophical Writings of Guanzi", in which he briefly introduced *Guanzi*. By 1896, the French sinologist Halrez published "A Chinese Chancellor in the Seventh Century B.C.: Guanzi of Qi State and the Book of Guanzi" in the Asiatic Magazine. In the late 1920s, the basic motivation for the study of *Guanzi* and the orientation of translations were mostly based on the field of personal interest, and the translation methods were mainly selected and abridged, which were insufficient in terms of both quantity and quality. However, the accumulated translated texts provided the basis for a larger scale of translations in the later period. In the 1950s, the study and translation of *Guanzi* was further deepened, and in 1952, Piet Van Delon, a scholar at Cambridge University, used bibliographic methods to examine the book, circulation, and authenticity of the editions of *Guanzi* from the perspectives of linguistics and philosophical thought in his work *On the Circulation of Guanzi* (published in the UK in 1952, Bulletin, Volume II, No. 41). In the article, the linguistic interpretation of many contents of *Guanzi* is covered, which in a certain sense provides inspirations for the translation method of *Guanzi*, and also has a certain influence on the subsequent research. From the 1980s to the present, academic research and cultural exchanges have continued to advance, so that the study of the translation of *Guanzi* has entered into a mature period, and the main motivation for translations has already been transformed into one based on the purposes of academic research and cultural exchanges. During this period, Allyn Rickett, a professor at the University of Pennsylvania in the United States, is the representative figure who specializes in the study and translation of *Guanzi*. Rickett published the first and second volumes of *Guanzi* by Princeton University Press in 1985 and 1998, respectively. Since then, a complete English translation of *Guanzi* has finally been produced in the Western countries, which marks that the translation of *Guanzi* in the West has risen to a new height. The publication of this complete translation has made it possible for *Guanzi* to move from partial and piecemeal translation to comprehensive and systematic translation in the Western world, completely changed the situation of insufficient attention to *Guanzi* in the Western and English-speaking worlds for a long time, and improved the situation in which there has been a mismatch between the significant value of *Guanzi* as classics and the influence of its Spreading to the world.

In 1995, China formally launched the project of "Library of Chinese Classics" (Chinese-English comparison), which is the first major national publishing project in the history of China to systematically and comprehensively introduce foreign language versions of Chinese cultural texts to the world, laying a solid foundation for the development of foreign translations of Chinese classics. The English translation of *Guanzi* was completed by Professor Zhai Jiangyue of Ludong University and was first published by Guangxi Normal University in 2005. This is the first full translation of *Guanzi* completed independently by a local Chinese translator, which is of great significance to the global promotion of the thought of *Guanzi* and Qilu culture.

9.5 Summary

Guanzi is a collection of state management ideas in the pre-Qin era, which is the result of the competition and integration of a hundred schools of thought. The system is very complicated, which not only involves the ideas of Taoism, Confucianism, Legalism, School of Yin-Yang, and the like, but also covers criminal law, civil law, administrative law, economic law, and procedural law according to the types of laws involved. *Guanzi* is an excellent representative of traditional Chinese culture, and its ideas on governance are extremely rich. The rule by law ideas presented in the book are characterized by inclusiveness and integration. The understanding and the practice of the law reflects the ideas of people-oriented thinking and ruling-by-law, and there are unique features in the legislation, law enforcement, justice, and compliance with the law, which is of great significance to the construction of the rule of law nowadays. At the same time, actively carrying out research on the translation and Spreading of traditional cultural texts, such as *Guanzi*, on the one hand, is conducive to keep Chinese cultures alive and enhance cultural confidence, and on the other hand, it is also conducive to strengthening the dialogue of civilizations, telling China's stories well, elevating the influence of Chinese culture, and shaping an objective and true legal image of China.

References

Chi, W. (2003). Research on Guanzi. Northwest Normal University.
Bodde, D., & Morris, C. (2004). *Law in imperial China*. Y. Zhu, Trans. Jiangsu People's Publishing House.
Liang, Q. (1996:56). *History of pre-Qin political thought*. Oriental Publishing House.

Chapter 10
A Case Study: Exploring the Path of Legal Image Self-Shaping—on Traditional Term Translation

Abstract This Chapter will mainly focus on the possible path of the legal image self-shaping through traditional term translation, including both ancient legal term and classic term. "The accuracy of the translation of traditional terms with Chinese characteristics created by other nations in the past will directly affect the authenticity and effectiveness of the international Spreading of the relevant discourse with Chinese characteristics and the reconstruction of China's cultural image" (Wei Xiangqing & Yang Ping, Wei, X., & Yang P. (2019). International communication of discourse with Chinese characteristics and standardization of terminology translation. Chinese Translators Journal, No. 1.). The self-shaping of China's legal image in the new era is to play the role of reforming from the bottom and uplifting the national cultural confidence. In the context of the new era of China's comprehensive promotion of the rule of law, China's legal subject consciousness is increasing and the construction of the rule of law is fully launched. China's image as a rule of law country in the world is increasingly becoming a subjective and conscious practice of the governmental institutions and departments under the leadership of the Communist Party of China (CPC). With the enhancement of China's comprehensive national power and its increasingly important role in the world stage, the situation where the image of Chinese law was previously shaped by Westerners is changing. Now Chinese themselves are beginning to shape their own legal image, which is no longer entirely determined by others. Criticism and exposure of legal orientalism, in essence, is to move toward "Oriental Legalism". The so-called Oriental Legalism is intended to reconstruct a new discourse and concept for understanding and interpreting law and the rule of law and to awaken the Orient, so that it can regain the subjectivity of dialogue with the West on an equal footing, and to make its own voice heard in the evolution of the world's civilization of the rule of law, which is a possible path to transcend the Legal Orientalism. In short, moving toward "Oriental Legalism" is a question of how to construct a new Chinese rule of law discourse system on the existing basis (Wei Leijie, Wei, L. (2018). The Chinese connotation of oriental legalism. Open Times, No. 6.). Behind the shaping of the image of the rule of law is ultimately a system of discourse composed of knowledge, ideas, concepts, and values. The construction of a logical and self-contained rule of law discourse system is the fundamental starting point for reshaping China's image of the rule of law. In its

X. Dong and Y. Luo, *The Legal Image of China in Chinese Legal Tradition*,
https://doi.org/10.1007/978-981-96-5797-1_10

pursuit of autonomy for the rule of law and culture as a whole, and in the development of its own legal model, China needs to be rooted in its own cultural traditions and world of meanings, but that does not mean that it is ignoring the trends in the development of human civilization and the differences between traditional and modern societies in terms of their basic organization (Lu Nan, op. cit.). In the nineteenth century, the ways and paths of China's legal image communication have given us full Enlightenment—the construction of the discourse system of the rule of law is a systematic project, which requires not only the awareness of innovation in the fields of ideas and concepts of law and the rule of law, but also the holistic and diversified forms and ways of translation and Spreading. The construction of the discourse is a system with communication effect built by social groups through a series of symbols, media Spreading, institutional operation, and social practice. It determines that the main body engaged in the construction of the rule of law discourse system needs the concept of great translation and broad Spreading underpinned by a large pattern and vision. Translation and Spreading have always carried an important historical mission and values of the times. Translation work in the new era is not only a correction of the misinterpretation of the historical image of the law created by foreign nations, but also a "self-shaping" and "reshaping" of the image of China's legal image in the new era. Due to the cultural differences between Chinese and Western languages, the translation of ancient Chinese laws faced many difficulties. Even Sir George Thomas Staunton admitted unashamedly the difficulties encountered in the translation, "The language of the text is so obscure and the structure so complex that even if the reader understands the meaning of individual words, he or she cannot figure out the meaning of the whole after combining them!" (Staunton,op. cit.,p.219). Some newspapers and magazines at that time also presented Chinese law in a one-sided and erroneous manner. For example, in *Chinese Repository*, the term "Yi Mu (夷目)", used to refer to a foreign leader in an official order, was inaccurately translated as "the barbarian eye", for the single character "夷" means "foreigner" and "目" means "eye" in English. Moreover, in reviewing the *Records of the Three Kingdoms*, there were instances where the author confused it with *The Romance of the Three Kingdoms* (Li Xiuqing 2015). The fundamental reason lies in the inherent limitations of the editors' and authors' knowledge, vision, language, cultural differences, ideology, and so on. This kind of "Chinese knowledge" translated and disseminated by Westerners, especially the cultural vocabulary with Chinese characteristics, will inevitably be misinterpreted in the process of translation. This exposes many limitations of China's legal image created by foreigners, which has brought many negative impacts on China's legal image.

10.1 Solving the Untranslatability of Ancient Legal Term

The Untranslatability of Ancient Legal Tradition is mainly reflected the translation of ancient legal terms. Different from modern legal terms, ancient legal terms has its unique cultural characteristics, including inheritance, creativity, and plurality.

The uniqueness of the Chinese legal system, the difference between the Chinese and Western ways of thinking, and the historicity of ancient legal terms are the main reasons leading to the untranslatability of ancient legal terms. The purpose of ancient law translation is to spread ancient Chinese legal culture and promote the foreign exchange of excellent traditional culture.

In recent years, the study of translation of professional terms has been a hot spot in the study of legal translation. The reason for this is that legal terminology "is a unique member of legal language, and it is precisely because of their existence that the legal language becomes professional and hence makes it different from general language" (Yang Shufang, 2003). However, the current research on the translation of ancient legal terminology is scarce, and there are few specialized articles focusing on how to translate the wisdom created by the people in the ancient cultural context. With the in-depth promotion of the national strategy of "Culture Stepping-out", the translation of Chinese classics is receiving more and more attention from the translation research community, and some scholars have spared no effort in calling for the translation of legal classics, which should reflect the value of cultural exchange. Against the backdrop, it is natural to emphasize the research on the translation of ancient legal terms, which deserves in-depth discussion.

10.1.1 The Characteristics of Ancient Legal Terminology

Ancient legal terms is a vocabulary extracted from the ancient legal and cultural context as well as codes and doctrines, and the examination of terms cannot be separated from the entire ancient cultural environment and legal system, and it is necessary to grasp its attribute characteristics from the whole Chinese legal system, the historical space, and the overall evolution of the legal system.

10.1.1.1 Inheritance

The legal system exists for the purpose of adjusting social relations and adapting to certain economic development and social changes and has its relative stability. The development of legal culture is always based on a certain cultural foundation for inheritance, transformation, and innovation and cannot be detached from the historical and cultural deposits, otherwise, it will be like water without a source and wood without a root.

Although China's ancient history has experienced a lot of changes of dynasties, however, the legal system and the codification of laws have shown continuity. Ancient people used their own wisdom to create a splendid traditional legal culture, the Chinese legal system is unique and brilliant codes as well as long traditions have been extended. From the *Book of Law* in the early Warring States period to *Qin Lü* in the Qin Dynasty, *Nine Chapter Law* in the Han Dynasty, *Bei Qi Lü* in the northern Qi Dynasty, *Kai Huang Lü* in the Sui Dynasty, and then the *T'ang Code* in the Tang Dynasty, the inheritance of the codes is obvious, and the inheritance of the language of the law, the concepts of the law, and the terminology of the law are even more self-evident. "The *T'ang Code* inherited some of the legal terminology of *Qin Lü*, such as '伪写*(Wei Xie)*(false writing of charges)', '受分*(Shou Fen)*(sharing of crimes)' and so on" (Wang Donghai, 2007, p. 68); "the *T'ang Cod*e and the Han Law also have a lot of similarities in terminology, such as '枉法*(Wang Fa)*' '主守*(Zhu Shou)*' '乘舆*(Cheng Yu)*' '服御物*(Fu Yu Wu)*' '大逆不道*(Da Ni Bu Dao)*', etc." (Ran Qibin, 2002a, 2002b, p. 1–2). "The structure and the content of *Song Xing Tong*(the Law of Song Dynasty) is almost the same as that of the *T'ang Code*, with twelve chapters, except for individual words to be avoided" (Liu Guzhen, 2004); "The titles of *Da Ming Lü(The Great Ming Code)* combine the essence of ancient laws, which originated from the Tang Law but is superior to it"(Huai Xiaofeng, 1998, p. ii); "*The Great Qing Code* are inherited from *Da Ming Lü* and the *T'ang Cod*e, and according to the Qing people's own words: I once examined the laws recorded in the laws of the Tang Dynasty, and there were more than eighty articles that differed from the decrees. Of these, most of them were the same, more than four hundred and ten, which are the present laws (referring to the articles of *the Great Qing Code*). Among them, those which are in conformity with the laws of the Tang Dynasty also account for three-fourths of one percent" (Chen Yu, 2016).

10.1.1.2 Creativity

Many of the core terms in ancient law are creative in themselves. For example, there is no conclusive evidence of the origin of the system of Bao Gu(保辜),[1] which is said to have been founded in the Western Zhou Dynasty, or inherited from the Qin and Han Dynasties. It is said that there are relevant records in the official history of the Han Dynasty, and in the chapter "DouSong" of the *T'ang Code*, a time limit was set for Bao Gu, which was used until the Qing Dynasty. The *Dictionary of Ancient Chinese Law* explains the term "保辜*(Bao Gu)*" as follows: "the ancient criminal law stipulated that if a person was injured as a result of an assault, the government would set a time limit and order the defendant to treat the injured. If the injured person died within the time limit, the defendant would be punished by death; if he did not die, the defendant would be punished by injury. The period of time set was called the Bao Gu Limit, and the period of time within the limit was called the Bao Gu Period" (Gao Chao & Ma Jianshi, 1989, p. 9).

Although the ancient legal system had its inheritance and closedness, it did not mean that there was no progress and development. Dynamically, in ancient times, the codification of law and the establishment of legal provisions always changed to meet the needs of social development and the needs of the ruling class to consolidate its position. At the same time, the language of the law varies with the development of society, legal thinking, and changes in legislative and judicial regulations. The creation of legal terminology in ancient times was reflected in two aspects.

[1] Bao Gu(保辜) refers to a system that protects victims in ancient Chinese criminal law.

One was the transformative inheritance of previous legal terms, that is, "old words retained their original form, but their semantic content was renewed, deepened and changed" (Wang Donghai, 2007, p. 69). The other is the creation of new legal words, for example, the *T'ang Code* included many new words of that time, such as "受分(Shoufen)", "定罪(Dingzui)", "元谋(Yuanmou)", "平赃(Pingzang)", "悬平(Xuanping)", "引虚(Yinxu)", "散禁(Sanjin)", "拷打(Kaoda)", "反拷(Fankao)", "取保(Qubao)", "诈冒(Zhamao)", "递加(Dijia)", "递减(Dijian)", "连累(Lianlei)", and so on (Ran Qibin, 2002b, p. 13–16).

10.1.1.3 Plurality

The plurality of ancient legal terminology has two meanings. Firstly, the terminology covers a diversity of social content, the legal system regulates social relations, and the ancient social relations are diverse, making the content of the ancient code norms and legal adjustments also diverse. The characteristics of the Chinese legal system are not static. With the development and progress of history, the content of the code is in the process of dynamic change in order to adapt to new social relations and consolidate the position of the ruling class. In the Ming Dynasty, with the rapid development of agriculture and handicrafts, and in order to adjust the new economic relations, the courtiers began to pay attention to economic legislation, further expanding the scope of the civil law, and elevating the status of the civil law, "the civil law and the criminal law in the *Da Ming Lü* are independent of each other, and do not relate to each other" (Xu Xiaozhuang, 2005). Statically, ancient codes are often labeled as "criminal law", but when examined over time, "although the codification structure of the main codes of ancient China was in the form of a combination of all laws, and there was no separation between civil law and criminal law, but in terms of the legal system, it was comprised of a variety of legal departments, such as criminal law, civil law, procedural law, administrative law, economic law, and so on" (Zhang Jinfan, 2007, p. 59).

Secondly, ancient Chinese legal terms came from a wide range of sources and a code of law might contain "thousands of terms" (Xiong Demi, 2016) or "about 8,000 articles" (Wang Donghai, 2007, p. 91), which leads to a certain degree of ambiguity in the boundaries of ancient legal terminology. "How to define ancient legal terms, or to narrow down the scope, is also a major problem faced by scholars of legal language at present" (Xiong Demi, 2016). Wang Donghai divided the archetypal category of legal vocabularies in the *T'ang Code* into three fuzzy zones: core archetypal, ordinary, and marginal. And continued to divide the legal words in the *T'ang Code* into domain-specific legal terms, borrowed general legal terms and legal narratives words, which are positioned in the three zones, respectively (Wang Donghai, 2007, p. 83). The plurality of ancient legal terminology is mostly reflected in the plurality of borrowed general legal terms. The legal vocabulary fully absorbed everyday terms, either "artificially formulating a particular meaning of a certain word" to legalize and standardize it, or "specifying or illustrating a legal manifestation of the term" to transform it into an "illustrative concept" (Chen Yu, 2016).

10.1.2 Reasons for the Untranslatability

The ancient Chinese legal system is different from the modern rule of law system in China, as well as the common law system and civil law system. This "difference between legal cultures creates a relative untranslatability of legal translations" (Liu Yingchun, 2009, p.102). The formation of any legal system is based on a specific cultural field, social psychology, customs, ways of thinking, etc. Ancient Chinese legal terminology "is a product of the unique legal culture of the Chinese legal system and a unique form of expression, the cultural factors that have a profound impact on the Chinese legal language, that is, the ancient Chinese social system, the mode of thinking and other cultural traditions" (Ma Li, 2009b, p. 17).

Uniqueness of the Chinese Legal System
The Chinese nation has created a splendid oriental culture over the course of 5,000 years of history, but "in the field of law culture, there has always been vertical output but no horizontal exchange and absorption" (Zhang Jinfan, 2007, p. 71). This independence, isolation, and conservatism made the formation of the Chinese legal system not only self-contained, but also rich in national characteristics. The Republican scholar Jiang Liquan once used "pure and clean" to describe the Chinese legal system, because "although the Han and Tang dynasties had the introduction of Western Buddhism and the Yuan and Qing dynasties had the rule of foreigners, the law remain the same. Without taking part in any miscellaneous elements, mixing the blood of other systems of law, and living as a parasite on other systems of law, it always supported its life independently and purely" (Zhang Jinfan, 2007, p. 371). However, in the late Qing Dynasty, the Chinese legal system was gradually disintegrated by the impact of Western legal culture, and the traditional Chinese legal system became lifeless. The Chinese legal system is characterized by the fact that its legislative thinking is an ethical code of law based on Confucianism. The distinctive features of the Chinese legal system that differentiate it from other legal systems are the "ritual-based", "unity of rites and laws", "patriarchal family-based", etc. The principle of "affection for one's kin" and "respect for elders and nobility" has always been consistent and regulates the ethical relationship of kinship rooted in blood and love. Language is the carrier of law, legal culture must be described by language. The most vivid characteristics of legal culture is manifested in the language of the vocabulary system. The uniqueness of ancient Chinese legal culture inevitably leads to the uniqueness of the legal language that goes with it and cultural difference makes it difficult to find the vocabulary equivalent to the cultural load words in other legal systems.

Differences in Ways of Thinking
Examining the characteristics of different nationalities and legal cultures, different ways of thinking are an important reason for the fundamental differences between different legal systems and cultures. The Chinese way of thinking is characterized by wholeness, intuition, and imagery and is mainly expressed in the legal language: firstly, the language is too general or generalized, with vague wording and a lack

of specificity, which can easily lead to ambiguity in comprehension; secondly, the language is overly concerned with linguistic simplicity, especially in ancient legislative techniques, where it seemed that the fewer words the better. Emperor Taizong of Tang Dynasty Li Shimin repeatedly emphasized that "the state decree must be simple, not a crime for several articles" (*The Political Program of Zhenguan Period·Sheling*). As a result, "*Yong Hui Lü* of the Tang Dynasty was too pressing for simplicity when it was formulated, but when put into practice, it was so difficult to operate that *Shu Yi* (explanation and supplement) was made, which turned out to be more complicated" (Hao Tiechuan, 1993). In terms of legislative language, "the body of the Tang law is too concise, and many articles are simply unreadable without notes and sparse comments; the second consequence is that the use of words is not standardised and inaccurate, and the phenomenon of multiple meanings of the word is more common" (Hou Xinyi, 1996). This difference in the way of thinking creates an obstacle to translation. On the one hand, ancient legal classics are based on traditional Chinese cultural and present a high degree of generalization, which will inevitably increase the difficulty of readers' understanding. American scholars D. Bodde and C. Morris have referred to the difficulty of translation, "The accounts of the cases in the *Xing An Hui Lan* (conspectus of criminal cases) are very terse in text, and there are many omissions, and a large number of sentences in which the subject and object are not clear, making it difficult to ascertain where the case took place and from whom a particular sentence came" (Bodde and Morris, 1995, p. 153). On the other hand, the phenomenon of multiple meanings of words in Chinese is also difficult to be expressed by the equivalent "multiple meanings of words" in English. Wang Donghai outlines 100 groups of synonyms from the correspondences between the legal texts, notes, and sparse texts of *T'ang Code*, constituting a spectrum of 100 synonyms (Wang Donghai, 2007, p. 275). The ambiguity of ancient legal terms leads to the inevitable "loss" of meaning in the process of translation, and it is difficult to achieve complete equivalence of vocabulary.

Historicity of Ancient Legal Terms

Language is a part of culture and a projection of historical and cultural attributes. "The ancient Han Chinese legal language has a set of ancient legal and jurisprudential concepts and terminology, which are not unrelated to the vocabulary system of the modern Han Chinese legal language, but the differences are enormous" (Ma Li, 2009b, p. 17). Ancient legal terminology was born in the context of history, reflecting the knowledge and attitude of ancient people toward environments, subjects, and social relations. Many words and modern legal terminology lack a platform for communication and cannot be directly linked and docked. For example, the words "行人*(Xingren)*", "转易*(Zhuanyi)*", "故杀*(Gusha)*", "回避*(Huibi)*", "主食*(Zhushi)*" in the *T'ang Code* have special semantic meanings, which are not the same as the meanings of modern words. There are also vocabularies that are not practiced in real contexts. Once removed from their historical, legal contexts, ancient legal vocabularies lose the basis on which they can be understood, exchanged, and used, and they also represent a void of meaning and a disconnect within the same culture for modern Chinese people, such as "斩衰*(Zhan Cui)*", "齐衰 *(Zi Cui)*", "

大功*(Da Gong)*", "小功*(Xiao Gong)*", "缌麻*(Si Ma)*".In the old days, mourning for relatives was differentiated according to the duration of mourning and the material and sewing method of the mourning clothes, and the connotations of these words were highly generalized and have long since disappeared in the modern context. Even in ancient contexts, the semantic integration of legal fixations varies from strong to weak, with some vocabularies having a strong dependence on the legal register and emerging as a whole in the register, and then transforming into free phrases in the domain of all people when they are separated from such a legal domain. In addition, the ancient legal vocabulary also appeared abbreviated words, small sentence type or long phrase type legal fixations, which further increased the complexity of the terminology, abbreviated words such as "二死*(Er Si)*", "三流*(San Liu)*", "五刑*(Wu Xing)*", "五服*(Wu Fu)*", "八议*(Ba Yi)*", "十恶*(Shi E)*", etc., long phrases such as describing the crime, the crime of "媒合奸通*(Mou He Jian Tong)*(adulterous intercourse)", "造畜蛊毒*(Zao Xu Gu Du)*(using a special poison to control everything about a person in order to serve a specific purpose)", "受财不枉法*(Shou Cai Bu Wang Fa)*(gain advantage through legal means)", "恐喝取人财物*(Kong He Qu Ren Cai Wu)*(forcible acquisition of property by intimidation)", "上书奏事犯讳*(Shang Shu Zou Shi Fan Hui)*(violating the taboos of the emperor's royal name and the temple name in the writing)", and so on, all of which have created heavy barriers to translation and to the understanding of the target readers.

10.1.3 Compensation Strategy

The relative untranslatability of ancient legal terminology determines that the translator should adopt some compensatory strategies and methods to fill the "vacancies" of lexical meanings in different cultural situations, to build a bridge between cultural barriers, and to effectively promote understanding and communication between different cultures.

10.1.3.1 Purpose of Ancient Law Translation

According to Hans Vermeer, a translation theorist of the German functional school, any translation has its purpose, and a clear and specific translation goal is crucial for the translator. The purpose of translation can also be called translation motivation, "the translator chooses different translation strategies due to the different translation motives" (Qu Wensheng, 2019). The purpose of translation directly determines the choice of translation principles and specific translation strategies, which is the major premise of the discussion of the translation of ancient legal terminology. The purpose of ancient legal translation is very different from that of modern legal translation. The purpose of modern legal translation is not only legal and cultural exchange, but also legal transplantation, legal borrowing, legal and cultural understanding and integration, and the promotion of judicial reform, with a view to achieving the same legal effect and practical effect in the target language environment. The language system of ancient law is already dusty history, and the main purpose of its translation is to disseminate ancient Chinese legal culture and promote the international exchange of excellent traditional culture. With the in-depth promotion of the national strategies of "Culture Stepping-out", "well-telling China's stories", and "strengthening international communication", the translation of ancient laws carries the important function of "cultural connection", "proclaiming Chinese cultural confidence", and "deepening and enriching the connotation of cultural translation of ancient Chinese classics". It is an important part of the plan to realize the "Chinese Dream" and the "Great Rejuvenation of the Chinese nation" (Xiong Demi, 2018, p. 5).

10.1.3.2 Compensatory Principle of English Translation of Ancient Legal Terminology

Linguistic symbols are the direct carriers of terminology in the legal conceptual system. "Legal translation is a real act of communication between two different symbol systems in different social cognitive, cultural and motivational scenarios" (Ma Li, 2009a, p. 166). Saussure proposed that the language system is composed of *signified* (or *concept*) and *signifier* (or *sound-image*), while Peirce put forward the "triad relation theory" of symbols, that is, "the symbolical relation formed by the representation (that is, the symbol), the object and the interpretation item, and only when a thing is in such a relation can it be regarded as a symbol" (Zhao Xingzhi, 2016). The translation of legal terminology is the conversion and reconstruction of meaning between different linguistic symbols in different cultural contexts, with both linguistic symbolism and legal specialization. For a long time "the term functional equivalence has been used not only in general translation theory, but also in comparative law" (Susan Sarcevid, 2017, p. 205). Searching for concepts in foreign legal systems that have the same function as specific concepts in domestic legal systems, that is, searching for equivalents, has also been regarded as a standard and norm by legal translation researchers. However, there are great differences between Chinese and English linguistic symbols in terms of both external sound images and internal references of meaning. Due to the aforementioned unique cultural background of ancient legal terminology, differences in thinking, and the historical nature of ancient Chinese, its translation is difficult to reach a completely equivalent linguistic sign in the target language environment, and the linguistic sign and cultural differences are the root of the principle of translation compensation.

Based on the general principles of translation and the generally accepted norms, statutes, and principles in the field of culture, literature, and aesthetics, Xia Tingde proposed six principles of compensation, namely the principle of demand, the principle of relevance, the principle of focus, the principle of proximity, the principle of equivalence, and the principle of consistency (Xia Tingde, 2006, p. 191). We believe that, based on the symbolic and professional nature of legal translation, the principle of demand, the principle of relevance, and the principle of functional equivalence are sufficient to apply to the translation of ancient legal terminology. The principle of demand is the premise of terminology translation. The "vacancy" of meaning caused by cultural characteristics is the just need of translation compensation, which helps the target language readers to better recognize and understand the cultural differences between each other. The principle of relevance means that the compensation should be related to the meaning of the terminology in the original text. As most of the terminology in the ancient legal system do not have actual effect, the principle of equivalence does not mean that it should have the same legal function as that in the target language environment, but rather that it should have the same or similar significance as that conveyed by the original text in terms of cultural information and linguistic symbols.

10.1.3.3 Compensatory Strategies for English Translation of Ancient Legal Terminology

The richness and diversity of ancient legal terminology also determine the diversity of its translation compensation strategy. Ancient legal terminology is no longer in circulation in the modern context, and its English translation is more about preserving to make the target language readers understand the Chinese culture. However, the uniqueness of the Chinese legal system will be more or less eroded by borrowing the terms of other legal systems, or by using the common language or daily language in the target language environment for the creation of terminology. In other words, using the vocabulary of a third legal system as a reference will lead to more misunderstanding of the Chinese legal system by the target language readers, not to mention that it is difficult to find equivalent vocabulary to the ancient legal terminology in other legal systems. Therefore, the strategy of "creating new words" is bound to be limited in translating ancient legal terminology, which is to a certain extent also deviating from the original source of cultural confidence and cultural exchanges. Given this, there are two main strategies to compensate for the translation of ancient legal terminology: to borrow functional equivalents to translate terms into terms; and to borrow neutral words in the target language for translation, which correspond to the translation of ancient legal terminology with different attributes, characteristics, and references.

In addition, the specific meaning of ancient legal terminology cannot be separated from the context of its historical text, and its vitality can be activated only in the text. In order to avoid the complete submergence of ancient legal terminology in the text of the target language expressed in the modern language, and to avoid the loss of its unique style and symbolic characteristics of the terminology in the original language, which can be transformed into the ordinary vocabulary or phrases in the target language, it is necessary to use the method of transliteration, and even the method of retaining the Chinese characters of ancient Chinese in order to compensate for the cultural gap. Mark a term in the target language that appears for the first time or calls for re-emphasizing it in order to indicate the original identity of the term and to ensure that the linguistic symbols maintain the unity of the object and the interpretive term in the target language.

Equivalent Literal Translation Legal translations need to convey cultural differences as well as consider reader acceptance. In the case of ancient terminology that has a common meaning with modern legal vocabulary and has a single univocal meaning, if a near equivalent can be found in the target language, "translation of terminology into terminology" is done as far as possible (Qu Wensheng, 2012). The purpose of borrowing functional equivalents is to achieve better cultural communication and make it easier for the target language readers to understand and accept. Of course, the specialized vocabulary for which a functional equivalent can be found represents only a very small portion of ancient legal terminology. Take the terms in *the Great Ming Code (Da Ming Lü),* for example, "人命*(Renming)*" can be directly translated into a neutral term "homicide [Renming]") and "谋杀人*(Mousharen)*" as "murder [Mousha ren]" which has the meaning of premeditated killing. In English, the suffix -cide often means "to kill", and words like "parricide", "patricide", "matricide", and "filicide" correspond to the meaning of killing a close relative, so these words can be directly borrowed to translate Chinese legal terms like "谋杀祖父母", "谋杀父母" "谋杀期亲尊长"(the murder of grandparents, parents, and ascendants). The word "诉讼*(Su Song)*" means "to sue, to bring a lawsuit, generally in relation to civil disputes" in *Dictionary of Ancient Chinese Law* (Gao Chao & Ma Jianshi, 1989, p. 325) so it can be directly translated as "lawsuit or suit [Susong]". The term "窃盗*(Qie Dao)*" in the *T'ang Code* reads "stealing other people's property, or hiding one's whereabouts and taking other people's property secretly", so it can be directly translated into a relatively common term in legal English as "theft [Qiedao]", which means " stealing or larceny".

Descriptive Interpretation Most of the ancient legal terminology is difficult to find a complete equivalent or approximate equivalent in the target language, and this "terminological inconsistency" prevails in every article of the ancient code and its legal names. The most effective way to compensate for terminological inconsistencies, from a legal point of view, is "descriptive interpretation, that is, using neutral language in the target language to express the intent and meaning of the source language" (Dong Xiaobo, 2015). The process of translation is the unity of understanding and expression; the premise of interpretation is to fully understand the original language. Ancient legal terminology has its cultural background and unique associative meaning. Most of them are highly generalized and fuzzy linguistic symbols with the characteristics of simplicity, and the symbols have a large space for interpretation. To interpret ancient legal terminology is to convey the complete meaning of the original text in the most concise language.

Describe the physical object behind the term for compensation. For example, there is a subtle difference between "笞刑*(Chi Xing)*" and "杖刑*(Zhang Xing)*" in the Five forms of punishment. The *Dictionary of Ancient Chinese Law* explains "笞刑*(Chi Xing)*" as "the punishment of hitting a prisoner on the back, buttocks or legs with a small bamboo board or thorns" (Gao Chao & Ma Jianshi, 1989, p. 37). The term " 杖刑*(Zhang Xing)*" is explained as "the punishment of hitting the back, buttocks or legs of a prisoner with a large bamboo board or thorns" (Gao Chao & Ma Jianshi, 1989, p. 437). The two types of punishment are uniform in kind, but differ in size, and can be translated respectively as "floggings with the light stick of bamboo or chaste-tree twigs [Chi]" and "floggings with the heavy stick of bamboo or chaste - tree twigs [Zhang]". And for the terms in "五服*(Wu Fu)*" like "斩衰*(Zhan Cui)*", "齐衰 *(Zi Cui)*", "大功 *(Da Gong)*", "小功*(Xiao Gong)*", and "缌麻 *(Si Ma)*". According to the *Dictionary of Ancient Chinese Law,* the difference between them is very subtle, and they can be translated as "garb of unhemmed sackcloth [Zhancui]", "garb of hemmed cloth [Zicui]", "garb made with greater coarseness [Dagong]", "garb made with lesser coarseness [Xiaogong]", "garb of plain hempen cloth [Sima]".

Describe the specific meaning of the creative and general terminology for compensation. The aforementioned term "保辜*(Bao Gu)*" refers to the period of time during which a person who has been injured by an assault is required to treat the injury and can be translated as "periods of responsibility for the consequences of a wound [Baogu]". The *Dictionary of Ancient Chinese Law*, defines "引虚*(Yin Xu)*" as "A false accuser affirms that the facts of the accusation are false". The *T'ang Code* contains a provision of "诸诬告人流罪以下, 前人未加拷掠, 而告人引虚者, 减一等" (Those who made false accusations were sentenced to exile. If the person falsely accused has not yet been punished, and the person confesses to the false accusation, the crime shall be reduced) (Gao Chao & Ma Jianshi, 1989, p. 411), so the term can be translated as "admitting making false accusations [Yinxu]". For another example, the *Dictionary of Ancient Chinese Law* defines the term "造意(Zao Yi)" as "first initiative" (Gao Chao & Ma Jianshi, 1989, p. 429). And *the Great Ming Code* contains a provision of "凡共犯罪者, 以造意为首, 随从者, 减一等" (For all co-offenders, the one who first initiated the crime shall be regarded as the principal offender and the follower, guilty of a lesser crime), so the term can be translated as "person who formulate the plan or original contriver [Zaoyi]".

Describe the clause or minor sentence expressing a charge or a crime. In the ancient legal terminology, there are a lot of crimes whose classification is relatively detailed, but they only exist in the ancient legal culture and couldn't find equivalent terms in modern legal systems. Therefore, interpretive approaches can be used to compensate for the vacancy of meaning through direct description. For example, "对制上书诈不以实*(Dui Zhi Shang Shu Zha Bu Yi Shi)*" refers to "the dishonesty in submitting reports or petitions to the Emperor", which can be directly translated as "replying to or memorialising the emperor untruthfully [Duizhishangshu zhabuyishi]". The phrase "出入人罪*(Chu Ru Ren Zui)*" contains two meanings of "出罪*(Chu Zui)*" and "入罪*(Ru Zui)*". "出罪*(Chu Zui)*" means "to convict a felony as a misdemeanour or to convict a guilty person as innocent" and "入罪*(Ru Zui)*" means "to convict a misdemeanour as a felony or to convict an innocent person as guilty"(Gao Chao & Ma Jianshi, 1989, p. 41). So the phrase can be translated as "exonerate the guilty and incriminate the innocent [Churu renzui]". For another example, the phrase "从驾稽违*(Cong Jia Ji Wei)*" refers to a crime in the Ming and Qing Dynasties, that is, if a person who was supposed to accompany the emperor on an inspection tour was overdue, or returned halfway, or fled in the middle of the tour, he or she would be guilty of this crime (Gao Chao & Ma Jianshi, 1989, p. 47). So this phrase can be translated as "delaying in escorting the 'carriage' [Congjia jiwei]".

Other charges have a high degree of generality and abstraction. For example, the phrase "造畜蛊毒杀人*(Zao Xu Gu Du Sha Ren)*" is not only a short sentence indicating an offense, but also contains a physical object that requires compensatory translation. The *Dictionary of Ancient Chinese Law* defines the phrase as "to cultivate poisonous insects or to create poisonous substances to harm people" (Gao Chao & Ma Jianshi, 1989, p. 428). The *Modern Chinese Dictionary* explains "蛊*(Gu)*" in more detail as "in the ancient legend, many poisonous insects were put in a vessel to eat each other, and in the end, the remaining undead poisonous insects were called Gu, which were used to put in food to harm people". (Division of Dictionary Compilation, Institute of Linguistics, Chinese Academy of Social Science, 2016, p. 469.) In fact, there is no way to translate this associative meaning completely and only approximate equivalence can be achieved. The phrase can be translated as "killing others by rearing venomous animals or making poisons [Zaoxu gudu sharen]".

10.1.3.4 Standardization of Ancient Legal Terminology Translation

The standardization of legal terminology translation is a major hotspot in the current research of legal translation. Compared with the attempts and practices that have been made in ancient legal translation, the standardization of ancient legal terminology translation has not yet been explored by scholars. The uniqueness of legal translation also determines the necessity of standardizing the translation of ancient legal terms, which is inseparably related to the difficulty of translating ancient legal terms. Professor Pan Wenguo once said, "It is difficult to accurately understand and translate the terms especially reflecting the world view, life view, philosophical outlook, and artistic outlook of the ancient Chinese. Many accomplished foreign translators are also intimidated by them, even if the translation is far from the original ones (Pan Wenguo, 2007) American scholars D. Bodde, C. Morris said in the preface to *The Law of the Chinese Empire* that "the ancient Chinese used in legal texts and cases is difficult to understand, which makes the translation work very difficult, especially the translator we invited lacks both an understanding of the *Ta Tsing Leu Lee* and basic knowledge of Chinese legal history" (Bodde and Morris, 1995, p. 3). It is precisely because of the difficulty of translating ancient legal terminology that the call for standardization of translation becomes more necessary.

The standardization of the translation of ancient legal terminology involves two levels of content, one is the establishment of the ancient legal terminology translation table, and the other is to strengthen the comparative and critical study of the translation of terminology. D. Bodde, C. Morris also provides a "Glossary" at the end of *The Law of the Chinese Empire*, with English translations of terms according to the "Wade-Giles Spelling System + Chinese + English translation", such as "cha wei诈伪(deceptions and fraud)" "chan斩(decapitation)" (Bodde and Morris, 1995, p. 475). The translations of the titles of the sections of *Xing An Hui Lan(Conspectus of Criminal Cases)* adopted the "Wade-Giles Spelling System + Chinese" approach, such as "Chih - kuan yu fan 职官有犯" Bodde and Morris, 1995, p. 486). Although the translations provided by D. Bodde and C. Morris are only a very small part of the ancient legal terminology, they still provide us with good examples. At present, the translation of ancient legal terms in the translation that have gone out of China is still inconsistent and even irregular, so it is necessary to establish such a glossary or dictionary for the translation of ancient legal terms, which requires the joint efforts of Chinese and foreign jurists, sinologists, linguists, and translators. Certainly, there is no such thing as a perfect dictionary, and any compilation of dictionaries is worthy of study and criticism. Now there are few comparative studies on the translation of ancient legal terms, and the related studies are only fragmentary and not systematic. "If everyone only cares about the translation, and nobody engages in comments and criticisms, it is difficult to improve the quality of translations" (Pan Wenguo, 2007).

10.2 Standardizing the Classic Term Translation to Boost National Image

Translation of Chinese classics is an important way of spreading Chinese culture internationally, and the quality of translation also determines whether Chinese culture can step out and be deeply understood by Western readers. Similarly, it also affects the impression and status of China in the eyes of the world. Classic terms are the indispensable pivotal expressions in a classic, and they play a fundamental role in supporting the establishment of the core concepts of classics the construction of an effective discourse, and the expression of the overall idea. On the one hand, classic terms tend to appear more frequently than ordinary words; on the other hand, classic terms play a unifying role for the secondary terms related to them, thus forming a network of intertwined relationships from the language symbols to the semantics in the texts. Due to the important position and role of classic terms in classics, a good translation of Chinese classics should not only consider the accurate expression of the terms, but also take into account their systematic, dynamic, and multi-dimensional nature, involving conceptual, linguistic, and communicative factors. Not only should we trace the root of the problem and make it justified, but we should also combine the points and consider them in a comprehensive manner. Only in this way can the translation of a classic be successfully marketed to the specific readers of a foreign culture.

In order to promote the overseas Spreading of Chinese traditional culture and the creation of China's national image, it is necessary to understand the essential characteristics and inherent requirements of classic terminology translation, and to pay attention to conceptual prominence, symbolic normativity, and the level of communicative choice.

Take *Master Lü's Spring and Autumn Annals*(《吕氏春秋》) as an example, it is an important cultural classic at the end of the Warring States period of China, compiled by the prime minister of Qin Dynasty Lü Buwei, who organized his disciples to write it. The book integrates the doctrines of various schools of thought, involving knowledge of astronomy, geography, Ying-Yang, and five elements, climate, music, education, military, agricultural production, and other aspects. It has formed a complete set of national governance doctrines and preserved a large number of pre-Qin documents and anecdotes, which have high academic value in the fields of philosophy, history, literature, economics, military science, and education. "Quanxue" is one of the articles in the "Meng Xia Ji" of *Master Lü's Spring and Autumn Annals*. The article encourages learning and stresses that the key to learning is to respect the teacher, and the primary task of a teacher is to convince people with reason and to promote benevolence and morality. These ideas reflect the importance that ancient Chinese society placed on learning to grow wiser and on respecting teachers, which are an important part of China's outstanding traditional culture. Their successful translation into other languages is of great practical significance for the Spreading of the excellent traditional Chinese culture and the creation of China's new national image on the world stage.

In the three existing English translations of *Master Lü's Spring and Autumn Annals* by Knoblock and Jeffrey(2000), Zhai Jiangyue (2005), and Tang Bowen (2010), the translators include famous overseas sinologists, experts in ancient Chinese literature of the pre-Qin as well as the Western and eastern Han Dynasties with experience in translating many Chinese classics, and experienced translators from important Chinese publishing houses who have translated a variety of historical, cultural, and philosophical texts. There are also senior translators from major Chinese publishing houses who have translated a wide range of historical, cultural, and philosophical texts. The three English translations are now available online at Amazon, and the Sinologist's translation has been well received by many English-speaking readers. Chinese scholars such as Zhou Heng (2012), Tian Xiaoyun (2013), Gu Wei and Luo Shutao (2014) have studied the translation of terms in these three versions separately. Because of the different research perspectives, these studies have not touched upon the essential features of classic terminology translation, not to mention taking into account the intrinsic requirements of terminology translation. Therefore, the conclusions are difficult to provide reference for other classic terminology translations, not to mention the lack of in-depth reflection on the role played by classic terminology translation in the "Stepping-out" of Chinese culture.

"Quanxue" is a typical expository essay,[2] pointing out that only through learning can a person know reason and morality; that the key to learning is to have a teacher who is "articulate and talented"; that the key to being a teacher lies in "胜理(Shengli)" (following the facts of the matter) and "行义(Xingyi)" (practicing the moral principles). The original text can be divided into three parts in accordance with the line of reasoning. The first part, from the beginning to "是入水而恶如濡也" (crossing the river without getting your shoes wet), expounds the importance of learning and the necessity of respecting the teacher. The core terms for this part include " *孝(Xiao)(filial piety)*", "*忠(Zhong)(loyalty)*", "*理(Li)(reason)*", "*义(Yi)*(morality)",

[2] The original text of "Quanxue" and its translation of modern Chinese can be found at http://ewenyan.com/articles/lscq/17.html.).

"圣人*(Sheng Ren)(a sage)*", "疾学*(Ji Xue)(studying hard)*", "尊师*(Zun Shi)(respect for the teacher)*", "道*(Dao)(the way)*". The second part from "凡说者，兑之也" (whoever truly preaches, speaks so as to make people happy) to "故师必胜理行义然后尊" (therefore, teachers must win by reasoning and promote morality before they can be respected). It mainly discusses the role a teacher should play. The core point is very clear, that is, the important thing for a teacher is to follow the reasoning and to implement the morality. "胜理*(Sheng Li)*" and "行义*(Xing Yi)*" are the core terms for this part. The third part, from "曾子曰"(Zeng Zi said) to the end of the text, elaborates on how to respect teachers by giving examples. The central meaning of this part lies in the last sentence "古之贤者，与其尊师若此，故师尽智竭道以教" (The ancient sages respected their teachers like this, so their teachers tried their best to teach them by all their talents and methods.) The core terms are "贤者*(Xian Zhe)(worthy man)*", "尊师*(Zun Shi)*", "道*(Dao)*" These three parts of the terminology as a whole form the semantic network diagram below:

The network relationship in Fig. 10.1 can be explained as follows: "孝*(Xiao)*" (2 times) and "忠*(Zhong)*" (2 times) are the basic moral qualities most highly regarded by "圣人*(Sheng Ren)*" (4 times) and "贤者*(Xian Zhe)*" (1 time) in ancient times. In order to achieve such qualities, one needs to know "理*(Li)*" (4 times) and "义*(Yi)*" (4 times), which can be acquired through "疾学*(Ji Xue)*". The key to "疾学*(Ji Xue)*" lies in "尊师*(Zun Shi)*" (4 times), which is why the ancient *Sheng Ren* and *Xian Zhe* all respected their teachers, with the aim of "胜理*(Sheng Li)*" (3 times) and "行义*(Xing Yi)*" (3 times) through teachers and hence acquiring "道*(Dao)*" (4 times), and thus the glory of filial piety(孝) and prominence in fidelity(忠) can be attained. The direction of the arrows in the diagram indicates the reasoning process, in which "疾学*(Ji Xue)*" and "尊师*(Zun Shi)*" are mutually exclusive, because to study hard, one must respect his teachers; conversely, a person who respects his teacher must also be a hard worker. That is why the arrows are two-way. All of the above terms are linked together to form the central idea of "Quanxue". It should be noted that the core terms mentioned here are repeated and consistent to a certain extent in the later articles of "Quanxue" and even in other chapters of the book. For example, there are "贤者", "尊师" and "义" in the chapter "Zunshi". In the chapter "Wutu", there are "理", "义", and "贤者". In the chapter "Yongzhong", there are also "尊师" and other terms. So, the following table presents the translations of these core terms in the three translations of "Quanxue" (Table 10.1).

10.2.1 The Essential Characteristics of Classic Term

Classic terms is the form of semantic representation of core concepts in classics, which involves the representation of knowledge system, the construction of discourse system and the effective Spreading of ideas in a particular classic. According to the "three-door" theory of terminology translation (Cabré, 2003a, 2003b), terminology translation is subject to the constraints of conceptual, semantic, and communicative factors, and the translation of classic terminology is naturally no exception. First of

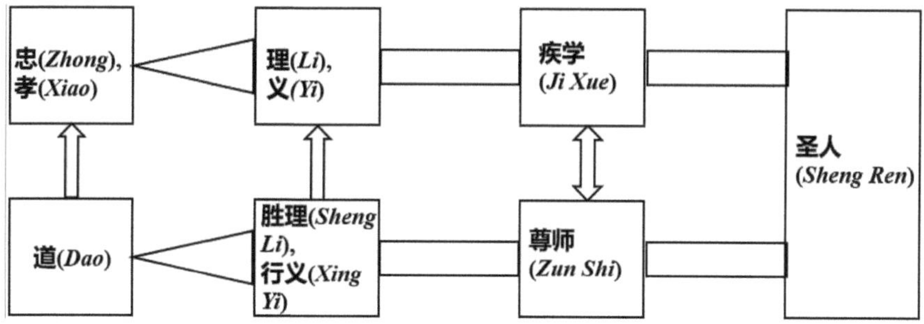

Fig. 10.1 Core Terminology Semantic Network Relationships in "Quanxue"

all, due to the age of most of the Chinese classics, many of the ideas and concepts in them have been imprinted with a specific history, which, coupled with several interpretations and a long history of transmission, has led to a semantic overlay of complexity; moreover, most of the classics, though in a simple form, are obscure and difficult to understand in language. The terminology in the classic contained the deepest spiritual pursuits of the Chinese people, and it is not easy for even native speakers to understand them accurately. For example, the term "道*(Dao)*" in "Quanxue", together with the terms "理*(Li)*", "气*(Qi)*", "势*(Shi)*", "情*(Qing)*" are all phenomena unique to the Chinese language, and it is actually difficult to understand them without the context of the Chinese language (Yang Lihua, etc., 2018). Secondly, the terms appearing in a classic as the form of specific discourse symbols are not only related to other terms in various parts of the whole classic, but also often have origins or corroboration relationships with terms in other classics of the same time, or even in previous classics. Some terms have been subject to multi-dimensional or multi-perspective divisions in the course of later interpretations, and these have led to the formation of complex refractive relations between classic terms at the level of discourse symbols, which must be taken into account in translation. For example, the term "贤者*(Xian Zhe)*" in "Quanxue" appears several times in the entire book, as one-fifth of its total length reflects the idea of "employing the virtuous" (Zeng Wenfang, 2016).

The meaning of this term varies with the context, and the ancient and contemporary meanings differ greatly, which requires special consideration when translating. Finally, in classic translation, the translation of specific terms is actually the expression and Spreading of specific ideas or concepts. As some scholars have pointed out, the process of terminology translation is the process of terminology cross-language application, as well as terms and the concepts they characterize, that is, the process of cross-language communication of related knowledge units (Wei Xiangqing, 2014). The English translation of these classic terms that are solidified as words or phrases concisely expresses their meanings in English words or phrases, constructing the conceptual terminology of Chinese thought and culture in the English-speaking world, which allows Western readers to truly understand the core connotations of ancient Chinese thought and culture; therefore, terminological translation is also a

Table 10.1 Treatment of Classic Core Terms of "Quanxue" in the Three Translations

Core terms	Translation of Knoblock and Riegel	Translation of Zhai Jiangyue	Translation of Tang Bowen
孝 (2)	filial piety (2)	filial piety (2);	be filial (1); filial piety (1)
忠 (2)	Loyalty (3)	Loyalty (2);	be loyal (1); loyalty (1)
理 (4)	reason (3); be provided with principles of rational order (1)	those principles (2); be at peace (1); these fixed principles (1);	principles of right (2); be in order (1); the logic of things (1)
义 (4)	morality (4)	(translated with "理" as "those principles") (2); morality and justice (2)	(translated with "理" as principles of right) (2); righteousness (2)
圣人 (4)	a sage (4);	a sage (3); sages (1);	a sage (3); sages (1)
贤者 (1)	worthy man (1);	sensible people (1);	man of virtue (1)
疾学 (3)	intense study (3);	study hard (3);	study hard (3)
尊师 (4)	honoring teachers (4);	respecting teachers (4);	respect teacher(s) (4)
胜理 (3)	promote reason (3)	stick to these fixed principles (1); adhere to the fixed principles (2)	follow the logic of things (3)
行义 (3)	practice morality (2); put moral principles into practice (1)	advocate morality and justice (1); adhere to morality and justice (1); practice morality and justice in person (1)	put righteousness into practice (3)
道(4)	Dao (3); their way (1)	what they are to be taught (1); his principles (1); his teachings; (omission) (1)	True way (1); his instructions (1); his principles (1); (omission) (1)

[10.1] The numbers in parentheses in the table indicate the number of times the term and its translation appear in the translation

"secondary construction" of the concept of terminology (Chen Haiyan. 2015). In the process of translation, the translator needs to exercise initiative and creativity to take the form that is most acceptable to the readers to communicate based on their understanding of the target language audience.

10.2.2 The Inherent Requirements of Classic Term Translation

Based on the above characteristics of classic terminology, in the process of translating classic terminology, translators have to consider the following points in order to meet the inherent requirements of classic terminology translation. The first one is the accurate grasp of concepts, which means the ability to reflect the most fundamental core meaning of the original terminology. This is not as simple as it seems some classic terms have undergone dynamic and multi-dimensional changes after being interpreted by different scholars over time. Therefore, their translation has to be considered from the diachronic and synchronic perspectives, focusing on their historical significance as well as their contemporary value. Although *Master Lü's Spring and Autumn Annals* is a "fairly well-preserved Chinese cultural classic" (Wang Lifen, 2005), in the course of its circulation, it has been systematically collated and revised by Gao Zhi of the Eastern Han Dynasty, Bi Yuan of the Qing Dynasty, and Xu Weiyu and Chen Qiyou in recent times, and the interpretations of the same terminology in different revisions may also differ. According to the preambles of the three translations, sinologists Knoblock and Riegel's translations were mainly based on Chen Qiyou's *Shi Chun qiu Jiao Shi*, while scholar Zhai Jiangyue's translation refers to several editions of Gao Zhi, Bi Yuan, Xu Weiyu, Chen Qiyou, and other commentaries, and the veteran translator Tang Bowen did not make this explicitly clear. There is a marked difference in the treatment of core terms in the three translations, and it is worth considering whether this is related to the referenced proof-texts. Although the three translations of "Quanxue" basically achieve consistency or similarity in the translation of the most common terms, such as "孝*(Xiao)*", "忠*(Zhong)*", "圣人*(Sheng Ren)*", "尊师*(Zun Shi)*", there is a clear difference in the treatment of terms such as "理*(Li)*", "义*(Yi)*", "疾学*(Ji Xue)*", "贤者*(Xian Zhe)*", and "道*(Dao)*".

For example, the term "贤者(*Xian Zhe*)" was respectively translated as "worthy man", "sensible people", and "man of virtue". The important thing is that, the inherent meaning or the contemporary value of the term should be presented in the translation. If the translator was unable to make a clear judgment, he or she must consider the entire translated text at the level of the linguistic symbols.

A successful translation of a classic can greatly reduce the reader's difficulty in understanding the original text, especially in grasping the core ideas of the whole text if the translator can maintain uniformity at the level of linguistic symbols in the translation of the same key terms. The difference between classic translation and general literature translation is that the translator needs to make some introduction on the text's production, main ideas, organization system, and so on before translation, so there are often preface, introduction, and the like before the translated text. Some translators will also preface each chapter with an introduction to make it easier for readers to understand some unfamiliar concepts. The terminology translation that appears at this time has already made preparations for the terminology translation in the translated text. Moreover, it is impossible for a serious translator to make arbitrary changes in the translation, unless the context makes it so, otherwise it destroys the consistency and systematicity of the terminology. As is customary in Western translation and publishing, the body of the translation should be followed by an index or glossary, notes or annotations, or other subtexts, so that readers can quickly find important translations of terms or phrases. It stipulates from another angle that translators must have certain norms when translating terminology, or else it is just not user-friendly for the readers. In specific chapters, it is also taken for granted to maintain consistency in terminology translation in the same text if the context has not changed greatly. Looking at the three translations of the core terms in "Quanxue", it can be found that the translations by sinologists Knoblock and Riegel did the best job in terms of consistency of terminology translation, as basically the same term is expressed the same way before and after.

Moreover, their systematicity is also most obvious. For example, taking into account the inter-referential relationship between "疾学*(Ji Xue)*" and "尊师*(Zun Shi)*", they translate the two terms as "intense study" and "honouring teacher" respectively, which is more systematic than the translation of "study hard" and "respecting teacher", which only indicated a one-dimensional relationship. Furthermore, they also explained the relationship between the two terms in the additional notes following the translations also by the two sinologists. On the other hand, in Zhai Jiangyue's translation and Tang Bowen's translation, there are a lot of inconsistencies of the same terminology, especially in Zhai's translation, where the use of the same terminology is treated in different ways, and with no clarification before and after the translation. For example, in the translation of "道*(Dao)*", Zhai chose four treatments of "what they are to be taught", "his principle", "his teaching", and an omission strategy. Obviously, the word was not treated as a term at all. Of course, it does not mean that fewer treatments are better, but if the context makes it so, corresponding changes are necessary. For example, in the translation of "理*(Li)*", there are three places in the original text where "理*(Li)*" appears as a noun ("此生于不知理义", "不知理义", and "遗理释义以要不可必") and there is only one place where "理*(Li)*" is used as a verb ("圣人之所在, 则天下理焉"), which is obviously not the same meaning as mentioned in the other three places, so some changes are necessary. All three translations have made corresponding changes here to be in line with the systematic use of terminology, namely be "provided with principles of rational order", "be at peace" and "be in order".

The third level of the inherent requirements for the translation of classic terminology is the consideration of communicative choices. As aforementioned, terminology translation is a process of cross-linguistic Spreading of relevant knowledge units and a "secondary construction" of terminology concepts. A good terminology translation should not only consider whether the source terminology has inherent meaning or contemporary value, but also the systematicity at the level of the linguistic symbols, and even more so, the acceptability of terminology concepts.

Translating Chinese classics to the world is essentially to disseminate the knowledge and concepts in Chinese traditional culture. Some of them are very profound and difficult to understand, far away from the target readers' life experience and knowledge, so it is very important to make the target language readers feel close to them and pleasant to them, or rather it is very important to take into account the target language readers' horizon of expectation. Since the number of contemporary Westerners who can easily read and understand literary and academic works translated from Chinese is small, and moreover, their "acceptance level is not very high" (Li Fengliang, 2017: 25). Classic translations must take into account the level of reception and reading interests of Western readers. As for the translation of terms of classics, it is necessary to simplify and concretize those esoteric knowledge and concepts. Among the three translations of the core terms in "Quanxue", we can see that the translations of Knoblock and Riegel are generally the simplest and most concise, and the translations of some terms can be specific enough for the general reader to perceive, such as the translations of "理*(Li)*"and "义*(Yi)*", which are characterized by the holistic, dialectical, subjective, and ambiguous thinking of the Oriental people, but they used the most familiar terms "reason" and "morality" for Western readers to create a sense of closeness.

Another example is the translation of "胜理*(Sheng Li)*" and "行义*(Xing Yi)*". "胜理*(Sheng Li)*" is translated as "promote reason" three times, and "行义*(Xing Yi)*" is translated as "practice morality" twice, and "put moral principles into practice" once. Except for one change in the translation of "Xingyi", the overall translation is very concise and fluent. On the contrary, in Zhai's translation and Tang's translations, many terms not only have more changes before and after, and some of them are quite complicated, making the terms abstract and vague. Of course, the translation of terminology is not that the simpler the better, the best translation is the one that can maximize the communicative effect. As French scholar (Daniel Gouadec, 2011: 6) said, "the quality of translation lies in the communicative effect, not in the way and method of expression". Such a terminology translation will attract readers, merge with the readers' expected horizons, and enhance the readability of the translated text, which will allow the knowledge and concepts of the original text to naturally cross the cultural and linguistic barriers and enter the readers' inner world.

10.2.3 Issues to Be Noted in the Classic Term Translation

According to the above analysis of the essential features and inherent requirements of classic terminology translation, especially combined with the horizontal comparison of the three translations of the core terminology of "Quanxue", we can conclude that the problems to be noted in the translation of classic terminology should include at least the following three aspects.

10.2.3.1 Conceptual Prominence

Conceptual prominence firstly refers to the fact that the translation of canonical terminology should be able to express the intrinsic ideas and contemporary values of classic terminology in the most profound way. As for the inherent ideas of classic literature at the time of writing, it is necessary for the translator to make accurate judgment on the background, historical significance, and value of the whole text, as the reason why classics are valuable is because it is engraved with the concepts and values unique to that era. Conceptual prominence is also manifested in the fact that the translation of classic terminology can inspire and motivate the readers today, thus giving it a cross-generational relevance. Because the translation of classic terminology is the process of cross-linguistic Spreading of the concepts and values embedded in ancient Chinese classic literature. It involves not only the Spreading of knowledge, but also the construction of traditional Chinese cultural values in foreign cultures, and even the process of striving for China's international right of speech in certain fields. Translators should not neglect the ideology in the translation of classic terminology, that is to say, translators need a certain view of classic terminology to clearly reflect the ideas contained in the original terminology in the translated text and fulfill its rightful function of knowledge Spreading and discourse construction. Sinologists Knoblock and Riegel and veteran translator Tong Bowen can be said to have made a significant contribution in this regard.

In the translation of many terms, they are very careful to deeply translate the specific historical meaning and values of the original terms. For example, in the translation of "道*(Dao)*", Knoblock and Riegel insist on using "Dao" to emphasize that it is a phenomenon unique to Chinese culture that cannot be replaced by English words, and that readers will inevitably have more associations with it when they read it. While Tang uses "The Way" to indicate its difference from the general expression "way". Another example is the translation of "理*(Li)*" and "义*(Yi)*", Knoblock and Riegel chose "reason" and "morality" to emphasize their contemporary values, while Tang used "right" and "righteousness" to reflect the unique meaning of the ancient time, namely the idea of moral construction from great chaos to great governance with "义*(Yi)*" as the core value (Hou Wenli, 2016).

10.2.3.2 Symbolic Normativity

Symbolic normativity refers to the consistency, systematicity, and completeness of the translation of classic terms. Without consistency, readers will often be faced with different interpretations of the same terminology, which is especially true for the communication of core concepts. Since different interpretations are difficult to produce a coherent and clear presence within the reader, the communication effect will be greatly reduced.

The systematicity is to take care of the possible variations of classic terms due to different contexts. In the same classic or even the same chapter, variations in the form of terminological expressions due to different contexts may occur both in the original text and in the translation. It is undoubtedly very favorable to the translation if the translator is able to keenly capture such dynamic and multi-dimensional information. In the translation of "Quanxue", the practice of Knoblock and Riegel can serve as a model. First of all, the explanation of relevant terms has been included in the introduction part and the pre-translation introduction of each chapter, which is basically the same as the expression of terms in the text. Then, in the specific chapters, they also noticed the contextual variation of the terminology, adjusted the translation accordingly, and listed the corresponding terms in the index after the translation. For example, in the translation of "道*(Dao)*", "Dao" is used in most cases, indicating that it is a specific concept, and "way" is used in a few cases, indicating that it is an ordinary word. Besides, the usage of "Dao" is detailed in the index after the translation. Completeness means that classic terms should be treated according to the terminology in the process of translation, and cannot be changed or taken away arbitrarily. For example, in the translations of the two sinologists, all the terms are given proper attention, while in the Zhai and Tang translations, there are two combined translations of "理义(Li Yi)". Regardless of whether this combined translation is correct or not, it is clearly lacking in terms of completeness of expression.

10.2.3.3 The Level of Communicative Choice

The level of communicative choice refers to the macro-strategies adopted in the translation of classics terms to meet the expectations of different target language readers, and to adapt to the ethical and aesthetic ideas of readers at different levels. Usually, the level of translation as we understand is always related to the purpose of translation, that is, every translation act has its basic level of translation purpose, and in addition there is likely to be the highest goal (or the final purpose) and some intermediate levels between these two poles (Fan Xiangtao, 2003). The translation of classic terms can also be divided into different levels according to the purpose of translation, such as the purpose level for the general public readers, the purpose level for the expert readers, and the purpose level for the readers who are in between the general public and the expert readers. In other words, the translator should start from the cognitive level of the readers, look for the expectations of the cross-language readers from the ethical and aesthetic levels, respect their habits and interests, and aim at the target. For expert readers, the terms in the original text must be treated as terms in the translated text, and additional explanations should be added when necessary; for general readers, the terms should be kept as simple as possible, and some of them can be simplified or even discarded without translation if they don't affect the understanding of the general meaning of the original text; for the readers in between, the terms in the original text can be retained without detailed explanations as long as the readers are made to know that it is a specific cultural concept.

According to Sinologists Knoblock and Riegel's description in the preface, their translation is intended to satisfy both the general public and the expert readers who have the requirement to study Chinese culture. Therefore, although the terminology is very concise in the text, there is an additional note after the main text of the translation, which explains some important terms in detail. For example, the title of this text "Quanxue" has a detailed explanation with 513 words attached to the translation. Since Zhai's translation is part of the "Library of Chinese Classics(Chinese-English Edition)" Project, which has the general public as the target audience and stipulates that footnotes and endnotes are not allowed, so she tried her best to translate the terms into what appears to be the most comprehensible English. Yet due to the limitations of the English language proficiency, it seems that many of these terms are not succinct, and sometimes counterproductive. Tang's translation clearly indicates in the preface that it is to spread Chinese culture to the English-speaking world as much as possible, so he pays great attention to the terminology translation. The annotations are exhaustive in many places, but some of them lack pertinence, which have not been able to achieve a better result. What's more, the reference source text version of his translation is unknown, so even there is false translation, we cannot know where it came from, leading to the reducing research value.

10.3 Summary

Ancient legal terminology translation is the core and main line of legal classic translation, and also a hard rock of in the legal classic translation. As long as the problem of terminology translation is solved, other problems will be solved relatively easily. With the deepening of culture "stepping-out", ancient legal classics will be paid more attention, and the translation of the terminology can escort the translation of the whole legal classics. Ancient Chinese language and modern Chinese language have a gap in time and space, cognition and psychology. To effectively compensate for translation, the premise is to better understand the hidden nuances behind the original text, and to use concise language as much as possible to convey sufficient information to compensate for the "loss" caused by cultural differences in the process of linguistic expression. Therefore, the translation of ancient legal terminology deserves more in-depth study and extensive discussion so that it can be more normalized and standardized. Terminology translation is an important part of classic translation. Without a correct understanding of the essential characteristics and internal requirements of classic terms, the translation of classic terms will lack due awareness of the principles. As a result, the quality of classic translations will be unsatisfactory, leading to translations that are not favored by readers, and even not being taken seriously for a long time. "Quanxue" advocates the important ideas of "studying hard" and "respecting teachers and emphasizing education" long practiced in Chinese traditional culture, which is of certain practical significance not only for the people of China, but also for the contemporary people of any nation or country. Therefore, successfully translating it into a language that other peoples are happy to see is an important part of the "stepping-out" of Chinese culture. Because of the typicality and complexity of the core terminology of "Quanxue", translators need to study the classic carefully and conscientiously before translation. The translation work must be based on systematic research, from the overall ideological expression of the classics to the conceptual cognition of individual terminology, from the specification of language symbols within the text to the choice of language symbols outside the text, as well as the interrelationships between the texts. Only in this way can translators be proficient in the translation of terms and effectively improve the quality of translation of classics, so as to contribute to shaping a new national image of China on the international stage.

References

Bodde, D., & Morris, C. (1995). *Law in imperial China*. Y. Zhu, Trans. Jiangsu People's Publishing House.

Cabré, M. T. (2003). Theories of terminology: Their description, prescription and explanation. *Terminology*, 163–199.

Cabré, M. T. (2003b). Theories of terminology: Their description, prescription and explanation. *Terminology, 2*, 163–199.

Chen, H. (2015). Analysis of the difficulties in the translation of Chinese ideological and cultural terms. *Chinese Translators Journal*, 13–17.

Chen, Y. (2016). The legal concepts and their provisions in the <Commentary on Law Codes of Tang Dynasty>—and comparison with the (statutes and regulations of Qing Dynasty). *Journal of CUPL, 5*.

Daniel, G. (2011). *Profession traducteur.* H. Liu, A. O. Wen, Trans. Foreign Language Teaching and Research Press.

Division of Dictionary Compilation, Institute of Linguistics, Chinese Academy of Social Science. (2016). *Contemporary Chinese dictionary* (7th edition) (p. 469). Beijing: The Commercial Press, 2016.

Dong, X. (2015). On the "equivalent" translation of English–Chinese legal terms. *Journal of Xi'an International Studies University*, No.3.

Fan, X. (2003). *Multidimensional portrayal of hierarchical purposes of translation. Foreign Language Education*, 44–47.

Gao, C., & Ma J. (Eds.). (1989). *Dictionary of ancient Chinese law*. Nankai University Press.

Gu, W., & Luo, S. (2014). A study on the translation of terms in *Master Lü's Spring and Autumn Annals. China Terminology*, 30–33.

Hao, T. (1993). The influence of traditional way of thinking on contemporary Chinese legislative techniques. China Legal Science, No. 4.

Here, "理(Li)(Reasoning)" and "义(Yi)(Morality)" have similar meanings, see Master Lü's Spring and Autumn Annals Dictionary (Revised) (p. 210).

Hou, W. (2016). Analysis of "Yi(义)(Morality)" in *Master Lü's Spring and Autumn Annals. Decision & Information*, 88–88.

Hou, X. (1996). Comparison of legislative techniques between Tang Law and Ming Law. *Science of Law (Journal of Northwest University of Political Science and Law)*, No.2.

Huai, X. (1998). *The Great Chinese Code: Statutes of Great Ming Dynasty*. preface (p. ii). Law Press.

Knoblock, J., & Jeffrey, R. (2000). *The annals of Lii Buwei: A complete translation and study*. Stanford University Press.

Li, X. (2015). *Perception and reception: Western understanding of the 19th century Chinese legal system based on the Chinese repository*. Shanghai Joint Publishing Company.

Li, F. (2017). *30 years of comparative literature development in China and the new pattern of international comparative literature*. Jinan University Press.

Li, X. Op.cit. p. 56.

Liu, G. (2004). An overview of the evolutionary laws of standardization of ancient Chinese legislative styles. *Journal of Guangdong University of Foreign Studies*, No. 1.

Liu, Y. (2009). *Ancient Chinese laws in English Translation* (p. 102). Dalian Maritime Publishing House.

Lu, N., op. cit.

Ma, L. (2009a). *Cultural constraints on legal language translation* (p. 166). Law Press.

Ma, L. (2009b). *Cultural Constraints on Legal Language Translation* (p. 17). Law Press.

Numbers in parentheses in the table indicate the number of times the term and its translation appear in the translation.

Pan, W. (2007). Chinese Foreign Translation, this is the time - macro thoughts on the problem of Chinese Translation and foreign translation. *Journal of Hangzhou Normal University (Humanities and Social Sciences)*, No. 6.
Qu, W. (2012). Reflections on the problems and causes faced by international translation of Chinese legal terminology. *Chinese Translators Journal*, No. 6.
Qu, W. (2019). A study on the English translation of Chinese feudal codes and the motivation of English translation. *Chinese Translators Journal*, No. 1.
Ran, Q. (2002). A study of the vocabulary of *commentary on Law Codes of Tang Dynasty*. Master's Degree Thesis, 1–2. Sichuan University.
Ran, Q. (2002). A study of the vocabulary of *Commentary on Law Codes of Tang Dynasty*, Master's Degree Thesis, 13–16. Sichuan University.
Staunton. op.cit. p. 219.
Susan, S. (2017). *New exploration of legal translation*. J. Zhao, Trans., et al. (p. 205). Higher Education Press.
Tang, B. (2010). *Lü's commentaries of history*. Foreign Languages Press.
The original English text reads: The principal difficulty in the transmission of knowledge and the pursuit of learning, as the Ru saw it, was getting students to treat their teachers with the respect proper to their calling. This was required, for only thereby could the Dao of the teacher be properly honored. And only when his Dao was properly honored, would the people realize the strict, reverent care that should be exercised in learning.
The original text and modern translation of the article can be found at http://ewenyan.com/articles/lscq/17.html.
Tian, X. (2013). A comparative analysis of the culture-specific terms in two major translations of *Lv Shi Chun Oiu* under postcolonial translation theory. Mongolia University.
Wang, D. (2007). *A study of the semantic system of ancient legal vocabulary: Taking Commentary on Law Codes of Tang Dynasty as an example*. China Social Science Press.
Wang, L. (2005). *A Study of Gao You's note on Master Lü's Spring and Autumn Annals*. Nanjing Normal University.
Wei, X. (2014). Explanation and reflection from the perspective of communication studies on terminology translation process. *Translation Forum*, 20–25.
Whether "Dao" is a term or not in *Master Lü's Spring and Autumn Annals* depends on the specific context. According to the explanation in Master Lü's Spring and Autumn Annals Dictionary (Revised Edition) (Zhang Shuangdi et al., The Commercial Press, 2010, p. 144), in many cases, "Dao" means "the origin of the universe, also known as essence, taiyi". There are many other explanations of "Dao" in the classics, which can be seen The Dictionary of Ancient Chinese (Second Edition) (The Commercial Press, 2017, p. 265).
Xia, T. (2006). *Research on translation compensation* (p. 191). Hubei Education Press.
Xiong, D. (2016). Characterization of the legal terminology of statutes and regulations of Qing Dynasty. *Journal of Southwest University of Political Science and Law*, No. 4.
Xiong, D. (2018). Study on the foreign translation of ancient legal codes and their criticism (p. 5). *China Social Science Journal*.
Xu, X. (2005). Discussion on the characteristics of *Statutes of Great Ming Dynasty. Journal of Tianzhong*, No. 1.
Yang, L., et al. (2018). How to make philosophy speak Chinese. *Dushu*, 52–61.
Yang, S. (2003). On legal terminology. *Journal of Political Science and Law*, No. 6.
Zeng, W. (2016). The sage view of *Master Lü's Spring and Autumn Annalss. Chinese Culture*, 21–24.
Zhai, J. (2005). *Library of Chinese classics: Master Lü's Spring and Autumn Annals*. Guangxi Normal University Press.
Zhang, J. (Ed.). (2007). *Review and prospect of the Chinese legal system*. China University of Political Science and Law Press.

Zhao, X. (2016). Discussion on "object" in peirce's semiotics, No. 2. Foreign Languages in China.
Zhou, H. (2012). Translation of culture-loaded words from the perspective of purpose theory—Taking *Master Lü's Spring and Autumn Annals* an example. *Huazhong Humanity Forum*, 84–86.

Chapter 11
Framework and Planning of the Chinese Legal Classics Spreading

Abstract China has a long history of about five thousand years. Chinese classics has stood the test of time and passed down from generation to generation with good comment, due to the amazing wisdom showed inside the classics. The report of the 17th National Congress of the Communist Party of China pointed out that it is necessary to "enhance culture as part of the soft power of our country", "do a good job collating ancient books and records", "strengthen international cultural exchanges", and "enhance the influence of Chinese culture worldwide". Xi Jinping, General Secretary of the Communist Party of China, mentioned at the Cultural and Artwork Symposium on October 15, 2014: "The international community's attention to China is increasing. They want to understand China, to know the Chinese people's worldviews, outlook on life, values, and to learn about China's historical heritage, customs, and ethnic characteristics". At the same time, he expressed expectations: "Cultural and artistic workers should promote and introduce our excellent cultural and artistic achievements to the world, allowing foreign people to feel the charm in the aesthetic process, deepening their understanding and appreciation of Chinese culture". Since the 18th National Congress of the CPC, leaders of the Party and the country have attached increasing importance to the cultural diplomacy. General Secretary Xi has also mentioned "cultural confidence" on many important occasions, promoting the process of carrying forward traditional Chinese culture. The report of the 19th National Congress of the CPC declared that socialism with Chinese characteristics has entered a new era, which is a new historic juncture. In addition, it proposed to improve our capacity for engaging in international communication so as to tell China's stories well, present a true, multi-dimensional, and panoramic view of China, and enhance our country's cultural soft power. Nowadays, Chinese culture has achieved significant success in going global. With the joint efforts of the government, scholars, and foreign Sinologists, many cultural classics have gained foreign language versions recognized by the public, contributing to the promotion of Chinese culture. The overseas promotion of Chinese legal classics is an important step for Chinese culture to go global. It embodies traditional Chinese legal thinking, legal wisdom, and legal doctrines, providing crucial guidance for China's comprehensive advancement of the rule of law today. However, it is essential to recognize that the efforts of the external Spreading of Chinese legal classics are still not as vigorous

X. Dong and Y. Luo, *The Legal Image of China in Chinese Legal Tradition*,
https://doi.org/10.1007/978-981-96-5797-1_11

as that of the Western legal culture. Currently, compared to the translation of other cultural classics, the promotion and study of legal classics are relatively scarce. The translation of legal classics still faces numerous challenges and there are many problems existing in this area.

11.1 The Current Situation and Existing Problems in the Translation of Legal Classics

Throughout the history of human cultural exchange, translation has served as the bridge for communication between different languages. Before the sixteenth and seventeenth centuries, Europeans gradually gained insights into Chinese legal culture through the introductions of missionaries, Jesuits, and the travelogues written by Marco Polo, Matteo Ricci, and Alvaro Semedo. However, these introductions or travel accounts did not directly quote the original texts of Chinese legal classics, significantly compromising the authenticity of the content (Hu & Dong, 2018a). Since the sixteenth and seventeenth centuries, the cultural exchange between China and the West have been continuously evolving. Even though the process is twists and turns, overall, it has kept the trend of progress.

In 1779, a French translated part of a Chinese classic of forensic science, the *Xi Yuan Ji Lu* (also known as the translated version of *Collected Cases of Injustice Rectified/ the Washing Away of Wrongs*), and published it in *Mémoires concernant l'histoire, les sciences, les arts, les molures, les usages,* etc. *des Chinois* in Paris. *Xi Yuan Ji Lu* has come into European's sight since then and was translated into other languages subsequently like Dutch, English, and German (Chen, 2016; Wang, 2018). In 1810, the first English translation of *The Great Qing Code* was published in the United Kingdom, titled as *TA TSING LEU LEE: BEING THE FUNDAMENTAL LAWS, AND A SELECTION FROM THE SUPPLEMENTARY STATUTES OF THE PENAL CODE OF CHINA,* marking the beginning of the century-long study of Chinese law by European and American scholars.

In 1997, the American sinologists Wallace Johnson completed the translation of *The T'ang Code, Volume II,* making it the first complete Western language translation of *The T'ang Code.* In 2005, the English translation of the *Great Ming Code* was officially published in the United States, thanks to the efforts of Professor Yonglin Jiang at Bryn Mawr College. The Spreading of Chinese legal classics abroad can be broadly summarized in three ways.

11.1.1 Learn About the Chinese Legal System for Proselytizing and Profit

Initially, missionaries, merchants, and Jesuits came to China with the purpose of trade and evangelism. They studied the Chinese language, culture, and classical works, aiming to discover the roots of Chinese culture or identify Chinese preferences to enhance their evangelistic and profit-making efforts. These foreign individuals came to China with clear purpose and spent a considerable time living in China. As a result, they grew a deep understanding of Chinese language and culture, introducing China to their home countries through oral accounts or travelogues. In this way, China, the mysterious ancient country of the East was unveiled, leading to a deeper understanding of China for the West. Travelers like Marco Polo, who lived in China for 17 years, praised its prosperity and advancements, depicted a well-functioning legal system, and organized market transactions. Spanish sinologist Juan González de Mendoza compiled *Historia de las cosas más notables, ritos y costumbres del gran reyno de la China (The History of the Great and Mighty Kingdom of China and the Situation Thereof)* based on European travelers' accounts, providing a detailed description of ancient Chinese legal culture. China's political system and laws thus spread to Europe, sparking Europeans' fascination with China. In the late sixteenth century, Jesuit Matteo Ricci portrayed various forms of ancient Chinese political and legal culture in an admiring tone (Gong, 2004).

In the nineteenth century, foreign sailors and merchants often came into conflict with local residents along China's coastal areas, and sometimes, the conflict could escalate into criminal cases, leading Europeans and Americans to pay particular attention to the related provisions in the *Great Qing Code*. After the Opium Wars, as the West established factories and churches in China, civil disputes emerged, which made the Westerners begin to focus on provisions in the *Great Qing Code* related to resolving civil disputes (Hu & Dong, 2018a).

11.1.2 Incomplete Translation by Sinologists

Sinologists disseminated Chinese legal texts abroad through compiling, selectively or partially translating them, a practice closely tied to the aim of translating Chinese legal classics. Sinologists refer to foreign scholars engaged in the study of ancient, modern, or contemporary Chinese humanities and social sciences. Early missionaries in China, such as Matteo Ricci, also belong to the ranks of Sinologists. For example, some early Sinologists compiled and selectively translated Chinese legal system, introducing China's social conditions to the West through publications like *Chinese Repositor* (Li, 2015a, 2015b). The Spreading of early Chinese legal classics abroad was mainly in the form of compilations, selected translations or partial translations, for the following reasons:

One is the purpose of cultural assimilation. Sinologists translated legal classics with the primary goal of "assimilating" Chinese culture. Eurocentrism led them to selectively translate only the parts of interest to fulfill their intentions. Reports with critical commentaries revealed the editors' aversion to aspects such as the large number of death penalty cases in China, frequent executions, and the cruelty of public executions (Li, 2015a, 2015b). The other is the complexity and length of Chinese legal classics. Most Chinese legal classics were written in classical Chinese, with lengthy, complex structures and extensive content. Translating them required a significant amount of time and effort, increasing the difficulty of translation. As a result, the number of complete translations was extremely limited. Sir George Thomas Staunton, in the preface to his translation of the *TA TSING LEU LEE*, openly stated that "the text has been found so obscure, and its construction so recondite" (Staunton & Qu, 2015). These two reasons contributed to the incomplete representation of Chinese legal classics abroad, leading to overseas readers' biases toward the legal system, legal wisdom, and legal cultural aspects showed in Chinese legal classics, creating a challenging situation for the Spreading of these classics abroad.

11.1.3 Spreading of Complete Translations and Research Papers

Regarding the number of the overseas publication of complete translations of Chinese legal classics and research papers by Sinologists and Chinese scholars, we can draw the conclusion that the number of full translations of Chinese legal classics is scarce. Within our reading scope, the currently available complete English translations include only *the Washing Away of Wrongs, the T'ang Code, the Great Ming Code,* and *the Great Qing Code.* The research on legal classics is primarily presented in the form of research papers. For instance, Wallace Johnson, the translator of the complete English version of *The T'ang Code*, took the translated text and introduction of the first three chapters of *the T'ang Code* as his doctoral dissertation (Johnson & Li, 1984). Similarly, the book *American Scholars on Chinese Legal Tradition* (《美国学者论中国法律传统》) includes 12 papers by American scholars on Chinese legal history, originally published in English journals. However, searching for the keywords "法律典籍" + "翻译" ("legal classics" + "translation") on the CNKI yields very few relevant results, indicating that domestic scholars may not prioritize research on the translation of legal classics. The "Library of Chinese Classics" project was officially launched in 1995, which is the first major national publishing project in China's history to systematically and comprehensively introduce foreign editions of Chinese cultural classics to the world. It plans to select 100 classic works from the most representative works in the fields of culture, history, philosophy, economy, military affairs, science, and technology from pre-Qin Dynasty to modern times. However, legal classics has been almost nonexistent in the selected works, which again showed that the current efforts in translating and introducing legal classics are insufficient. Overseas individuals have a limited understanding of Chinese legal classics and traditional legal wisdom. To the extent that some scholars are calling for it, the translation history of Chinese cultural classics overseas should not be confined solely to the Four Books and the Five Classics (authoritative and important books associated with Confucianism, written before 300 BC.), and literary works. It should also encompass a broader range of works, including Chinese legal, medical, historical, ethnic, and technological texts.

In general, four significant representative Chinese legal classics of the traditional Chinese legal family have been fully translated and published overseas. This development plays a crucial role in promoting the introduction of legal classics, providing overseas readers, scholars, and sinologists with the opportunity to gain insight into the entirety of the traditional Chinese legal family. It also provides primary research materials for researchers interested in studying traditional Chinese legal systems. However, in the process of translating legal classics, several problems still exist: (1)There is a scarcity of translated works covering a broad range of legal classics; (2) Complete translations of legal classics are rare, and the initiative for translation is often controlled by foreign Sinologists and scholars; (3) Lack of diversity of translated languages: translations of legal classics are predominantly concentrated in European and American languages, with a noticeable gap in translations for countries along the Belt and Road initiative; (4) Insufficient emphasis on academic research, that is, both domestic and international scholars show inadequate attention to the translation and academic research of legal classics.

11.2 The Feasibility and Necessity of Chinese Legal Classics Going Global

Since the onset of reform and opening-up, China has been dedicated to translating literary works and actively promoting its cultural heritage. In the early twenty-first century, the "Going Global" strategy for Chinese culture became a cultural development guideline, fostering social and cultural prosperity. In 2013, the Belt and Road initiative was proposed, aiming to establish a community of shared interests, destiny, and responsibility with political trust, economic integration, and cultural inclusiveness. This provided a solid platform for Chinese culture to go global. Subsequently, leaders at all levels, led by General Secretary Xi, have emphasized the importance of Chinese culture going global, implementing projects such as the "China Classics International Project", the "Silk Road Book Translation Project", and the "Chinese Cultural Works Translation and Publishing Project". Against such a backdrop, it is worth contemplating whether Chinese legal classics can leverage the "Going Global" strategy and the Belt and Road initiative to achieve internationalization and garner international recognition, and whether such an approach is necessary.

11.2.1 Feasibility

One of the feasibility is based on the homology of legal culture with some countries along the "Belt and Road". Although ancient legal classics originated in feudal China and were almost completely discarded during the legal reforms of the late Qing Dynasty, it does not mean that they lack scientific and rational elements. The Chinese legal traditions, with its unique and highly identifiable national characteristics, pure texture, and the exclusive absence of elements from other legal systems, have consistently influenced various countries in Southeast Asia. The legal system of the Tang Dynasty represented the mature form of feudal legal systems. The *T'ang Code*, as the representative legal code of the traditional Chinese legal family, one of the world's five major legal systems, influenced the traditional legal systems of countries including Japan, Vietnam, Korea, and Ryukyu. Japan's *Taihō Code* and *Ōmi Code*, Korea's *Koryo code*, Vietnam's *Quốc triều hình luật (the Le Code),* whether in terms of structural composition or content principles, all based on *the T'ang Code* (Zhang, 2007). *The Great Ming Code* inherited *the T'ang Code* and continued to influence the legislation of East Asian countries such as Japan and Korea profoundly.

In the nineteenth century, Japanese domains began to emulate the legal codes of the Ming Dynasty, with many legal categories directly adopting from *the Great Ming Code.* Representative works of Korean legal culture, such as *Jing Guo Da Dian(경국대전) (the State Code)* and its successors like *Xu Da Dian(속대전)* and *Da Dian Tong Bian(대전회통),* were also influenced by the *Great Ming Code.* All these show that China and Japan, as well as China and Korea, share a common legal cultural roots in aspects such as "尚礼仪(*Shang Li Yi*) (valuing ritual propriety)", "敦族仪(*Dun Zu Yi*) (emphasizing unity and harmony within families and kin)", "重公权(*Zhong Gong Quan*) (emphasizing public authority)", and "兴专制*(Xing Zhuan Zhi)* (promoting absolutism)". It also underscores that the' guiding ideology of Confucianism, legislation principles emphasizing the three cardinal guides and the five constant virtues, the normative content of the combination of ritual and law, and the system of emphasizing public authority and strict judicial governance were in line with the social needs of Japan and Korea at that time (Li, 2004).

The other feasibility comes from the certain influence of Western countries. Chinese legal classics, through translation and Spreading by Western scholars, have exerted a certain historical influence in Occident. According to statistics, there are 21 different translations of *The Washing Away of Wrongs* in 9 countries, including three in Korean, eight in Japanese, one in Vietnamese, one in Dutch, two in German, three in French, two in English, and one in Russian (evaluation version) (Chen, 2016). This is sufficient to demonstrate the influence and leading position of Chinese forensic medicine in the world at that time. As for the *Ta Tsing Leu Lee,* after its publication in the United Kingdom, several major British review publications, including *the Edinburgh Review, the Eclectic Review, the Monthly Review, the Critical Review,* and *the British Critic*, all provided reviews for this translation. This contributed to the second Spreading of traditional Chinese legal codes in the United Kingdom (Staunton & Qu,

2015). The English translation of *the Great Qing Legal Code* also attracted the attention of scholars in other European countries. In 1876, French scholar P. L. F translated it into French, and in 1924, G. Blès translated it into French again (Bodde & Morris, 1995). Since the nineteenth century, many sinologists and domestic scholars have written research papers on the Chinese legal system. Numerous foreign students have also used the Chinese legal system as material for their doctoral dissertations. Although the current number of studies and perspectives may not be extensive, it indicates that legal classics are gradually attracting the attention of overseas scholars and general readers. In other words, there is considerable potential for the acceptance of legal classics in the international market.

With the government support, it is entirely possible to make great progress in the translation and introduction of legal classics, allowing them to objectively take the international stage and show the objective form of China's traditional legal system to the world.

11.2.2 Necessity

Firstly, it's necessary to advance the rule of law in an all-round way by drawing on the essence of traditional legal culture. The 19th National Congress of the Communist Party of China proposed in its report that we will draw on China's fine traditional culture, keep alive and develop its vision, concepts, values, and moral norms and do so in a way that responds to the call of our era. With this, we will see that Chinese culture maintains its appeal and evolves with the times. In the process of socialist legal system construction, it is essential to not only learn and draw from modern legal systems in the West but also deeply study the traditional Chinese legal system, from which we can extract legal thinking, theories, principles, systems, experiences, and lessons that remain applicable even in the present. It is crucial to scientifically summarize the patterns of the occurrence and development of the traditional Chinese legal system, find its points of convergence with contemporary rule of law, and seamlessly integrate it into the present legal system construction. The contemporary culture of socialist rule of law with Chinese characteristics not only inherits traditional legal thinking but also finds its origins in ancient legal culture in the practices of legislation, judicature, and legal supervision (Hu & Dong, 2018a, 2018b).

The blending of traditional legal culture with modern legal culture forms the "cultural soil" for contemporary rule of law advancement. This interaction influences the effectiveness of contemporary rule of law advancement, giving rise to China's unique legal psychology, legal consciousness, and legal behavior. In the development of the rule of law, we should take the needs of legal development of our society as the foundation. Considering our national conditions and relying on our own legal culture, we aim to create an advanced Chinese legal culture and form a new type of traditional Chinese legal system, preventing the situation where the practice of the rule of law is influenced by other countries. Under such a background, the value of traditional Chinese legal culture should be highly regarded. This underscores the important significance of advocating the translation of legal classics. It plays a crucial role in strengthening the country's cultural soft power and resisting cultural hegemony (Liu, 2012).

Secondly, it's necessary to reshape the international image of traditional legal culture and boost national cultural confidence.

Legal classics depict the traditional legal image of China. When Westerners were first exposed to traditional Chinese legal system, they had a great prejudice against the traditional Chinese legal system, and even used it as a tool to demean the image of China. Up to now, there remain biases and criticisms in the West toward China's traditional legal system. In such a context, the translation of Chinese legal classics becomes crucial. To gain recognition from other cultures, comprehensively display China's legal image, and reshape the image of the traditional Chinese legal family, it is essential to actively translate and introduce these legal classics to the outside world in contemporary times. Taking the translation of *the Great Ming Code* as an example, its status has been a subject of controversy in the Western academic circles. In the eyes of most Western scholars, *the Great Ming Code* is a tool of imperialist China to wield power, characterized by oppression and power orientation. They hold serious biases against the traditional Chinese legal system. Scholar Jiang Yonglin, in an effort to counteract Western biases against Chinese legal civilization, translated *the Great Ming Code,* seeking to reshape its classical standing in Western academic and legal circles (Xiao & Wang, 2017).

In the context of the new era, only by proactively providing objective research materials to overseas scholars can the biases against China's traditional legal system be further eliminated worldwide. In addition, Chinese traditional legal culture embodies the main spirit of traditional Chinese culture, possessing its own unique value judgments and cultural structure. China's modern legal culture construction is also based on the inheritance of traditional culture. In the transitional period, Chinese society accommodates both modern and traditional aspects. If divorced from the foundation of traditional culture, the construction of modern rule of law culture becomes like a tree without roots and water without a source. Culture is a comprehensive, overarching, and inclusive concept. Ancient legal classics are not only an important part of traditional culture but also integral to the "going global" strategy of culture. By translating fine parts of traditional legal culture, we provide new choices for those countries and nations who both hope to accelerate development and maintain their independence. This contributes Chinese wisdom to global governance, overall enhancing the appeal and persuasiveness of traditional Chinese culture. It helps earn respect and recognition for the values of Chinese culture worldwide, thereby boosting the cultural confidence of the Chinese nation.

11.3 Strategic Planning on Content and Framework for Chinese Legal Classics Going Global

Translation has always been an indispensable condition for communication between two languages, serving as a bridge for interaction among people from different linguistic backgrounds and laying the foundation for mutual cultural understanding. The "going global" national strategy of culture can open up a broader translation market for the internationalization of Chinese culture. The introduction of the "Belt and Road" initiative has also laid down extensive development space for Chinese culture to go out. Over the past century, there are more practices of translating from foreign languages into Chinese in the field of legal document translation. Therefore, promoting legal classics to go global cannot directly apply the above practical model, for it needs experiences of translating from Chinese into foreign languages. Moreover, the endeavor of promoting legal classics to go global beyond selecting and translating texts; it also involves knowledge and practices in legal history and communication studies. It is an interdisciplinary and cross-cultural undertaking, making it essential to elevate the translation of legal classics to a strategic level and plan comprehensively. In the 1970s, foreign researchers proposed that the output of language planning, besides specific policies, would also manifest in strategic forms. The theory of language strategic planning stems from the practice and development of the discipline of language planning. It includes language status planning, language ontology planning, language acquisition planning (or education planning), language prestige planning, language function planning, and discourse planning (Shen & Xia, 2018). Strategic planning is not only a political act but also a research activity. Different from the personalized and fragmented individual actions of a few foreign translators out of academic interests and preferences in the past, the strategic planning for the translation of legal classics is now more comprehensive and holistic. It involves not only supporting policies of government at the macro level but also the selection of specific texts, translators, and the Spreading strategies at the micro level. Besides, the planning content and tasks vary at each level. Based on the theory of language strategic planning, we propose a multi-agent systematic research and analysis framework in different problem domains from macro, meso, and micro perspectives, as illustrated in the diagram below:

11.3.1 Basic Content of Strategic Planning

The Basic Content of Strategic Planning for the Translation and Introduction of Legal Classics can be divided into four parts, including status planing, ontology planing, education planing, and Spreading planning.

Status Planning In January 2019, President Xi emphasized in a congratulatory letter on the establishment of the Chinese Academy of History that, in the new era, the perseverance and development of socialism with Chinese characteristics require systematic research on Chinese history and culture. It is more necessary to profoundly grasp the laws of human development history, draw wisdom from in-depth reflections on history, and move toward the future. Legal classics have continuously provided abundant thoughts and wisdom for advancing the rule of law in China, thus demanding a more systematic and in-depth exploration. However, the translation of legal classics is not receiving the attention it deserves, mainly because of a limited understanding of the value of the traditional Chinese legal family and traditional legal culture within academic circles. Strategically planning the status of legal classics translation involves placing a high emphasis on its significance in effectively narrating Chinese history and disseminating Chinese culture. In terms of ideological understanding, it is essential to achieve consensus and agreement. This involves not only a reevaluation of the value of the traditional Chinese legal family but also a comprehensive recognition of the strategic significance of translating legal classics. In practical terms, relevant government departments should take the lead in organizing and, when implementing major national projects, include legal classics translation projects within the scope and perspective of research. This involves granting legal classics and other cultural classics equal status and policy support to attract more researchers, gradually elevating the level of attention given to the translation of legal classics.

Ontology Planning Legal classics translation is characterized by its uniqueness, professionalism, and cultural significance. Legal terminology constitutes a fundamental element of legal texts, and the ancient Chinese legal terminology is a system that incorporates the form and meaning of the cultural symbols of ancient legal language. Ancient legal classics are a manifestation of the cultural spirit of a nation, and the ancient legal language along with legal terminology serves as an externalization of the national spirit. The translation of ancient legal terms needs to transcend the constraints of time, space, and cultural contexts, posing significant challenges. This necessitates that the translation of legal classics cannot simply adopt the discourse system used for other types of texts. Instead, it must be based on the ontology of the translation of ancient legal classics, which means to make careful internal system planning and build a distinctive and compatible disciplinary discourse system. Ancient Chinese legal classics encompass a wealth of achievements, ranging from codes, systems and their supplementary forms, to thoughts, doctrines, and the fruits of national legal wisdom. To navigate through this vast cultural heritage, it is imperative to systematically sift through, distinguishing the authentic from the spurious and extracting the essence from the course. This requires meticulous selection of both original works and translators. Additionally, there is a need to enhance the development of standards, principles, strategies, criteria, evaluations, and critiques in the field of legal classics translation. In addition, conducting critical research on the translation of ancient legal classics not only enriches translation theory but also contributes to the external translation and Spreading of modern legal language and culture (Xiong, 2019). This approach helps overcome language and cultural barriers, prevents the production of low-quality language and translations, and ultimately enhances the overall quality of legal classics translation.

Education Planning According to existing records, from the beginning of translating Chinese classics to the present, the primary contributors have consistently been Western missionaries, sinologists, and others. Undeniably, Western sinologists have played an indispensable role in the process of translating Chinese classics. However, in the historical juncture of the new era, to promote the "going global" of traditional culture', it's more necessary to grasp the initiative and introduce China fairly and truthfully' from a comprehensive, multi-dimensional, and objective perspective of Chinese people. As international cooperation increasingly become a consensus in the field of classic translations, it is imperative to make forward-looking, long-term education plans. This includes identifying and nurturing potential practitioners, theorists, and critics in the field of legal classic translations, ensuring an ample reserve of talents, enabling China to take the initiative in shaping the discourse on the translation of Chinese legal classics. Legal classic translation places exceptionally high demands on translators. Translators must not only have a profound understanding of Chinese culture, history, and ideology but also possess strong proficiency in English expression. The education planning of legal classics translation is inherently interdisciplinary, which is of great benefit to the communication and transformative development of various disciplines. It is necessary for foreign language majors, law majors, and history majors to cooperate with each other and try to promote the education system of translation of ancient legal classics from the aspects of talent training objectives, knowledge system construction, and the combination of theory and practice.

Spreading Planning It can actually be viewed as prestige planning. The global recognition of Chinese legal classics is cultivated through international Spreading, highlighting the interdependence of Spreading planning and prestige planning. Translation and Spreading complement each other; the purpose of translation is to facilitate better Spreading. It serves as both the logical starting point and the method and means of Spreading. Simultaneously, Spreading broadens the scope of translation research. The Spreading of a translated work is not automatic or spontaneous. The completion of the translation does not signify the completion of Spreading; it invariably relies on the use of Spreading methods and technologies. Through specific Spreading channels, complete information and signals are sent to the audience. Spreading planning is a systematic undertaking that involves the active involvement of Spreading agents. It also requires comprehensive consideration of Spreading objectives, target audience, content, media, effects, and the Spreading environment, among many other aspects of planning and research (Xie & Liao, 2016). Due to variations in the Spreading environment and the cultural needs and levels of target readers, it is necessary to tailor different Spreading strategies based on the intended audience. This ensures precise positioning of media methods. Additionally, it is essential to conduct feedback and evaluation of the communication outcomes, assessing the effectiveness of the Spreading, which allows for adjustments and decisions related to new translation projects, text selection, and potential changes in communication methods.

11.3.2 Main Components of Strategic Planning

The strategic planning for legal classics translation is mainly embodied in four levels, including government level, industry level, academic level, and media level.

Government Level The government plays a crucial role in translation planning. While government-led translation activities boast a controllable regulatory framework, the ultimate translated works often fall short of the expected impact due to internal factors within the source culture, thereby limiting their effectiveness in cultural diplomacy (Wu & Jiang, 2018). For instance, in the 1980s, only about 10% of the translations of the "Panda Book Series" managed to capture the interest of readers in the English-speaking world, while the majority of translated works fell short of achieving the goal of culture communication (Geng, 2010). In the new era, the translation and introduction of classics should give equal consideration to both market discourse and political discourse. The government's role in the translation and introduction of classics should shift from the original "rule maker" to a "supporter" or "promoter". In future efforts to translate legal classics, the government should enhance its attention to external translations of legal classics. Drawing lessons from practices in other fields, leveraging collaborative platforms established by the government with external partners, such as supporting and funding collaborations with international publishing houses, can further increase the exposure and acceptance of translated legal classics overseas. This approach aims to provide a broader understanding of China's traditional legal system to people worldwide and actively promote cultural exchange between China and the world.

Industry Level At the industry level, the focus is primarily on publishing institutions. Collaboration between domestic and foreign publishing institutions should be promoted. Through the joint efforts, they should be responsible for essential tasks, such as determining the original classics to be translated, translated languages, and suitable translators, as well as thorough research on the reading habits and preferences of target readers, the publishing and distribution models in the target language country. This comprehensive approach facilitates the distribution and marketing of translated versions of classics in overseas markets. Establishing Chinese cultural centers abroad has proven to be an effective method in recent years for academic diplomacy and promoting Chinese culture to go global (Feng, 2019). It is worth noting that well-established publishing institutions have the capability to support the development of publishing institutions in countries along the "Belt and Road". Alternatively, they can directly establish branch offices overseas, achieving a localized operation in terms of publishing and distribution. This approach enables a more effective understanding of the cultural psychology and atmosphere of the target environment, allowing for timely feedback and adjustments.

Academic Level The academic level, comprising academic associations and research institutions, serves as the "think tank" to drive Chinese legal classics to go global. Historically, there has been a notable absence of scholarly exploration into the translation of legal classics. A statistical analysis of 500 papers published in academic conferences and journals over the past decade, focusing on ancient classics translation, revealed a mere six articles related to the translation of ancient legal classics. Furthermore, these articles were confined to the two English translations of legal texts from the Tang and Qing Dynasties (Xiong, 2018). To play a more significant role in the translation and introduction of legal classics at the academic level, there is a need to strengthen multi-dimensional, interdisciplinary, and systematic research on the translation of legal classics. Research could start from macro perspectives such as policy considerations, or from micro perspectives like translation techniques and talent cultivation; interdisciplinary and collaborative research can also be paid attention to from the perspectives of communication studies and legal history. Such comprehensive research effort aims to provide theoretical support for legal classics going global.

Media Level Media serves as the carrier for cultural transmission, playing the pioneering role in Spreading. Structurally, media can include both domestic and foreign outlets, establishing bridges for cultural communication and exchange through collaboration. In terms of methods and carriers of communication, it encompasses professional academic journals as well as mass media and audio-visual platforms such as the Internet, television, radio, newspapers, and magazines. This paves the way for a diversified and multi-tiered Spreading channel for legal classics to go global. In recent years, China has utilized media to spread academic ideas, producing films and TV dramas with a strong Chinese cultural essence, employing modern techniques to spread Chinese culture worldwide (Feng, 2019). As a creative approach, there is potential in integrating the translation of legal classics with television or film productions to enhance communication. For example, historical dramas like *The Legend of the Condor Heroes*, *Demi-Gods and Semi-Devils*, *The Return of the Condor Heroes*, and *Return of the Pearl Princess* have gained popularity and acclaim in Vietnam. Utilizing concurrent promotion of relevant ancient legal classics in conjunction with television and film productions can help audiences gain a more multi-dimensional understanding of authentic traditional Chinese culture. The influence of film and television can thus drive the acceptance of legal classics.

11.3.3 Principles of Strategic Planning

The strategic planning of the translation of legal classics also needs to follow four principles, including the principle of scientificity, systematicity, pertinence, and openness.

Scientificity Strategic planning is one of the crucial manifestations of public policy, and a well-developed strategic plan must possess scientific and rational qualities. Policy investigation and policy debates are essential prerequisites for attaining rationality. Without investigation, there is no right to speak. In the past, the "going global" of classics was more driven by government initiatives, without sufficient consideration for the psychological acceptance of the target language country and the reading habits of the readers. The prerequisite for scientific planning is to achieve completeness, sufficiency, and truthfulness of information. Whether in goal setting, option selection, or the optimization, supplementation, and adjustment during policy implementation, a comprehensive and accurate information base is essential. The scientific nature of planning is directly proportional to the comprehensiveness and truthfulness of information. Planning is not a work in a vacuum; we cannot come up with a fine plan through mere imagination. Investigation and research lay the foundation for planning and are essential for achieving success. To formulate a scientific plan, it is essential to center it on the needs of the readers and conduct thorough investigation and research. The translation and introduction of legal classics necessitates familiarity with the cultural psychology, reading environment, legal discourse environment, legal discourse expression methods, and the Spreading channels of legal discourse in the target language country. Formulate a scientific plan and clarify goals and targets based on facts, thereby increasing the chances for the legal classics to go global.

Systematicity Strategic planning is a systematic endeavor. Fragmented or scattered planning cannot integrate information and resources nor achieve overall goals. A specific policy is always complementary to other policies at parallel levels, while interacting and connecting with policies within the same framework, forming a cohesive and integrated approach (Hu, 2000a, 2000b). Strategic planning requires consideration from a holistic perspective as well as an examination of the logical relationships among its various components, so as to construct an internally logical, interconnected, and systematically coordinated planning framework. The serious disconnect between discourse translation and discourse Spreading is one of the significant reasons behind issues such as low translation quality, outdated modes of communication, and unsatisfactory Spreading outcomes (Hu & Li, 2018). Essentially, translation is an act of communication. The translation and Spreading of culture and discourse form a closely interconnected whole. It requires us to study translation from the perspective of communication, conducting a more comprehensive and objective analysis of translation and communication activities. Additionally, in practice, it is crucial to strengthen communication, connection, and collaboration between translation and communication departments, ensuring the close integration and convergence of policy planning.

Pertinence Planning is meant to be implemented, and facing different audiences and target readers, it requires feasibility and pertinence. The translation of legal classics should not only align with the strategic considerations of national culture going global but also be grounded in the practical demands of the target country, demonstrating a high degree of pertinence. Having pertinence means avoiding blindness and generality. There are essential differences between the civil law system and the common law system. In view of the different legal culture sources in different countries, the planning of translation and introduction of legal classics should have regional and national consciousness. That is to say, the modes of communication should vary when targeting developed countries in Europe and America compared to developing countries along the "Belt and Road". There should also be consciousness of different groups, which means that the cultural reading needs of elite and mass audiences differ. Even within countries along the "Belt and Road", there are differences in the common foundation of legal culture. Therefore, it's necessary to develop specific and targeted strategies on a one-to-one basis and promote the "going global" of legal classics step by step with focus and clear goal in an organized way. Pertinence is also a crucial prerequisite for achieving flexibility in cultural communication methods.

Openness The formulation, execution, and evaluation of any public policy are subject to changes in the policy environment, resources, and effectiveness (Hu, 2000a, 2000b). Therefore, whether in the formulation of policies or planning, it is essential to embody a certain degree of openness, dynamism, flexibility, and interactivity. The formulation of translation plans for legal classics is not a one-time task; it always evolves with the progress and outcomes of the "going global" of legal classics and make adjustments, modifications, and enhancements continuously, which reflects the dynamic nature of the plan of translation and Spreading that adapt to the changing times. Furthermore, there are no rigid boundaries or distinctions between the research subjects and the research content. Solely focusing on one's own field may lead to a narrow perspective and dispersed efforts. The realization of national strategies requires the coordinated efforts of various disciplines, departments, and subjects. The interdisciplinary nature of strategic planning research also demands lateral intersections and integration between research subjects and research content. In terms of structure and mechanism, there should be a certain degree of flexibility and openness to facilitate effective interaction among different elements and structures within the overall plan.

11.4 Summary

Cultural exchange involves various aspects. The traditional Chinese legal family, with its unique charm and value, has historically exerted significant influence on the world, acknowledged by observers from third countries. Tradition holds enduring value as a mirror and reference for contemporary times. Even today, traditional legal culture, with its profound historical and cultural essence, continues to embody the spirit and elegance of national culture. Exchanges in the legal field are of great significance to China's comprehensive advancement of the rule of law and the development of a modern rule of law culture. Since the 18th National Congress of the Communist Party of China, General Secretary Xi has delivered a series of important discourses on advancing rule of law comprehensively.

In the process of strengthening the advancement of the rule of law, the internationalization of legal governance is indispensable for China. Legal classics constitute the traditional source of China's legal system. Promoting Chinese legal classics to go global is a crucial step in reinforcing the development of the rule of law in China. As socialism with Chinese characteristics enters a new era, in the context of the national strategy of cultural globalization and the Belt and Road Initiative, how legal classics can go global and gain international recognition is a matter deserving serious consideration. With the historic juncture in the new era, promoting the outstanding traditional Chinese culture requires harnessing the power of the main roles. Dust-laden classical works need to be brought into the sunlight, revealing profound cultural richness to the world. We must uphold cultural confidence, cultivate long-term awareness, and attach great importance to the translation and introduction of ancient Chinese legal classics. We should also comprehensively plan and actively promote excellent ancient legal classics to go global in time. It is not only to contribute Chinese solutions and wisdom to global governance but also to make efforts to improve the socialist legal system with Chinese characteristics and construct a discourse system for the international Spreading of Chinese ancient legal culture.

References

Bodde, D., & Morris, C. (1995). *Law in imperial China*, 74. Y. Zhu, Trans. Jiangsu People's Publishing House.

Chen, H. (2016). The washing away of wrongs: A magnum opus in ancient Chinese forensic medicine. *Chinese Rule of Law Culture*, (6).

Feng, Y. (2019). Chinese culture 'going out' in the new era: Realistic problems and strategic paths. *Journal of Chongqing University of Technology (Social Science)*, (1).

Geng, Q. (2010). *Chinese literature walking towards the world through literary translation—A study of English translation in panda books series*. Shanghai International Studies University.

Gong, P. (2004). Legal exchanges between China and foreign countries before the 19th century. *Jin Ling Law Review*, (1).

Hu, B., & Dong, X. (2018). Drawing from the essence of traditional legal culture to build a country of socialist rule of law. *Chinese Social Sciences Today*, 2018-12-12:005.

Hu, B., & Dong, X. (2018). Emphasizing the research value of the English translation of the Ta Tsing Leu Lee. *Chinese Social Sciences Today*, 2018-11-27:003.

Hu, K., & Li, C. (2018) Translating and disseminating the discourse on 'major-country diplomacy with Chinese characteristics': A study of the undertaking's substantive, methodological and axiological aspects. *Chinese Translators Journal*, (4).

Hu, N. (2000a). *Modern public policy research, 39*. China Social Sciences Press.

Hu, N. (2000b). *Modern public policy research, 46*. China Social Sciences Press.

Johnson, W. (1984). The legal philosophy in the Tang code. M. Li, Trans. *Peking University Law Journal*, (4).

Li, Q. (2004). Examining the historical significance of the Great Ming code through its influence on East Asia. *Journal of Comparative Law*, (3).

Li, X. (2015a). *Western interpretation of Chinese law: 19th century western perspectives on Chinese law based on Chinese repository, 52*. Shanghai Joint Publishing Company.

Li, X. (2015b). *Western interpretation of Chinese law: 19th Century western perspectives on Chinese law based on Chinese repository, 94*. Shanghai Joint Publishing Company.

Liu, J. (2012). Soft power and discourse right in translating Chinese classics: The case of Legge's I Ching, book of changes. *Henan Social Sciences*, (7).

Shen, Q., & Xia, T. (2018). Fundamental issues of language strategic planning for 'the belt and road initiatives'. *Journal of Xinjiang Normal University (Edition of Philosophy and Social Sciences)*, (1).

Staunton, G. T. (2015). Memoirs of Sir George Thomas Staunton, Bart, 219. W. Qu, Trans. Shanghai People's Publishing House.

Staunton, G. T. (2015). Memoirs of Sir George Thomas Staunton, Bart. , 45–49. W. Qu, Trans. Shanghai People's Publishing House.

Wang, H. (2018). The output track of translating Chinese legal literature and its enlightenment. *Political Science and Law*, (11).

Wu, Y., & Jiang, M. (2018). China's foreign translation planning and national image construction since the reform and opening-up. *Foreign Languages in China*, (6).
Xiao, H., & Wang, J. (2017). A descriptive translation study of the legal text. *Journal of the Staff and Worker's University*, (1).
Xie, K., & Liao, X. (2016). 'Translation-communication studies': Name and reality. *Shanghai Journal of Translators*, (1).
Xiong, D. (2018). Translation of ancient legal classics and criticism studies. *Chinese Social Sciences Today*, 2018-10-19:006.
Xiong, D. (2019). The practical significance of critically studying the translation of legal classics: A trivial discourse on the English translation of the Ta Tsing Leu Lee. *Chinese Social Sciences Today*, 2019-2-12:007.
Zhang, J. (2007). *Retrospections and prospects of Chinese legal system, 46*. China University of Political Science and Law Press.

Epilogue China's Image in the West: From "Civilization Hegemony" to "Civilization Mutual Learning"

China, as one of the oldest countries in the world, boasts a splendid culture and a glorious revolutionary tradition. Throughout its development, China has experienced numerous challenges and ups and downs. Even though going through crisis after crisis, this nation has thrived with a firm belief in fairness and justice, demonstrating unwavering dedication to development. It has cultivated the great Chinese legal culture, earning a well-deserved place in the global family of legal cultures. Each dynasty has enacted its own laws and regulations. Scholars including politicians, philosophers, legal scholars, and historians have written numerous essays, articles, and books, expounding their theories on law, justice, and state governance, which leaves us with a rich collection of legal classics. Legal classics constitute a vital component of Chinese legal culture. They document the legal practices of our ancestors, summarize experiences and wisdom in governance, inherit traditional values and thoughts, and contribute to the development of civilization (Zhang & Dian, Zhang, The Journal of Jiangsu Administration Institute 2:130–136, 2013). In terms of the translation of legal-related works, as early as the seventeenth century, the Western world engaged in intense discussions and debates about ancient Chinese political and legal systems. However, "none of the Western individuals involved in such discussions, including famous thinkers, scholars, and jurists in the age of Enlightenment, could truly understand Chinese law through written laws and legal codes" (Wang & Xi, Wang, J. (2001). The eastward spreading of western culture: Study of the early history of the correspondence of legal concepts between China and the West. Tsinghua Forum of Rule of Law, 296–359.). For instance, when it comes to Chinese law, the renowned Italian missionary Matteo Ricci believed, "Once someone ascends to the throne, regardless of his background, he will enact new laws and regulations that he deems appropriate" (He, G., Wang, Z., & Li, S. (2010) De Christiana expeditione apud Sinas. Shanghai: Zhonghua Book Company.). The kind of translation by Western sinologists under the influence of cultural hegemonism has brought a dual crisis: firstly, it has created a rigid image of Chinese legal culture internationally, hindering the promotion of Chinese legal classics; secondly, the

X. Dong and Y. Luo, *The Legal Image of China in Chinese Legal Tradition*,
https://doi.org/10.1007/978-981-96-5797-1

insufficient influence of domestic legal culture has led to certain issues of national identity confusion. Furthermore, while the translation of Chinese legal classics has achieved commendable results, it still faces challenges such as numerous errors and misunderstandings in the translations, a lack of comprehensive and systematic examination and research on existing translations, and a limited number of versions provided by Chinese translators. President Xi emphasized in the report of the 19th National Congress of the Communist Party of China: "We will improve our capacity for engaging in international communication so as to tell China's stories well, present a true, multi-dimensional, and panoramic view of China, and enhance our country's cultural soft power" (Xi, J. (2017). Full text of Xi Jinping's report at 19th CPC National Congress. http://cpc.people.com.cn/n1/2017/1028/c64094-29613660.html.). Effective communication can only occur on the basis of equality. In the new era, to truly enhance China's capacity for international legal and cultural exchange, sufficient attention and additional resources should be allocated to the translation of Chinese legal classics. This ensures that China holds the initiative in interpreting its legal culture, challenging stereotypical impressions held by Western Sinologists regarding Chinese rule of law, and consciously safeguarding the cultural sovereignty of the country. From the perspective of mutual learning between civilizations, it is crucial to inherit and disseminate new translations of legal classics.

Overview of the Translation of Chinese Legal Classics

Culture is the absorption and transformation of the natural environment by a nation in the course of historical development. It reflects the unique creativity and practical abilities of humanity and is manifested through a series of material and spiritual works, which ultimately became classics. Legal classics, as an integral part of legal culture, are an undeniable source of a nation's legal creativity. They inherit the values of our ancestors, summarize past experiences, and propel the development of our legal civilization. President Xi Jinping made an important speech before regarding the value of outstanding traditional legal culture and the legal wisdom it embodies, as well as its significant importance for current efforts in legal modernization and mutual learning between civilizations. The contents are as follows: "How to govern and control humanity has been a major issue that our ancestors have been exploring". During the pre-Qin period, the Legalists proposed the idea of "the rule of law". In the Spring and Autumn period, systematic legal codes were formulated and promulgated. In the Han and Tang Dynasties, relatively comprehensive legal codes and systems were established, among which, the Tang Code, in particular, having a widespread influence. The core values and ideological imprints of Chinese culture and civilization are deeply embedded in the extensive legal codes. The ancient legal system contains abundant wisdom and resources, making China's legal system distinctive among law systems worldwide. "We should attach importance to the study of our ancient legal traditions, learn from the successes and failures of legal practices, explore and inherit Chinese legal culture, extracting its essence and discarding its dross" (Xi,

2015). In summary, legal culture research should emphasize the reinterpretation of legal classics and the study of their modern significance.

In the exchange and communication of legal cultures, translation is an essential topic that cannot be ignored. Since the fourth century, China has attracted attention and interest from the West, but their understanding and comprehension of China and Chinese culture have been more subjective. More than a thousand years later, in the latter half of the thirteenth century, Marco Polo traveled from Italy to China. In his famous travelogue, *The Travels of Marco Polo*, he made introductions and descriptions of various aspects of China. He introduced China's political and legal systems, praising the dedication and competence of Chinese judges and the profoundness of the legal system. Westerners first gained conceptual understanding of Chinese legal life (He & Xu, 2000). After the first Industrial Revolution, the flourishing trade between the East and the West facilitated vibrant cultural exchanges, marking a phase of selected translations and abridged translations of Chinese legal classics. With more and more Westerners coming to China, they inevitably encountered various legal affairs, compelling them to explore and become familiar with local laws and legal traditions. In order to grasp the overall picture of Chinese legal life, some scholars chose to translate selected works of legal culture to meet their practical needs. Abridged translation was carried out under Eurocentrism and Ethnocentrism. It wasn't until 1810, when Sir George Thomas Staunton published the translation of *the Ta Tsing Leu Lee* in London, that the translation of Chinese legal classics entered a phase of complete translation.

The translation of Chinese legal classics has a long history, but the results have not always been satisfactory. According to incomplete statistics from the *Introduction to the History of Chinese Legal System* published in 1957, there were 932 works and documents related to law (Legislative Affairs Office of the State Council of the People's Republic of China, 1957). Over half a century later, in the *Bibliography of Chinese Legal History* published in 2019, this number increased to 2,352. This book classifies traditional Chinese legal literature according to norms, systems, theories, and practices (Institute for Chinese Ancient Legal Documents of China University of Political Science & Law, 2019). It provides a comprehensive overview of Chinese legal classics for readers both domestically and internationally. However, in the over 200 years since 1810, out of the 2352 Chinese legal classics, only four have been fully translated. Not to mention the cultural and artistic classics that contain rich legal thoughts and legal affairs. The four legal classics that have been fully translated are *the Ta Tsing Leu Lee, The Washing Away of Wrongs, The Tang Code,* and *The Great Ming Code.*

The *Ta Tsing Leu Lee* is the first fully translated official feudal legal code. Sir George Thomas Staunton, a renowned British Orientalist, translated it into English, and published it in 1810. He introduced Chinese legal system and thoughts at that time in detail, meeting the needs of Western society to understand the legal environment in China, and attracting widespread attention (Qian & Cao, 2015). Many scholars and translators subsequently retranslated this English version into Spanish, Russian, Italian, and French. In 1876, Paul-Louis-Félix Philastre translated *the Ta Tsing Leu Lee* into French. In 1924, P. Gui Boulais published another French version

(Su, 2003). In 1994, Oxford University Press published the second edition of *the Great Legal Code (the Ta Tsing Leu Lee)*, and it is the latest English edition. William C. Jones, a renowned scholar at the University of Washington specializing in Chinese law, did this translation. The second legal classic that received active promotion and had a significant impact on the West is *The Washing Away of Wrongs*. It is a ground-breaking work, a first ever written book of forensic science and legal jurisprudence worldwide. Song Ci, known as the foremost forensic scientist, was hailed as the father of forensic science. He published *The Washing Away of Wrongs* in 1247, which was his life's work and the world's earliest book on forensic medicine. The translation of this book began in 1779, but only a few chapters were translated. De Groot did the first complete translation in 1862 in Dutch. In 1873 and 1981, Herbert A. Giles and Brian E. Mcknight published English versions respectively, titled as *The His Yuan Lu, or Instructions to Coroners* and *The Washing Away of Wrongs: Forensic Medicine in Thirteen-century China* (Qu & Huang, 2021). The book has been translated into 19 different languages, influencing the establishment and development of modern forensic medicine in countries and regions such as the United Kingdom, the United States, France, Italy, and Japan. The other two codes, *The T'ang Code* and *The Great Ming Code*, each have only one complete English translation. As for the former, Wallace Johnson translated it into two volumes, which were published by Princeton University Press in 1979 and 1997, respectively. Professor Jiang Yonglin of Bryn Mawr College translated the latter into English, which was published by the University of Washington Press in 2005 (Wang, 2018).

Chinese Legal Image Constructed under Cultural Hegemonism

Translation plays a pivotal role in promoting the exchange of legal cultures between the East and the West. "Unlike the translation of literary works, the structure of legal texts is rigorous and complex, thus translators have limited freedom in translating. The identity and motives of the translator significantly impact the final rendition of the translation" (Qu & Wan, 2019). As is well known, translation, as a form of cross-cultural communication, inevitably serves specific purposes. The translation of Chinese legal classics is no exception. Translator's motivations or goals determine which text to translate, which translation theory or method to employ, and which strategy to adopt for publishing and promotion. Hence, in order to provide some insights into the translation of contemporary Chinese legal classics, it is necessary to summarize and analyze the motivations behind the translation practices of Western sinologists in the past.

The *Ta Tsing Leu Lee* is the last and most representative feudal legal code in Chinese history, and the first Chinese legal classic directly translated from the source language into the target language. The translator of this book, Sir George Thomas Staunton, was one of the prominent thinkers and Orientalists on China during the nineteenth-century period of Sino-Western exchanges. He is also considered as one of the founders of British Sinology. In 1793, the British government appointed Lord Macartney to lead a diplomatic mission to China to celebrate the 83rd birthday of Qianlong Emperor. At that time, Staunton was only 12 years old, and this was his first visit to China as a Page to Lord Macartney, accompanying his father, who had been appointed secretary. During the long journey, he learned Chinese from the hired native translators of the mission and quickly acquired the ability to communicate in Chinese for daily interactions. On September 14, 1793, Qianlong Emperor received the British mission. Young Staunton, as a foreign child who could speak basic Chinese, caught the interest of Qianlong Emperor, who rewarded him with an embroidered bag and a piece of jade. This unique experience left an indelible mark in Staunton's mind, inspiring him to pursue Sinology research. In January 1800, seven years after his first visit to China, Staunton returned to this country. However, this time, he took a position as a clerk at the East India Company's Guangdong office, where he worked for over a decade. On the evening of February 10, 1800, the British ship Providence violated regulations by entering Humen. Crewmembers on the ship fired shots at Chinese fishermen, resulting in one death. During the trial and negotiation process of this case, the British authorities noted that the Chinese government was handling the case in accordance with relevant provisions of the *Ta Tsing Leu Lee*. Therefore, they have submitted a request to the Chinese government, demanding copies of current laws. Stanton was appointed as the translator for this case and successfully translated the six guidelines designated by the Chinese authorities. His translation skills were highly recognized, and he was soon assigned to translate the entire text of the *Ta Tsing Leu Lee* (Hou, 2009).

Stanton spent nearly a decade completing the first comprehensive translation of the *Ta Tsing Leu Lee*. His translation was driven by the pragmatic needs of the British at that time to understand and use Chinese law for the protection and safeguarding of the interests of British merchants and citizens in China. As for the motivation behind the translation, Stanton believed, "Under all circumstances he flattered himself, that a faithful version of the Fundamental Laws of the Penal Code of China might, with the addition of some supplementary matter, not only prove interesting as far as regards its immediate subject, but likewise afford a more compendious and satisfactory illustration, than any other Chinese work that could have been selected, of the peculiar system and constitution of the Government, the principles of its internal policy, its connection with the national habits and character, and its influence upon the general state and condition of the people in that country" (Staunton, 1810). Qu & Wan indicate that the fundamental purpose of Westerners translating Chinese legal classics was to gain an in-depth and comprehensive understanding of Chinese society and its inner operating mechanism. In this way, they can assist authorities to have a say in Sino-British trade and diplomacy, gaining an advantage in legal conflicts and preparing for the next wave of colonial expansion (Qu & Wan, 2019).

Staunton's evaluation and judgment of China and its legal system bear a strong cultural hegemony bias. On the one hand, Staunton compared the national characters of Chinese and Western countries. He believed that superior geographical conditions and abundant natural resources ensured China's prosperity but also led to a lack of "the adventurous pursuits of trade with foreign nations". As he stated, "With little opportunity of becoming generally acquainted with the state of the rest of the inhabited world, ... Thus the Chinese, although they certainly became at a very early period a rich, populous, and, comparatively, an enlightened nation, have not been at any time enterprising, warlike, or commercial, and therefore have been in fact deficient in those qualities which, of all others, are the most conducive to the extension of the fame of any people among distant countries" (Staunton, 1810). Furthermore, Staunton believed that the more civilized a society, the less restraint the law imposed on individuals. He thought that China's legal regulations restricted personal freedom, impeded social progress and development, and concluded that "the Chinese would rank very low indeed in the scale of civilized nations" (Staunton, 1939). However, such criticism may actually be unfair, as it is one-sided to judge a country or its people without delving into historical origins or the inner operating mechanism of the society. By dismissing the Chinese as vain, arrogant, lacking spirit of adventure and enterprise, Staunton reveals his own "undisputed sense of superiority".

On the other hand, Staunton also recognized the significant importance of the *Ta Tsing Leu Lee* in social life. He pointed out that Chinese legal history, with its long history, had undergone continuous "cautious and clumsy" modifications and supplements, allowing the laws and regulations to better adapt to the specific national conditions. "There are certainly many points upon which these laws are altogether indefensible. We shall look in vain, for instance, for those excellent principles of the English law, by which every man is presumed innocent until he is proved guilty; and no man required to criminate himself. Such maxims the Chinese system neither does nor indeed could recognize. But it will scarcely escape observation, that there are other parts of the code which, in a considerable degree, compensate these and similar defects, are altogether of a different complexion, and are perhaps not unworthy of imitation, even among the fortunate and enlightened nations of the West" (Staunton, 1810). In this argument, Staunton compared Chinese laws and legal principles with those of Europe. Although he praised the intrinsic complementarity and consistency of Chinese laws, it is not difficult to discern subtext of statements such as "those excellent principles of the English law" and "the fortunate and enlightened nations of the West" is that Chinese laws, legal principles, and systems are inferior to those of the West. It is not surprising that the early translation of Chinese legal classics by Sinologists would be influenced or even dominated by Eurocentric cultural hegemony. The reasons are apparent. Firstly, the direct power imbalance between Western countries and China resulted in a cultural advantage for Westerners, as China at that time was indeed a vast but relatively weak nation. It was only natural for knowledge to flow from the superior to the subordinate, and the reverse would be rather unusual. Secondly, translations were often undertaken to assist authorities in gaining a relatively comprehensive understanding of Chinese laws and systems, facilitating their trade activities and colonial expansion. The primary task of translation was to convey the terms of information in a clear and straightforward way, rather than promoting Chinese legal culture. The pragmatic meaning of the translation outweighed its value for legal research. Thirdly, this style of translation aligned with the ambitious global colonial strategies of Western nations and was an integral part of the entire cultural expansion process. While the wording of the translation may seem objective, it was sufficient to evoke Western desires for conquest. The more they knew about China, the more eager they became to exploit it. In conclusion, Sinologists' translations of Chinese legal classics were more or less, overtly or covertly, influenced by deep-rooted cultural hegemonism and Western-centrism. Such translations struggle to provide a genuinely objective depiction of Chinese laws and legal culture.

The Self-shaping of China's Legal Image Under Oriental Legalism

In the new era of comprehensively advancing the rule of law in China, the legal subject consciousness has been increasingly strengthened, and the development of the rule of law is in full swing. The endeavor to shape the image of a rule-of-law state on the world stage has become a conscious and proactive practice for government agencies and departments led by the Communist Party of China. As China's comprehensive national strength continues to ascend, it assumes an increasingly significant role on the global stage. The era characterized by the Western-crafted image of Chinese law is gradually giving way to a period of self-shaping. Criticizing and exposing legal Orientalism essentially represents a shift toward "Oriental Legalism". The concept of "Oriental Legalism" is designed to reconstruct a fresh understanding and interpretation of legal discourse and concepts. Its objective is to rouse the East, facilitating the restoration of subjectivity in equitable dialogue with the West. In the ongoing evolution of global legal civilization, it strives to articulate its perspective, presenting itself as a potential path beyond Legal Orientalism. In short, moving toward "Oriental Legalism" is the question of how to construct a new discourse system for Chinese rule of law on the existing foundation (Wei, 2018).

Behind the shaping of the rule of law image is ultimately a discourse system composed of knowledge, ideas, concepts, and values. Building a logically compelling and self-contained discourse system for the rule of law is the fundamental starting point for the reformation of China's legal image. In the legal model of pursuing the rule of law, the cultural autonomy, and continuous development, China needs to be rooted in its own cultural traditions and the meaning world. However, this does not mean disregarding the trends of human civilization development or ignoring the fundamental differences in the organizational structure between traditional and modern societies (Lu, 2017). In the nineteenth century, the methods and pathways through which the image of Chinese law was disseminated have provided us with ample insights. The construction of a legal discourse system is a systematic endeavor, requiring concepts of legal and rule of law, and innovative ideas. It also necessitates diverse forms and approaches in translation and Spreading. The construction of discourse is a communicative system developed by social groups through repeated employment of a series of symbolic representations, media Spreading, institutional operations, and social practices. This determines that the subjects engaged in the construction of the rule of law discourse system not only need a broad perspective and vision but also require a concept of grand translation and broad Spreading.

Translation and communication have always carried significant historical missions and contemporary values. The translation work in the new era serves not only as a correction of misinterpretations of Chinese legal images in the history, but also as a self-construction and reconstruction of the image of the rule of law in contemporary China.

Due to the cultural differences between Chinese and Western languages, the translation of ancient Chinese law faces numerous challenges. Even renowned translators like Sir George Thomas Staunton acknowledge the difficulties encountered in translation. Staunton notes that, "the text has been found so obscure, and its construction so recondite, that no effort of attention was adequate completely to reconcile the apparent sense of the words, when considered individually, with their collective meaning, such as it was unanimously declared to be, by the most intelligent of the natives whom the Translator had an opportunity of consulting" (Staunton, 1810). Chinese knowledge translated and disseminated by Westerners, especially culture-specific vocabulary with Chinese characteristics, is inevitably prone to some misinterpretations in the translation process. It exposes many limitations in the "he shaping" of the Chinese legal image, bringing about numerous negative impacts on the image of Chinese law.

"The accuracy of the past translation of traditional Chinese terms with distinctive characteristics made by western translators will directly impact the authenticity and effectiveness of the external Spreading of relevant Chinese discourse and the reconstruction of the cultural image of China" (Wei & Yang, 2019). The "self-construction" of the rule of law image in contemporary China aims to play a role in radically reform and rejuvenating national cultural confidence.

From the perspective of international communication and the construction of national image, an international platform requires a collective discourse construction, necessitating a grand narrative, and calling for extensive translation and Spreading. This approach aims to enhance overall influence and visibility. "Grand translation should be a collective and cooperative translation activity conducted at the macro level, involving multiple semiotic codes. It is a comprehensive intersemiotic translation, which can constitute diachronic cultural memory" (Luo, 2019). The concept of Grand translation and broad Spreading represent a development concept for the panoramic and multi-dimensional construction of national image and cultural communication. It involves the participation of multiple subjects in various forms, emphasizing the need to construct intersemiotic translation comprehensively. This approach aims to achieve a multi-dimensional impact across roles, media, and eras. The construction of China's rule of law national image and the Spreading of legal culture requires cross-disciplinary participation. This responsibility extends beyond government departments and transcends the tasks of translators alone. It calls for the collective involvement of legal literary writers, critics, directors, scholars, internationally renowned figures, translators, and others. In terms of communication format and structure, it can involve the translation of laws and regulations, the translation of rule of law discourse, as well as the creation, critique, painting, and academic research of legal literature. Additionally, collaborative documentation through music, drama, film, micro-videos, and other mediums is also important. Also, various mediums such as books, audio-visual materials, stages, radio, television, the Internet, newspapers, and short video platforms can all be fully utilized. We can not only rely on the extensive domestic media resources but also leverage influential international media institutions. Through diversified and collaborative communication, these platforms can play an immensely significant role.

In the context of the new era, the construction of China's legal image aims to tell the story of Chinese rule of law to the world through a comprehensive legal discourse system. It involves multiple subjects, channels, and forms, working together on all fronts. The goal is to present a panoramic, true, and multi-dimensional image of China's rule of law. This is not only a current research topic but also an ongoing concern for the future, requiring continuous and collaborative efforts from generations to come.

Facilitating Mutual Learning of Civilizations Between China and the West

The legal culture developed by a nation undoubtedly reflects a strong national character. However, it is equally indisputable that, whether in the East or the West, the core principles and values of law share considerable similarities (D. Xiong, 2018). Such similarities make translation possible. With regard to these differences and divergences, only through communication and mutual learning can diverse cultures flourish and people truly understand each other. The translation of Chinese legal classics has made a significant contribution to legal cultural communication and the promotion of legal civilization among different countries and regions. China has entered a new era of modernization of legal system, with a relatively comprehensive legal system gradually being developed. Therefore, we should encourage domestic translators and researchers to retranslate and reinterpret Chinese legal classics from the perspective of promoting mutual cultural exchange to examine and evaluate China's legal culture, and to take the initiative in constructing and promoting our national culture, while respecting and preserving the individuality of our national culture, fostering legal culture exchanges objectively and truthfully.

To achieve mutual learning of civilizations, it is essential to look into a culture from a relatively objective and rational perspective. Chinese legal classics constitute the collective memory of the Chinese nation regarding law, rules, and justice, which help to shape the legal and cultural identity of the Chinese nation, laying the foundation for our confidence and belief in the current modernization of the rule of law (Dong & Zhang, 2021). In the new era, conducting the new translation of Chinese legal classics provides us with a rare opportunity for self-reflection. It allows us to understand our legal history, analyze the strengths and weaknesses of our legal culture, reflect on the successes and failures of past experiences in external translation and promotion, and innovatively explore practical strategies and approaches to address the problems and obstacles encountered. In order to promote Chinese legal culture internationally, it is essential that we possess a sufficient understanding of legal culture, have full confidence in its strength and vitality, and harbor a determined belief in the bright prospects of legal culture. Only with such confidence and determination can we successfully project legal culture onto the global stage.

Secondly, mutual exchange of civilization must take place on a fair platform where all parties actively interpret and promote their own ideologies, cultures, and ways of life.

As mentioned above, the long-standing trend of translating Chinese legal classics has been predominantly led by Western scholars, leading to some presumptive misunderstandings. This has resulted in a stereotyped and rigid image of Chinese law and legal culture, along with biases rooted in a Western-centric perspective on legal culture. To thoroughly address these issues, it is crucial for domestic translators to have their say in retranslation. Through "flexible and vivid communication, rational critique, and thoughtful innovation" (Y. Xiong, 2019), we can trace our legal origins, summarize the development path of our legal culture, promote our legal discourse on the international stage, and display our past legal achievements and future goals. In the new era, continuous translation of Chinese legal classics serves two purposes. On the one hand, it helps further explore the unique implications of Chinese legal discourse, contributing China's legal wisdom and strategies to the rapidly changing international landscape. On the other hand, it assists China in gaining the discourse power for legal modernization on the international stage, maximizing the integration of all forces conducive to the development of both China and the world (Dong, 2018).

Thirdly, domestic translators translating Chinese legal classics again can offer more materials for relevant research and create a fair platform for legal cultural exchange and mutual learning. Modern history indicates that the translation of Western legal literature and the promotion of legal thought have been of significant importance in the development of Chinese modern legal system. However, it seems evident that there is a notable deficiency in the importation of Western legal culture and the exportation of Chinese legal culture. Entering the twenty-first century, the improvement of the socialist legal system with Chinese characteristics, rapid economic growth, and robust national strength have fully demonstrated the vitality and unique charm of Chinese legal culture, law, and regulation. Secondly, China should actively introduce excellent legal works, outstanding legal scholars, translators, historians, and legal experts to the international community while continuously learning advanced legal ideas, experiences, and practices from other countries and regions.

Conclusion

China is the Other's mirror image in the West. In the Western Other-oriented imagination of China, there exists a recognition of certain realities in China, as well as anxieties and expectations regarding the China-West relationship. Moreover, it serves as a metaphor for Western cultural self-identity and ideologies. The Western image of China is a comprehensive set of discourses about "the Other" in modern Western history, constituting a discourse system exerting power (Zhou, 2006). Law is a discourse of state power and a form of subjectification. When words like "barbaric" and "backward" become labels of Chinese law in Western perceptions, this discourse gains global Spreading, evolving into a form of epistemology. Simultaneously, it continues to develop into rational legal discourses of Westerners' rather than discourses of objective truth. This process can legitimize the exclusion of China from international legal rights. In the nineteenth century, the Western portrayal of the Chinese legal system laid the groundwork for the emergence of "legal Orientalism". Examining the depiction crafted by Westerners and the Spreading of Chinese law during this era not only provides insights into Western intentions but also facilitates an exploration of the underlying thought patterns or discourse structures embedded in these literary materials. It illuminates the dominating influence generated by these discourse structures. Even today, these notions continue to exert a certain influence, shaping the field of Chinese legal studies in the United States, Europe, and even within China. Taking "legal orientalism" as a perspective to study and explore the construction and Spreading of the image of Chinese law in the nineteenth century provides insights and reflections for the self-shaping of the image of China as a rule-of-law nation in the new era. "Oriental legalism" fundamentally aims to construct China's image as a nation governed by the rule of law comprehensively, within the context of advancing legal principles in China. Rooted in the principles of cultural exchange, mutual learning, and cultural equality, it seeks to present and widely disseminate China's image as a rule-of-law nation on the international stage, thus overturn the biased Chinese legal image shaped by Westerners in the history.

The traditional Chinese legal classics passed down through the ages are a concentrated reflection of Chinese legal culture. Over the past two centuries, Westerners have overwhelmingly dominated the translation of Chinese legal classics. In the new era, to adapt to the global trend of cultural globalization and the modernization of legal culture, "the focus of translation should shift from translating Western works into English to translating Chinese works into English. This means translating masterpieces that best represent China and Chinese culture and delivering them to a broader audience" (Wang, 2006). Whether translated by Sinologists or other translators, there should be active efforts to reconstruct and reinterpret Chinese legal classics. Namely portraying Chinese legal culture from the perspective of Chinese people, rectifying intentional or unintentional misinterpretations and distortions made by previous translators and researchers. It also involves seizing control of the initiative and the right to say in elucidating the domestic legal culture, fostering the establishment of an equitable platform for cultural exchange. This aims to introduce outstanding Chinese legal culture and exemplary legal works to the international community. Not only draw on advanced experiences from other countries, but also contribute China's unique governance wisdom to the world, which will help achieve mutual learning and equal dialogue among different civilizations.

References

Dong, X., & Zhang, Y. (2021). Translation and research of traditional Chinese legal classics. *China Legal Science, 9*(3), 23–58.

Dong, X. (2018). Legal translation contributing Chinese wisdom to global governance. *Chinese Social Sciences Today*, 2018-06-26.

He, G., Wang, Z., & Li, S. (2010). *De Christiana expeditione apud Sinas*. Zhonghua Book Company.

He, Y., & Xu, G. (2000). *History of sinology abroad*. Shanghai Foreign Language Education Press.

Hou, Y. (2009). The first attempt by Europeans to fully translate Chinese legal classics: Staunton and his translation of 'the Ta Tsing Leu Lee.' *Historical Archives, 4*, 97–104.

Institute for Chinese Ancient Legal Documents of China University of Political Science and Law. (2019). *An overview of ancient Chinese legal classics and documents*. Shanghai Classics Publishing House.

Legislative Affairs Office of the State Council of the People's Republic of China. (1957). *Introduction to reference books on the history of Chinese legal system*. Law Press.

Li, X. (2015). *Western interpretation of Chinese law: 19th Century western perspectives on Chinese law based on Chinese repository, 56*. Shanghai Joint Publishing Company.

Lu, N. (2017). Review of Teemu Ruskola's legal orientalism: Towards oriental legalism?" *SJTU Law Review*, (3).

Luo, X. (2019). Big translation and cultural memory: The construction and transmission of national images. *Foreign Languages in China, 16*(05), 95–102.

Qian, L., & Cao, P. (2015). A literature review of English translations of Chinese classics by translators of British East India Company. *Journal of Huaihai Institute of Technology: Humanities & Social Sciences Edition, 13*(10), 66–69.

Qu, W., & Huang, S. (2021). The western translation of the washing away of wrongs and the narration of the 'other.' *Chinese Translators Journal, 42*(01), 48–58.

Qu, W., & Wan, L. (2019). What has motivated English translation of the codes of pre-modern Chinese dynasties. *Chinese Translators Journal, 40*(1), 51–59.

Staunton, G. T. (1939). *Narrative of the Chinese Embassy to the Khan of the Tourgouth Tartars in the years of 1712, 13, 1 4 & 15*. The Emperor's Authority.

Staunton, G. T. (1810). *Ta Tsing Leu Lee: Being the fundamental laws and a selection from the supplementary statutes of the penal code of China*. T. Cadell and W. Davis.

Staunton, G. T. (2015). Memoirs of Sir George Thomas Staunton, Bart., 219. W. Qu, Trans. Shanghai People's Publishing House.

Su, Y. (2003). Another perspective: A study on the Chinese legal and cultural traditions through the eyes of modern England and America. *Global Law Review, 25*(126), 76–83.

Wang, J. (2001). The eastward spreading of western culture: Study of the early history of the correspondence of legal concepts between China and the West. *Tsinghua Forum of Rule of Law*, 296–359.

Wang, N. (2006). *Cultural translation and classic interpretation*. Zhonghua Book Company.

Wang, H. (2018). The output track of translating Chinese legal literature and its enlightenment. *Political Science and Law, 11*, 117–126.

Wei, L. (2018). The essence of oriental legalism in the context of China. *Open Times*, (6).

Wei, X., & Yang, P. (2019). International communication of discourse with Chinese characteristics and standardization of terminology in translation. *Chinese Translators Journal*, (1).

Xi, J. (2015). Accelerating the establishment of socialist rule of law in China. People's Daily, 2015-01-01.

Xi, J. (2017). *Full text of Xi Jinping's report at 19th CPC National Congress*. http://cpc.people.com.cn/n1/2017/1028/c64094-29613660.html.

Xiong, D. (2018). An interpretive approach to different English versions of Chinese classics of legal culture from ancient China. *Journal of Southwest University of Political Science and Law, 20*(5), 13–21.

Xiong, Y. (2019). *The eastward spreading of western culture and the social changes in modern China*. Shanghai Educational Publishing House.

Zhang, S. (2013). Classics: The indispensable source of legal culture. *The Journal of Jiangsu Administration Institute, 2*, 130–136.

Zhou, N. (2006). *Faraway celestial empire: Western images of China* (Vol. 1), 14. Peking University Press.

FSC www.fsc.org
MIX
Papier aus verantwortungsvollen Quellen
Paper from responsible sources
FSC® C105338

If you have any concerns about our products,
you can contact us on
ProductSafety@springernature.com

In case Publisher is established outside the EU,
the EU authorized representative is:
Springer Nature Customer Service Center GmbH
Europaplatz 3, 69115 Heidelberg, Germany

Printed by Libri Plureos GmbH
in Hamburg, Germany